ADG-7543

GP

D1616088

BIO   Provost, Jon,
PROVOST   1949-

             Timmy's in the well.

2007

DATE			

GP 308

BAKER & TAYLOR

Timmy's in the Well

Timmy's in the Well

THE JON PROVOST STORY

JON PROVOST and LAURIE JACOBSON

CUMBERLAND HOUSE
NASHVILLE, TENNESSEE

TIMMY'S IN THE WELL
PUBLISHED BY CUMBERLAND HOUSE PUBLISHING
431 Harding Industrial Drive
Nashville, TN 37211

Cover design: Gore Studio, Inc.
Book design: Mary Sanford

Library of Congress Cataloging-in-Publication Data
Provost, Jon, 1949–
  Timmy's in the well : the Jon Provost story / Jon Provost and Laurie Jacobson.
     p. cm.
  Includes index.
  ISBN-13: 978-1-58182-619-7 (hardcover : alk. paper)
  ISBN-10: 1-58182-619-2 (hardcover : alk. paper)
  1. Provost, Jon, 1949– 2. Actors—United States—Biography. I. Jacobson, Laurie. II. Title.

PN2287.P75A3 2007
791.4502'8092—dc22
[B]
                                                          2007039002

Printed in Canada
1 2 3 4 5 6 7—13 12 11 10 09 08 07

This book is lovingly dedicated

To my children, Ryan and Katie, whom I love more than life itself

To my wife, Laurie, who made this book happen

and

To Mom, who made it all happen

Contents

Foreword

I had made a guest appearance in an episode of *Lassie* as a runaway young man kicked out of a dishwasher's job at a small town greasy spoon. I escaped on the tailgate of an old truck. I sat on the paw of a dog and quite easily said "'scuse me"; such was the reality of the individual. Little did I know a year or so later I walked into the magic cave, the yawning mouth of a soundstage off Sunset Boulevard in Hollywood. There again was the truck, the farmhouse, the dog, my new family, the family of millions who loved, cared, and dealt with life in the innocence of another time.

That "innocence" was the start of the series, the purity of coincidence that revealed a new story every week, where wrong was quickly discovered and right had to win. The story was told in the wonderful eyes of Jon Provost and in the actions of Lassie. This genuinely good actor and his loving partners surrendered themselves "well prepared and on time" to the relentless pursuit of a camera that really knows them, really liked them.

Decades do what they do. I know Jon Provost, man and boy, and willingly give him love and admiration. The picture memory of that first day for me was the human dream: the farm, the truck, the mother and father, the dog, the boy, perhaps the sweet promise of immortality. I like him a lot, a most lovable fellow. I can hardly wait to read how it all happened.

JON SHEPODD
"PAUL MARTIN," 1958
LONDON, MARCH 2007

Acknowledgments

First, we'd like to thank our family, especially my brother and sister, William Provost and Fran Rubin, for revisiting some difficult times.

We are grateful to many people for their time, their help and inspiration, and for their stories, among them:

Lee Aaker, Laurie Ackerman, Dan Altenes, A Minor Consideration, Mary Badham, Dick Bakalyan, Rand M. Bard, Bill Beaudine Jr, Ralph Benner, Debbie Bond, Cathy Jones Brazil, Jody Brisken, Ron Brown, Gary Brumburgh, Dal Burns, Al Burton, John Michael Caffey, Bonnie Ray Webb Campbell, Canine Companions for Independence, Angela and Marjorie Cartwright, Diane Sherry Case, David Cassidy, Sue Chantry, Arnie Cohen, Stephen Cohen, Ace Collins, the Conflenti family, Laura Connolly, Janice Coville, Wendy Hagen Cox, Jim Dalton, Catherine Deeney, Cherrie Dolloff, Ed Donahue, Bruce Dzieza, Will Estes, Todd and Ann Ferrell, Abel Fernandez, Tracy Ford, Jenna Girard, Cheryl Gonroski, Susan Gordon, Ruthel Hawkins, Marsha Heckman, Lonnie Hill, Connie Hines, Billy Hinsche, Billy Hughes Jr., Whitey Hughes, Frank Inn, Darlene Rettig Insley, Davy Jones, Grace Kuhn, Susan Ladin, Sheilah Lee, Linda Lewis, Living Legends Ltd., Stanley Livingston, Anne Lockhart, June Lockhart, Mary Lou Lueken, Ace Lundon, Betty Lynn, Brother Phil Mandile, John Mangoni, Tyler Mark, Belinda Meyer Marcum, Anne Moses Marino, Flip Mark (Philip Goldberg), Sandy McClusky, Patty McCormack, Mike McGreevey, Ralph Millero, Karen McCoy Montecillo, Bill Mumy, Roger Nakagawa, Lloyd Nelson, Danny Nero, Jay North, Paul Petersen, Jessica Peterson, Karen Pfeiffer, Sydney Pollack, Jerrie Potterville, Dom Priore, B.A. Provost,

Vivien Provost, Hugh Reilly, Deane Rettig, Tom Rettig, Trina Robbins, Robert Ross, Leslie Rugg, Bryan Russell, Jeanne Russell, Don Schoenfeld, Evelyn Schultz, Keith and Kevin Schultz, Rosemary Hilb Shaw, Jon Shepodd, Lynne Shepodd, Marvin Silverman, Craig Smith, Sharon Smith, Brent Sohn, Frank Stafford, Jerry Stahl, Stan Stamper, Susie Space Swan, Keith Thibodeaux, Sondra Space Thiederman, Lou Tylee, Joey Vieira, Dee Wallace, Marc Wanamaker, Bob Weatherwax, Daniel J. Webster, Dodie White, Lana Wood, Alan Young, Ray Zollen.

Thank you to Classic Media.

Much gratitude to our manager and dear friend, Anne McDermott.

Last, but by no means least, our deepest thanks to the fans who continue to hold Timmy close to their hearts.

Introduction

The biggest thing I learned writing this book was that as Timmy, I never fell down a well. Really. I thought I had. I'd heard the phrase all my life, both from people I knew and people I'd never met before: "What is it, Lassie? Timmy's in the well?" In my seven years on *Lassie* and in more than 260 half-hour episodes, I fell off cliffs, into abandoned mines and storm drains, culverts and caves, rivers and creeks, but never a well. And yet, "Timmy's in the well" became a catchphrase that crossed generations and cultures and is still used by owners of dogs and cats around the world today.

So, why did I choose it as the title of my memoir? Because we all fall into wells—those holes on the road of life. Some we stumble into, others we're thrown into, and some we dig ourselves. Some are nothing more than potholes and we easily pick ourselves up, but others are deep and dark and how we climb out of them can change everything. Don't worry. This book isn't a "how to" or an "inspirational something." It's my journey along with my family's—a typical American family irrevocably altered by my fame—and the wells we encountered while living through a time in Hollywood and beyond.

Jon Provost
Santa Rosa, CA
August 2007

The only time you will hear me use the words *divorce* and *my husband* in the same sentence is when I tell you that it was easy to divorce myself from the fact that my subject is also my husband. Sure, at the beginning, I felt extra pressure. I mean, this wasn't just any book; it's my husband's one-and-only memoir. And then there's the fact that it marks the fiftieth anniversary of his debut as Timmy Martin, one of classic television's most iconic characters. OK, all right, I admit it. I was intimidated. If I screwed this up, it would be bad on so many levels.

All my concerns dissipated when I began hearing the stories. Ultimately, I am a fan of Hollywood, always have been. I've been researching and writing about it for close to thirty years—more if you count all those hours glued to *The Late, Late Show*. But as much as I've learned, as many times as I have peeked "behind the veil," I was surprised by so many things in Jon's professional life. And I was astonished by things in his private life. While Jon portrayed part of an idyllic television family, his relationship with his own family was deeply affected as a result of his skyrocketing career. Did you know the suicide rate amongst the siblings of child stars is far higher than among "normal" siblings? Neither did I. That's the tip of the iceberg. For anyone considering putting a child in show business, there's plenty to learn.

The late '50s–early '60s is such a fascinating period, not only in Hollywood, but in our country: the collapse of the studio system, the burgeoning industry of television, the civil rights movement, JFK, rock and roll, Vietnam, the sexual revolution, and the Sunset Strip. Peppered with names like Grace Kelly, Bing Crosby, Jane Wyman, Anita Ekberg, William Holden, Lucille Ball, Elvis Presley, Natalie Wood, Kurt Russell, Sal Mineo, Davy Jones, David Cassidy, Jay North, and many more, Jon's path from toddler to television to teen idol is a pioneer's trek across some amazing territory. And in the fashion of that time, it has a Hollywood ending: He and his family find their personal happiness and their way back to one another. And Jon and I ride off together into the sunset.

Laurie Jacobson
Santa Rosa, CA
August 2007

"Outside of a dog, a book is a boy's best friend.
Inside of a dog, it's too dark to read."

GROUCHO MARX

Prologue

Several members of the crew held ropes connected to the raft to hold it in place while Lassie and I climbed on board. The water was shallow and calm—but frigid—in this bend of the Sonora River, high in the Sierras. I wore a wetsuit underneath my clothes. It was awkward, but it helped keep the cold out. The shot had been carefully planned and explained to me. It could only be done once. Lassie and I were to navigate downriver toward the white water by means of a long pole I would use to push the raft forward. When we hit the current, we were to jump into the rapids. I should act like I'm in trouble, fighting for my life. Downstream, out of camera range, there was a safety line across the water. All I had to do was go with the flow of the water, then reach up and grab the line as I passed under it. My stunt man, Whitey Hughes, didn't think this was a good idea; he wanted to go in for me. Director Bill Beaudine disagreed. Sure, it was dangerous, but they'd all be there if something went wrong. Besides, they only had one raft and it would disintegrate in the rapids. "So do little boys," thought Whitey. Beaudine insisted that everything would be fine. Since they could only get the shot once, it had to be me out there, not Whitey. I enthusiastically agreed. I was a twelve-year-old boy looking to break the monotony of a film shoot—this sounded exciting. Beaudine ignored the warning and decided to risk letting both Lassie and me do the stunt.

I boarded the raft and pushed it along in the shallow water. Lassie sat next to me, alert and ready. I felt like Tom Sawyer or Huck Finn, making my way downriver. A few moments later, everything changed. The water swirled around us in all directions. Lassie and I got the cue to jump and we leaped into the water. Even with the wet suit, the water felt like pins and needles stabbing my neck, hands, and feet. My wet jacket and jeans were heavy and difficult to move in. My leather boots filled with water. I struggled to keep my head up as I hurtled downriver. The raft hit a rock and splintered into a hundred pieces. White water spun me in circles. I couldn't see the cameras anymore. The shore rushed by. I tried to focus on the safety line stretched across the river. If I missed that, I'd really be . . . BAM! I slammed chest-first into a sharp rock hidden beneath the water. Instantly, all the air was knocked out of me. I couldn't breathe. I was swallowing water. Panicked, I flailed my arms wildly. I went under. Out of the corner of my eye, I saw two of the crew get in the water. I gasped for air, weak from the fight. They reached out their arms and scooped Lassise out of the rapids as I sailed by. I went under again. "The kid is great," someone said. "What a performance." I couldn't hear them. Exhausted, choking, I went under for the third time.

Timmy's in the Well

Part One: Opportunity Knocks

"Will I Get to See a Movie Star?"

—Cecile Provost

"Will I get to see a movie star?" my mother asked.

"You just might," answered the young woman who looked after me in the nursery at the Pasadena Episcopal Church where Mom, a Southern Baptist, taught Sunday school. She picked up the *L.A. Times* and showed her. "It says right here in Hedda Hopper's column they need a two- to three-year-old boy with blonde hair and blue eyes to be Jane Wyman's son. That's Jon, and he minds so well. I think you should take him."

"Jane Wyman? Oh, I would love to see Jane Wyman. I saw her in *Johnny Belinda* and it was wonderful. OK, I'll take him there. Maybe I can get her autograph."

That was it—the spark that started my career. The woman who told Mom about the audition that Sunday in October of 1952 couldn't have had any idea her suggestion would change the entire course of my life and the lives of my family. In the Provost household, of course, everyone knows the story. We heard Mom tell it a thousand times.

> Mom: I went home and asked my husband to draw me a map to Warner Bros. He said, "What's Warner Bros?" I told him it's a movie studio and asked him if he could find out how to get there from our home in Pasadena because they were looking for a little boy to play little "So Big." Edna Ferber wrote that story and it's a good one. B.A. said he'd find out where it was, but he told me I was wasting my time on a wild goose chase. I didn't expect Jon to get the job, but I hoped I might get to see Jane Wyman, and she's great. So I took him. There were about 300 children; it was what they call a "cattle call" audition. Anybody who had a two- to three-year-old boy could bring him. Some even had their little girls' hair cut so they looked like a boy.

In short, it was a zoo; kids crying and yelling and running around. I was a third child, and my brother and sister were a bit older than me—eight and six—all of which probably played a part in my calm disposition. Mom said I never cried. Whatever the reasons, I was a good little boy who did what he was told. That would serve me well this day.

The casting people took ten kids at a time into a room. I went in and didn't come out. Nine more children went in and nine came out. That happened a few times before a rotund woman in her sixties wearing a flowered dress and a floppy hat approached Mom. She said her name was Lola Moore.

"Which one is your little boy?"

"He's the one who hasn't come out yet."

"Oh?" Lola said. "Who's your agent?"

"Agent? What's an agent? We aren't selling our house."

"I think your son is going to get this job, and if I say he's with my talent agency, I can get him more money—maybe $70 a day. Can I be your agent?"

"$70! Does it cost money?" Mom asked. Lola explained she gets just 10 percent of whatever I earn; otherwise, Mom pays nothing at all. "Do I have to sign something? Because I don't think my husband would like that." Lola said they could just shake on it and so they did.

> Mom: And sure enough, a lady who'd been taking all the children in came out with Jon and said, "Whose child is this?" I held up my hand and said "I'm his mother." And Lola said, "I'm his agent." She motioned us both in and told us Jon got the job.

My career was off to a great start—my first job and an agent all in one day. At two and a half, I'm sure I didn't even realize it had begun. All I'd done was to behave. Mom ran home to tell Dad. As she remembers it, he was up on a ladder working outside.

"Well, what do you think?" she asked.

"Wild goose chase."

"It wasn't; he got the job. What do you think he'll make?"

"I don't know; how much?"

"$70.00"

"Is that a month?"

"That's a day," I told him.

> Mom: I never saw him come down off a ladder so fast!

So Big

So Big was based on Edna Ferber's Pulitzer Prize–winning 1924 novel. It tells the story of the struggles of a widow to support herself and her son Dirk—the "So Big" character. I portrayed Dirk early on, when his

father was still in the picture. Actor Steve Forrest played Dirk as an adult. Enormous Sterling Hayden played my father, Pervus. We Provosts were little. Mom was a petite five-foot-two and Dad couldn't have been more than a couple inches taller. That was part of the key to my success; because I was small, I looked younger, but I understood more.

February 1953 I worked two weeks on *So Big* out in Orange County at sprawling Tustin Ranch the following February. I was not quite three. The highly acclaimed Robert Wise directed. I appear in a sweet scene with Jane Wyman before Sterling Hayden and Richard Beymer interrupt with bad news. My first in a long line of "mothers," Miss Wyman danced for me in a field wearing vegetables as earrings, causing me to squeal with laughter as I sat and played in the muddy field. In the scene she asks me how big I'll get, and I respond with my first movie line. I stretch my arms wide and say " . . . soooo big."

Mom: Robert Wise was a famous director, but nobody told me he was so important so I was over there asking him questions all the time . . . but he took the time to answer them. The other mothers told me I wasn't supposed to talk to the director. "What's the big deal?" I answered. "You stay in the background, don't go talking to people." Well, I wasn't used to that . . . but I got by with it.

Mom got by all right; what she didn't know never hurt her. For someone who didn't know much, she got an article about me in both a local Pasadena paper as well as in her mother's hometown paper in Arkansas where Grandma had a

Mom is on the far side of the camera next to the director.

farm. In the coming years, what she would learn about promotion in general and promoting me in particular could fill a book by itself. She and I attended the West Coast premiere of *So Big* on Tuesday night, November 3, 1953, at the Paramount Theater across from Grauman's Chinese Theater on Hollywood Boulevard. Jane Wyman received many accolades. Steve Forrest received the Golden Globe Award for Most Promising New-comer. And, oh yeah, Mom *did* get Jane Wyman's autograph.

If it was fate that day the nursery teacher mentioned the audition, *So Big* also seemed touched by a similar hand. I played Dirk as a baby. As a boy of eight, he was played by Tommy Rettig, the boy from whom I would inherit Lassie. And the dog on the set was owned and trained by Rudd Weath-erwax, the owner and trainer of Lassie. He would become a father

WEST COAST PREMIERE
Warner Bros. Pictures presents
EDNA FERBER'S PULITZER PRIZE-WINNING NOVEL
"SO BIG"
starring JANE WYMAN
STERLING HAYDEN • NANCY OLSON
Tues. Eve., November 3, 1953 at 8:30
PARAMOUNT HOLLYWOOD THEATRE
6838 Hollywood Boulevard, Hollywood, California
583 ☆ SPECIAL SECTION

figure to Tommy and, for me, the grandfa-ther I never knew. Within a year, they would be working together. I would join them three years later. By then, I would be a sea-soned professional.

The Beginning

No one in my family was "in the business." My mom was from a tiny town in Texas called Wolfe City. The road sign as you entered read: *The Blackest Land, the Whitest People.* She never spoke much about her father, Grandma's second husband. Or the one that came after him. Whenever one of us asked, Mom and Grandma would say, "They all died," giving us the impression Grandma was a widow three times. Decades later, I found out that Mom's dad, my grandfather, was actually very much alive when Mom and Dad married, but he was not invited to the wedding, and I don't believe she ever saw him afterward. Grandma's third husband had come and gone by then. She kept his name, McClure, but that's all anyone knows about him. Grandma was a survivor who knew how to cut her losses, pack up, and move on . . . and on, and on. Mom inherited her resourcefulness, her sense of adventure, and her ability to keep a secret. They moved from Texas to Oklahoma to Arkansas, close to Hot Springs, a remote town in the Ouachita mountains. All kinds of people went to "the Springs" for a variety of recreation: the mineral baths, the casinos, and the moonshine. During Prohibition, Al Capone came from Chicago to strike deals with bootleggers, and when the heat was on in the Windy City, he cooled his heels in Hot Springs at the casinos and the baths. Family lore has Mom and her half-sister, Dolly, riding around Hot Springs with Capone.

> *Mom:* I was always movie-struck. I took my 10 cents to see the movies where a lady sat down in front and played the piano. The movies were nothing but cowboys on Saturdays. . . . We'd stay all day and watch it over and over and finally Daddy'd come and get me out. In college, I was a home economics major, but I also did a little theater on the side because I liked it. If I had an extra quarter, I'd buy *Photoplay* magazine, but a quarter was a lot of money in those days. My mother had to sell two or three dozen eggs to get a quarter.

Mom—born Cecile Priscilla Edwards—went to Ouachita College (now Ouachita Baptist University) in '34 and '35. Voted "cutest girl" both years, Mom was movie-star pretty—a petite blonde with twinkling blue eyes. In 2004, three years after she died, I got a letter from a woman who wondered if Mom had ever mentioned her first husband. After I picked myself up off the floor, I realized it made complete sense. Seems she and a handsome football player at Ouachita were married sometime around 1935.

> Fran: I always knew it in my heart. Once, when I was a newlywed, I borrowed a platter from Mom. She wasn't home, but she'd told me where to find it. In the same drawer was a picture of her with a man I'd never seen before and instantly, I knew they were a couple . . . you know how you can just look at people and know they're together? I never said anything about it, but when I returned the platter a week later, the picture was gone and I never saw it again.

I'm told the marriage didn't work out and she left him a year later for someone else, breaking his heart. Later, alone, Mom and Grandma went back to North Carolina, where Grandma still had family—including an identical twin sister none of us ever met. Southern women and their secrets—these two took them to their graves. And what actresses they were too, regrouping and adapting to whatever life put in their path.

Cornelia Hardin Edwards McClure and her daughter, Cecile, moved to Los Angeles in 1939. They bought a two-story home near the Ambassador Hotel, and Mom went to work designing and making dresses for Lanz on Wilshire Boulevard near Fairfax.

Like all good Daughters of the Confederacy, Grandma attended a national convention of the UDC, where she met a very nice lady from Alabama. Achie Provost had traveled from Mobile to attend the convention as a delegate. The two got to talking—you

November 1941

know: I have a daughter. I have a son. Is she married? Is he married? Days later, Cornelia invited Achie and her son to Sunday dinner.

On the appointed day, Achie and her son, B.A. (Bion Archibald, but no one called him that) arrived, but Mom refused to come downstairs. Seems she thought Dad was a "wolf," though nothing could've been further from the truth. But curiosity finally got the better of her.

July 18, 1942

Dad: Cecile and I hit it off at first sight. We dated constantly during the "blackouts," and six months later we got married.

Fran: Mom always said she was twenty-seven, the same age as Dad, when they got married. Years later, she admitted she had shaved a few years off. My guess is that she was about five years older. One night at a family gathering, someone was joking about it and I joined in, saying, "Yeah, Mom, how old are you, anyway?" She snatched my arm and dragged me into the kitchen. "You are going to kill this family with your questions. Leave it alone." She scared me plenty and I never mentioned it again.

Dad's mother was very conservative. She'd never have allowed Dad to marry an older divorcée. So Mom and Grandma kept the past a secret. It didn't hurt anyone. My parents were the love of each other's lives for sixty years.

Mom moved into Dad's bachelor digs near the L.A. Coliseum, then after a month or two she suggested they buy a house. He told her to look near the Northrop Corporation, where he worked as an aeronautical engineer—a wing and tail man. Back then, you came to L.A. to be in show business or the aerospace industry. That's why he wasn't overseas, he was needed here building aircraft. Mom found a sweet little two-bedroom in Morningside Park and another nearby for Grandma, the beginning of her Midas touch with real estate. If I hadn't come along, she'd have made a fortune with it. They moved in, adopted a stray kitten, and joined a number of social clubs.

November 15, 1944

My brother William Bion was born. Early on, he developed asthma, and his doctor suggested my parents move from the

damp coastal side to the east side of Los Angeles. Mom hit the house-hunting trail again and soon found a nice two-bedroom with a second house in back for Grandma in Maywood. Dad did all the remodeling and home improvement, a life-long practice. He learned to fix just about anything.

My sister Francile Ann was born. Her name was the combination of Mom's name and the name of her best friend, Frances . . . a very Southern tradition.

March 30, 1946

Dad celebrated another spectacular event that year, a career milestone. While at Northrup, he spent years helping to design an aviation marvel, the precursor to the Stealth Bomber, called the Flying Wing. The B-35 was designed to have a 10,000-mile range, allowing it to fly from the United States to Europe, drop its bombs, and return. On June 25, the XB-35 Flying Wing Bomber made its maiden flight out of Northrup Airport to Muroc Army Air Base—one of the greatest achievements in modern aviation history.

Mom fell in love with a four-bedroom Victorian in Pasadena and found a house for Grandma there, too. Built in 1901, the place needed a complete overhaul, which Dad did evenings and weekends, tearing the place apart: electrical, plumbing, plaster, flooring. Mom took William and Fran to Huntington Beach for the summer until it was livable. Dad put the finishing touches on it just before Christmas and they celebrated with a huge New Year's Eve party. Mom

June 1947

loved having people in the house, a true Southern belle with hospitality for all.

Always enterprising, Mom looked at the large carriage house and hayloft in the back with a beautiful pitched roof and saw apartments. Dad designed two one-bedroom apartments and got to work. By the summer of 1949, they had renters paying $35 a month.

March 12, 1950 My parents woke at the usual time that Sunday. Mom began having labor pains and off they went. Dad drove Mom from Pasadena to downtown L.A.'s Methodist Hospital—more than half an hour—for my birth.

Dad: It was close, but I didn't get arrested.

I was a surprise . . . a diaphragm baby. And if Fran's guess about Mom's age is right, she had to be close to forty, so I was a "change of life" baby, but no matter. She never missed a step.

Mom: I was always a club woman. Just because I had little children was no excuse to miss my clubs. I put him in a basket and I went.

Fran: To this day, I don't think she wanted Jon . . . or maybe it's that she wanted Jon but not me because I was too close to William, only months apart; it was very rough for her. She was just starting to get a full breath when Jon was born. I don't know if she was ready for him.

Dad: As the summer of 1950 approached, Cecile and her mother decided they would like to take the kids and go back to Arkansas for the summer. They all piled into our brand new 1950 two-door Plymouth sedan with Jon in a baby basket and left me home to work.

That summer, Grandma bought a 160-acre farm just outside of Fayetteville in Elkins. We spent every summer there for the next ten years. Sometimes Dad would come for a week, but not often. He'd put the swamp cooler—the predecessor to air conditioning—on the passenger window of the Plymouth, and we'd drive Route 66, stopping along the way at every attraction: rattle snakes, big jack rabbits, buffalo, petrified wood, alligator ranches. The farm was miles of dirt roads. At first, the main house was unlivable. Dad designed a log cabin and sent the plans to some new friends, Homer and Eula Clark, who lived just up the road. Homer built it and had it ready for us the next summer. The cabin was tiny and rustic, with kerosene lamps and even an outhouse. Outside was a well with a bucket we dropped to get water.

> *William:* My mom would drive us out and leave us there for the summer, then she'd come back and get us at the end of the summer. Jon would normally only be there for a few days because he was working. We called the Clarks "Aunt" and "Uncle." They had a horse for Fran to ride. I went hunting and fishing. Uncle Homer was real good at showing an equal amount of time and interest in each of us. He didn't favor one of us over the other. Fran and I were very close, but even in Arkansas, she stayed with Homer and Eula and I stayed up the road with Grandma.

Fran once dressed me as a little girl for Halloween before my first haircut.

Whatever Lola Wants...

After the *So Big* cattle call, Lola told Mom she would send me on other auditions, but it would never be a big mob like this again, so Mom agreed. What did she have to lose? I really think Mom and Dad believed they'd never hear from her again, but they didn't know Lola Moore.

A first generation American born to German immigrants outside Chicago, Lola made her way to Hollywood and blazed a trail as one of the first agents for children. There was only one other in the '20s, Harry Weber, a former vaudevillian who repped Mickey Rooney for a while. She also wrote stories for Western serials at Universal. By the '30s, she worked solely for the kids, a difficult road in early Hollywood because most kids didn't need an agent unless they worked regularly. Hungry stage moms found out on their own about auditions. Mom didn't know anything about the business. She put herself—and me—in Lola's hands.

Paul Petersen: Lola was an institution here in our era. She and Jeanie Halliburton handled virtually all of the children in the entertainment business. The only ones they didn't handle would be people like Natalie Wood and Brandon de Wilde who had jumped up to another level. Lola was a truly huge woman, probably three hundred pounds, with the ankles dripping over the shoes . . . a grandmotherly figure of enormous girth. Her office was out of her home—9172 Sunset Boulevard. All the kids really liked her. She wore these flamboyant, wide-brimmed, flowered hats, and everywhere she went, she had her handkerchief mopping her brow because she sweated profusely. But she had the kids and she knew one talented kid from another.

Mom was keeping the highways hot, running me into Hollywood for auditions. Television attracted attention. Few were lucky enough to have one at home. Most people stood in front of appliance store windows to catch their favorite shows like *Fireside Theater* on NBC, a dramatic series featuring a different cast and story each week. My next job was in an episode called, "Sergeant Sullivan Speaking," shot in 1953 at movie pioneer Hal Roach's studio in Culver City. William Bendix and Joan Blondell played my parents, but the episode is lost and Mom never shared any stories or photos with me about it. That's a surprise, since a press release from BBD&O's New York office said that Fran and William appeared with me in this one.

The Country Girl

1954

Mom: Sometime later, Lola called about an audition. She said there'd be a total of four little boys and to dress Jon in a navy suit with short pants. I took him to Paramount Studios. They told me which stage to go to, and in come one, two, three little boys. They all have on navy suits with short pants. To me, they all looked alike. One of them had been working a lot, so I figured he'd get the job.

The job was playing Grace Kelly and Bing Crosby's son in the screen version of the Clifford Odets play *The Country Girl*.

"I'm George Seaton, the director," said a voice. Mom looked up. Six feet tall, broad shouldered, with kind eyes, Seaton he was at the top of his game in Hollywood. He looked at the four boys and said, "I can't make this decision. Hold on a minute. . . . Hey, Bing!"

> *Mom*: I almost fainted. I never thought I'd see Bing Crosby. We mothers didn't say a word. We stood back behind our boys and were quiet. Bing walks over, looks at the four kids, puts his hand on Jon's head and says, "George, don't you know my son when you see him?" Mr. Seaton said, "Maybe you're right, but I don't know. I should give Her Majesty a chance to see who is going to be her son, too." He hollers, "Grace!" and out walks Grace Kelly. She came over to Jon and says, "Bing, don't you know our son when you see him?" So it had to be.

Grace Kelly, the gorgeous socialite cover girl and movie star who would one day be a princess, had not yet met her prince. She spent most of the movie in plain, dowdy clothes and horn-rimmed glasses as a desperate, battered wife. Bing Crosby was, of course, a world-class crooner, an Oscar-winning actor, and a popular comedian, especially when paired with his best pal, Bob Hope. He played a washed-up, alcoholic actor—just the opposite of his public image. The film's other star, William Holden, had just gotten the Oscar for *Stalag 17*.

I played Johnny Elgin in two scenes with "my parents" in happier times. Mom was with me on the set every day. At four, I was only allowed to spend twenty minutes of every hour in front of a camera. I wanted to work longer. I was a ball of energy. At ease with grown-ups, I

struck up a conversation with Mr. Crosby while we waited for technicians to light the set. Whatever I said made him laugh. "Say, this kid ad libs better than Bob Hope!"

In my first scene, "Mother" and I listen (I conduct) as "Daddy" records a ballad, "The Search Is Through," in a studio. Afterward, he holds me while he talks to Mom, then he puts me on a chair between them, in the process accidentally giving me a wicked wedgie—which was not in the script. I stop to pull on my shorts—another of my ad libs—then Dad and I take off, hand in hand. We stop for him to pose for a photographer, and I wander away. Sound of screeching tires, a woman's scream. Cut to Bing screaming "Johnny!" My only death scene and it's offscreen.

October 24, 1954   *The Diamond Jubilee of Light* was part of an unprecedented nationwide public relations event put on by General Electric to celebrate seventy-five years of electric light. The two-hour extravaganza aired on all four networks, ABC, CBS, NBC, and DuMont, and it was produced by none other than David O. *Gone With the Wind* Selznick. The show was shot by legendary cinematographer James Wong Howe, written by men like Mark Twain and John Steinbeck, and directed by King Vidor and William Wellman. I was a guest along with President Eisenhower, Helen Hayes, Lauren Bacall, David Niven, Kim Novak, Debbie Reynolds, and many more. And all for a budget of $150,000.

These occasional roles and print work didn't disrupt our home life much. Mom got ladies from church to supervise William and Fran after school or to cook dinner.

Two years earlier, we had moved from Pomona to a huge house in Pasadena, a white elephant to everyone but Mom and Dad. They collected income from tenants on the second floor and over the garage, plus the Raymond house and the two apartments in the rear. The only problem was Dad worked in Pomona at Convair and the drive was exhausting. He asked Mom for help. She quickly found a pretty Victorian. They sold the house in Pasadena for six times what they paid and bought the Pomona house plus five additional acres nearby for cash.

Since we were now living somewhat in the country, we acquired some animals: a white Arabian horse named Golden Boy for Fran; a Nubian goat Mom named Ballerina because she kneeled and pranced; a duck that responded like a dog; a dachshund, Schultzy, named after Ann B. Davis's character on *Love that Bob*; some tumbling pigeons; and a cat for Dad. We lived in a very friendly neighborhood where everybody knew everybody. Mom and Dad helped at the school across the street. Dad and William got involved with Scouts. We had plenty of oranges from the lot next to us and Mom had a large rose garden.

I made a personal appearance at the United Artists Theater in Pomona where *Country Girl* was playing. According to the *Pomona Progress Bulletin,* I ate five cans of Camp Fire Girls peanuts that night. Just two nights earlier, Grace Kelly had won the Academy Award for her performance. In all, *The Country Girl* garnered seven nominations, including Best Director and Best Picture. Mr. Seaton also won an Oscar for Best Screenplay. Within a year, he would be president of the Motion Picture Academy.

> April 1, 1955

Six weeks later, at the Cannes Film Festival where *The Country Girl* was shown, Grace Kelly met Prince Ranier of Monaco. Within a year, she would be a princess.

RKO

Aviator and Hollywood mogul Howard Hughes sold RKO Studios to General Tire Corporation. Hughes also sold RKO's film library to television, making RKO the first studio to do so. It marked a turning point: Television was here to stay. The new owners made veteran producer William Dozier head of production. He offered me a seven-year contract and, after some discussion, my parents signed.

> Summer 1955

RKO had me in a succession of roles of growing importance. Now that I was a contract player, I no longer had to audition. At most, I was sent to meet with people. I was in at least three films and possibly two others whose titles are now lost. The first, *He Laughed Last,* was an early effort for writer/director Blake Edwards, a "crime comedy," but *The Pink Panther* it was not. I appear in only one brief scene in this Columbia Pictures release. I'm not sure if RKO loaned me out or if this was shot before I signed with them.

The film begins in the mid-1930s, with a nightclub owner played by Frankie Laine reminiscing about the good old days with an old gangster pal. The rest is a flashback to the Roaring Twenties about a young couple, played by Richard Long, later of *Big Valley* fame, and Lucy Marlow. In the last scene, the gangster asks Frankie Laine what ever happened to them. Laine leads him from his office into the club and there they are, Long and Marlow, with four children, William and me along with Dana Dillaway and Charles Herbert.

> *William:* I still have my original paycheck stub from it. We had to eat cold spaghetti while Frankie Laine sang *Danny Boy*. Mom signed me up with Lola after that. The whole thing for me was that I had other interests. It would be fun if it just happened and I didn't have to work at it, but going out on interviews was a drag. "OK, you'll be hearing from us," and you never do. It was disheartening. I'd rather be playing with my friends.

My next role was in *Toward the Unknown*, the story of a former test pilot, William Holden, who cracked under torture, and his journey to redeem himself. It was directed by the great Mervyn LeRoy and written by Beirne Lay Jr., a B-17 pilot and the coauthor of the book *12 O'Clock High*. The air sequences in the film were phenomenal. I play the son of James Garner, in his big-screen debut, and I have one scene in which Holden comes over to tell my mom, gorgeous cover girl Karen Steele, that Dad has cracked up in his plane.

I also worked in a television show that year. *Kiss for a Lieutenant* starred Kim Novak and Guy Madison. We have notes from Miss Novak and other items from our paths crossing, but no photos or script, and the show is lost, but I know one thing: I sure was racking up some good-looking parents.

Back from Eternity

March 1956

My third film released in 1956 was shot early the same year. I know because there's a photo of me celebrating my sixth birthday on the set—the first of a dozen or so birthday/photo opportu-

nities. The producer had more to celebrate than I did: At six, I could now work longer than I could when I was five.

In *Back from Eternity*, a plane crash strands an assortment of people in a remote jungle, and not just any jungle, but South American cannibal territory. It was a remake of the 1939 film *Five Came Back*, and both versions were directed by John Farrow, an elegant man of fifty-two who wore ascots and "talked funny," (he was from Australia). He married Tarzan's Jane, Maureen O'Sullivan, in 1936 and they had seven children, daughter Mia among them. Maybe that's why he worked so well with me; he had kid experience.

The cast was wonderful. The tough pilot was played by Robert Ryan, with Keith Andes as his co-pilot. Anita Ekberg played a prostitute, Rod Steiger a killer on his way to execution, Phyllis Kirk a wealthy socialite with a weakling boyfriend played by Gene Barry. Adele Mara was the brave flight attendant, Cameron Prud'homme played a college professor and the legendary Beulah Bondi played his wife. (In an uncredited role, Barbara Eden played one of the professor's students.) Fred Clark was a bounty hunter escorting Steiger, who later becomes lunch for the cannibals. Jesse White played a gangster who worked for my mob boss dad; his job was to escort me to the home of friends in South America. And I played Tommy Malone.

The men are able to repair the plane, but in its weakened state it will accommodate only five of the eight who remain. As the cannibals close in, Steiger and the old couple are left behind with a gun and only two bullets, leaving Steiger to his terrible fate.

Paramount Studios was huge compared to the RKO lot. We used two soundstages to create the jungle set and the crashed plane. Even though Dad was an aeronautical engineer, this was my first time seeing a real plane up close, inside and out. It was neat. Beulah Bondi was very kind and grandmotherly. Jesse White was wonderful, so friendly and sweet. He made friends with Mom, too. Later, when we moved to Beverly Hills, we went to his house a number of times. In late 1996, after many years, I saw him at an autograph show just a few months before he passed away. Of all his many films and the many stars he worked with, one of the ten photos on his table was the shot of us together on that plane. He embraced me warmly. "Jon, my dear old pal . . ." That's one of the great things about those autograph shows—the reunions they provide. Jesse White was the real deal from the moment I met him and I'm grateful I had the opportunity to tell him.

But first and foremost in *Back from Eternity,* I remember Anita Ekberg.

If you look up *va-va-va-voom* in the dictionary, her picture would be there. Miss Sweden of 1950 immediately caught Hollywood's eye . . . and mine. It wasn't that at five-foot-six-and-a-half Miss Ekberg was so tall; maybe it was the $39^{1}/_{2}$–22–36 that went with it that made her seem larger than life . . . at least any life I had had up until that time. And, as luck would have it, she loved me! I fondly remember how she constantly pulled me onto her lap to hug me tight. Neither Mom nor Dad were big on hugs. I relied on moments like these.

Anita Ekberg: "I wanted to cuddle him, but it's like cuddling a string of little firecrackers."

I remember the crew offering me money, "Hey, kid, we'll give you five bucks if you'll trade places with us." I didn't quite get what all the commotion was about. I just thought she was really nice . . . and really soft.

When a reporter asked me if I liked working with her, I replied, "Who wouldn't? She gave me a rocket ship and some 'Xs' and 'Os.' Xs are kisses and Os are hugs. She gave me lots of both of them and all the men on the set said they wished they were six years old."

As for the filming, I remember the simulation of the crash. Of course, they used a model for the actual crash, but they used shots of us holding on for dear life inside the cabin. I was wearing one of those yellow life preservers that inflates when you pull the cord. Boy, that was neat. I really wanted mine. I asked for it a dozen times, but I never got it.

My big scene comes when the entire cast is gathered around the campfire and I lead the group in the Lord's Prayer. We were praying to be rescued from the jungle. Although I'm certain I already knew the Lord's Prayer from church, I know I had no idea what a cannibal or a shrunken head was.

We wrapped at the end of April. In mid-May, Miss Ekberg wed actor Anthony Steele. In hindsight, I realize what a great shield I made for her on the set, keeping all the guys at bay, especially with her impending (first) marriage. But I like to think she liked me a little bit too.

Variety liked me, calling me "an appealing moppet" and calling the film "solid," "tensely suspenseful," and "hotly romantic." The tag line for the advertising became "O-o-o-h that Ekberg!" My sentiments exactly.

All Mine to Give

Later that summer, RKO cast me in a real tear-jerker, *All Mine to Give,* sometimes called *The Day They Gave Babies Away,* based on a true story of a young Scottish couple played by the vivacious Glynis Johns and Cameron Mitchell, a lovable bear of a man. They immigrate to Wisconsin in 1856, build a life, have six children—that's where I come in— but both tragically die young. The oldest son finds homes for all his siblings on Christmas Day. I played the oldest son as a toddler. The film was vetoed by Howard Hughes, but the senti-mental story appealed to RKO's new owners, General Tire, and every year at Christmastime, it plays somewhere in the world, a cult classic.

Back from Eternity and *Toward the Unknown* opened, but we had no time to pay attention. RKO cast me in another film right away, my biggest role yet. Looking back, I realize that there were no family outings to see me in the movies, nothing to bond us

September 1956

together over them. Instead, they represented temporary interruptions in family life, a life they'd established before me but one I barely remembered. And now I was cast in the starring role in an incredibly ambitious project that would take Mom and me halfway around the world for more than three months.

Fran: The movie that made a big difference was *Escapade in Japan,* because that was the first time my mother went *away,* away. She went to Japan.

Escapade in Japan

As one of the first American films to shoot almost entirely in Japan and the first since the end of World War II, *Escapade in Japan* was a huge deal. I played Tony Saunders, flying from the Philippines to Japan to meet my parents, played by Teresa Wright and good old Cam Mitchell. In the story, the plane ditches in the ocean and I am rescued by a fisherman whose son, Hiko, played by Roger Nakagawa, speaks "American." He and I mistakenly believe that I am in trouble, and we lead police on a travelogue chase through Japan that includes ancient temples, geisha girls, and a burlesque house before Roger and I are returned to our frantic parents.

Winston Miller (writer): Before anything could be done, all kinds of people and officials had to be interviewed and asked for permission and cooperation. . . . Boys had to be found who were just right, who could carry the story. Then there's all the big exteriors from the Inland Sea to Kyoto festivals, the plane crash and rescue, the language problem, finding a suitable fishing village.

Dad: "What's going to happen to me and the other two children and the animals?" I asked my wife. She told me not to worry. She'd already arranged for an old lady to take care of things. What a gal!

Mom: I made sure she was old. I wasn't going to have some pretty young thing around my husband all that time.

Fran: Oh, gosh, Mrs. Olsen. Mrs. Olsen. She was rough. Boy, that was terrible. I've tried to block it out.

William: One thing that was easier on me was, being a male, I had a little better rapport with my dad. Fran, with Mom being gone a lot, didn't have the mother-daughter relationship.

Of course, I didn't have any idea of the turmoil our impending departure was causing at home or even that Fran and William were upset. I was isolated from them both by work and by our age difference. Plus it was September, and they were entering the fifth and seventh grades. I would have started first grade that year, but learning to read would have to wait. Mom and I had a million things to attend to: passports, over a dozen inoculations, press photos, wardrobe fittings. My passport was easy enough, but Mom had a problem.

Mom: They asked if we had passports because they were sending us to Japan with Cameron Mitchell and Teresa Wright. I had to get my passport where I was born. I wasn't born in a hospital; my mamma had a lady down the road, seventeen miles from town. In those days, they ran a buggy to come out there.

Mom had to go to Texas with Grandma to straighten it out. Grandma and a cousin swore to the birthdate and year, August 30, 1915. And so the mystery of my mother's age was forever sealed. While she was at it, she upgraded her birthplace from Wolfe City to Greeneville. Fran gets a big kick out of that.

Next we had to get something like fifteen different inoculations. Every day for a week we went to the studio infirmary for injections of malaria, cholera, yellow fever, typhus, you name it! One day it was right cheek, left cheek; next day, right arm, left arm. Talk about a pin cushion! We had a drastic reaction to one with both our temperatures soaring to 104 within minutes of the shot. We felt like we'd been hit by a train.

The flight to Tokyo took almost twenty-four hours. We left Los Angeles on a TWA Constellation. All futuristic streamline curves, the Constellation was the biggest, the best, the most modern in the days before jets. The entire plane was filled with our crew and cast—close to a hundred people. And RKO brought more than forty tons of cameras and equipment.

September 27, 1956

We landed in Hawaii first, Honolulu, with me glued to the window. I had never seen anything so lush and green and so isolated. During the long layover, we left the plane. A pretty lady gave us leis, and we crossed the tarmac into the terminal to a special cordoned off area. We passed an enormous World War II memorial with big antiaircraft guns and crashed Japanese Zeros right in the middle of the airport. I've still never seen anything like it. Eventually, we flew on to Wake, then Guam,

and finally we landed in Tokyo on September 28. The shoot would begin in four days in Kyoto.

Turning Japanese

From the moment I walked outside, everything was overwhelmingly different except one thing—the people were little just like Mom and me.

But the clothes, the hair. All the women wore kimonos and all the children of school age wore uniforms. We looked pretty different ourselves. Whenever Mom and I walked outside, groups of people, old and young, swarmed around us. Mom was a striking blonde. People just reached out and touched our hair. We adjusted and went places on our own, unafraid. That was Mom, so adaptable.

The crowded streets provided lots of hustle and bustle: street vendors, bicycles, cars, and three-wheeled trucks. I loved how the tiny vehicles maneuvered easily through the alleyways and side streets.

Hotel rooms don't stand out in my mind as a rule, but I remember the one in Tokyo because the bathtub was missing. When Mom called the front desk to inquire, she was told that everyone uses the communal baths . . . so that's what we did.

I don't think I'll ever forget the experience. The indoor bath looked like a large swimming pool, but was only three feet deep and surrounded by giant aquariums filled with tropical fish. A nice Japanese lady guided me to a low, wooden stool just perfect for me and took my robe. I sat while she poured warm water over my shoulders and bathed me with sponges. Mom, too. It was great— at least I thought so. Then we got in the tub and soaked. I had seen my mother naked, but there were women Grandma's age and men, too. Boy, was that an eye-opener for a six-year-old kid. After that, we used someone's private bathroom until we could change rooms. Something else I won't forget: Mom wanted to experience a Japanese massage and called for a masseuse. Two escorts accompanied the masseuse; she was blind for complete privacy. I really have to give Mom credit. She was a true adventurer and passed that "when in Rome . . ." ethic on to me.

Two days after we arrived, there was a luncheon for all of us to meet the local dignitaries and VIPs. I was always at home in a room full of adults, and the language barrier wasn't much of a problem. I asked for the shrimp. What they brought me was a whole prawn with feelers sticking up and a pair of eyes looking back at me. I couldn't imagine how I was supposed to eat it. By the time we left Japan, I loved sushi. Chopsticks were easy; I mastered them quickly—maybe Roger showed me.

Cameron Mitchell was playing my dad again. This time, my mom was Teresa Wright, the only actor nominated for an Oscar for her first three film roles, two of them in the same year. That's pretty impressive. She and Cam both were bright, warm, sensitive, not showy onscreen or off, lovely people to be with.

Roger Nakagawa: I came to be in *Escapade* through pure luck. The producer and director came to Japan and went to all these different schools including mine, ASIJ—American School in Japan—asking for the names of any eight-year-olds who could speak Japanese and English fluently. I gather my name was on the list. Three hundred boys auditioned for this part. I got a call at home: "Hello, do you want to be in a movie?" That night there was a discussion. My parents didn't want me to be in a movie because in those days to be in the entertainment world was not appropriate. But they discussed it again and the conclusion was they would give it one shot.

In the summer, on the way to a family vacation, we stopped at one of the studios and I had about a twenty-minute screen test. We didn't hear another word until September or October. We got a call and they said, "Yes, you got the job." It was no big deal to me, just something different that came along."

Producer-director Arthur Lubin was big and blubbery and very engaging. His forte was light comedy. He'd directed an Abbott & Costello film and six of the *Francis the Talking Mule* series. The first week, we made our way to Saigasaki, a quiet fishing village a hundred miles from Kyoto on the Pacific coast. So much of Tokyo had been bombed and rebuilt, it appeared all brand new. Outside of the city was distinctly different, dark and ancient. The

clothing changed to more of a working man's garb, dirt roads, no plumbing. One day as we drove from our hotel to the location, we passed a man with a long bamboo pole across his back and a bucket hanging from each end . . . the "honey bucket," I was told. Apparently these homes left their . . . buckets out for this man to empty and carry away. One hundred miles in Japan was definitely worlds away.

People lined the streets to watch the 21-vehicle convoy carrying the 121-man crew and tons of equipment, including 2 nine-ton generators that had to be parked an eighth of a mile outside of town because they were too large to get through the streets. A 50-man crew worked all day repairing a road washout to get them across.

Two identical Japanese fishing boats were held in readiness, a speedboat buzzed between the ships and shore, a special radio hookup was opened for communication with the camera boat. For part of the journey on land, we used a special train. On moving night, they loaded it up like a circus and transported the entire company and the bulk of the equipment to the next location overnight.

International News Service: Japanese tradition dating back to the 13th century was shattered Wednesday by a Hollywood motion picture company intent on showing the real Japan to the world. RKO moved into one of ancient Kyoto's most spectacular temples which had not seen a ray of light since it was constructed in 1266 A.D. Light of any

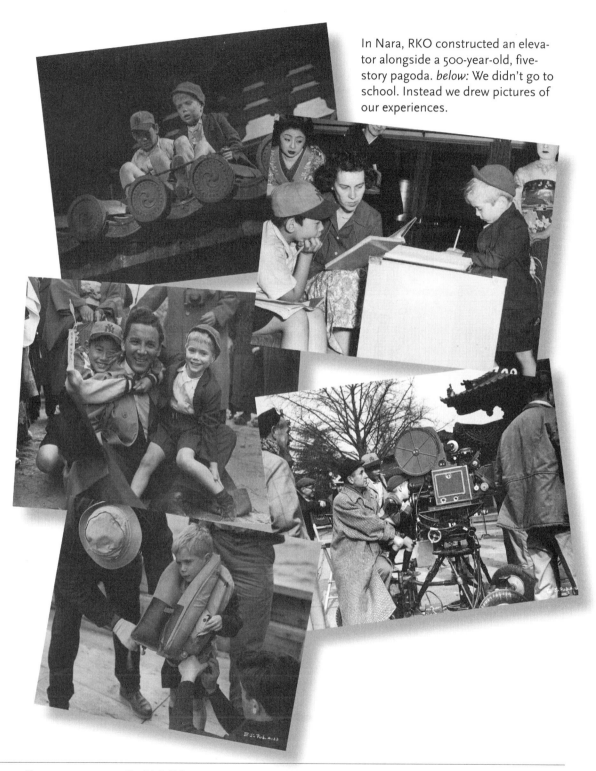

In Nara, RKO constructed an elevator alongside a 500-year-old, five-story pagoda. *below:* We didn't go to school. Instead we drew pictures of our experiences.

kind, with the exception of small candles, had never been permitted in the "sanjusangendo" or temple of 1001 gods. Tourist-minded Kyoto Mayor Gizo Takayama placed a welcome mat in front of the 396-foot temple. Says Lubin: I don't think there's a thing in Japan left out of this picture.

Miss Wright loved her first trip to Japan and spent every free moment roaming the countryside with her two cameras. Cam, a topnotch athlete, was made honorary captain of the swank Kyoto Racquet Club tennis team. He also learned the painful art of Kendo, where two opponents go at each other with heavy bamboo poles. The makeup man worked overtime covering all the bruises on Cam's face after his first session. I'm not sure Mr. Lubin allowed a second session.

In *Back from Eternity*, I had gotten to wear one of those yellow life vests that inflate around you when you pull the ripcord. I wanted to keep mine at the time, but couldn't get it. Now I really had my eye on the one I wore in *Escapade*. I asked Mr. Lubin if I could have my life preserver when we wrapped. He leaned down, all his blubbery rolls shifting, and promised me the vest. I never got it, but weeks later, back in Los Angeles, we realized he had bigger things on his mind.

Back in the USA

Mom shot home movies of everything and sent a roll home to Dad every week. Transatlantic calls were very expensive and not spontaneous. Mom and I missed Halloween, William's twelfth birthday, and Dad's forty-first, and Thanksgiving. The separation was especially hard for Fran.

Fran: I got my period. Mom had never told me about menstruation, so I had no idea what was happening to me. I thought I had cancer. I was so scared. I couldn't go to my dad or my brother. On the third day, I fainted in class and was sent to the school nurse. I broke down crying and told her I had cancer and was dying. "Oh, honey," she said, "you're not dying." I was so relieved, I mean, it was huge. . . . It was the biggest crisis in my life and I felt completely alone.

William: Before this job, we were all one family.

In Japan I was going all day, six days a week. At the end of each day, I was like a zombie, but I'd have to work on lines. I didn't know a leading role from a supporting one. I just learned what they gave me every night and went day to day. It was all a blur: one day, shivering on the waterfront in our underwear, the next running through an ancient temple. I got pretty sick. Mr. Lubin sent me to the hospital. Mom undressed me in a private room and a short time later, a lady came in. She introduced herself in English, asked me a few questions, and began to examine me.

"Where's the doctor?" Mom asked.

"I am the doctor," the lady replied.

I think Mom and I both did a double take. A woman doctor? Neither one of us had ever heard of that before. If Mom was concerned, she didn't say anything. When in Rome. . . .

A gorgeous little Japanese girl named Hideko Koshikawa appeared in a few key scenes in the film and won everyone's

Hideko and I went to an amusement park on top of a department store!

heart. I fell head over heels in love with her. She was nearly a head taller than me, and I reached up to hug and kiss her every chance I got.

Back at Universal Studios, a struggling contract player named Clint Eastwood got one line in *Escapade* as a pilot named Dumbo.

Mom and I saw *Back from Eternity* in Tokyo. In a world that was far from any "global" concept, in a country with which we were recently at war, how surreal that must have been for Mom to be in a movie theater in Japan watching her son on-screen.

Roger: I had fun making the movie. I never intended to make another; that was the deal my parents made. Years later, Dad told me I had several more offers, but they never told me anything about them.

That doesn't surprise me; Roger was a natural.

I said Arthur Lubin had a lot of other things on his mind besides my life vest, and I meant it. RKO was collapsing around our heads. Deep in the red after eighteen months, General Tire shut down production at RKO. One problem: we were still in Japan. Mr. Lubin frantically worked to get us home before the ax fell. Over 1,200 residents turned out at the Kyoto railway station to say goodbye when we left. The studio literally dissolved while we were in the air.

Mom: When we got off the airplane [in Los Angeles], a man met us and said "You don't have a contract any more. All contracts with RKO are gone." It was all over just like that. This wasn't a big deal to me. It had only been an occasional thing, not like we worked there five days a week. I told B.A., "I guess I'll stay home from now on." He said, "That suits me fine."

December 19, 1956

Getting Lassie

Mom must have been humoring Dad. First of all, she was not a woman to stay home. Besides, I was working more frequently, not only in movies, but in television and print work. In fact, Dad passed a billboard for Weber Bread with my face on it every day on his way to work. I had been signed by a studio. Clearly I was hurtling toward something.

My fate would be determined over lunch between girlfriends. Ann Rutherford played Scarlett O'Hara's sister, Careen, in *Gone With the Wind* about the same time she played Polly Benedict in twelve *Andy Hardy* movies with Mickey Rooney and Judy Garland. She retired in 1950 and three years later became Mrs. William Dozier.

Ann Dozier and Bonita Granville went way back. Bonita grew up on the stage, was nominated for an Oscar at age eleven as the evil child in *These Three,* and charmed fans as the star of the *Nancy Drew* series. In 1946, Jack Wrather produced two of her films. They married in 1947.

Jack Wrather, a Texas oil millionaire with visionary genius, recognized the potential of the new television industry early on. He already owned *The Lone Ranger.* Now he wanted something for Bonita to get involved in. He called Robert Maxwell.

Robert "Bob" Maxwell was nervous. The producer of *Lassie* sensed his hit show was in trouble. After three years and twenty-nine shows a season, he felt all the original plots had been used, that there was no new territory for a boy and his dog. Worse, he had a restless cast. TV audiences had fallen in love with the Miller family: Gramps, Ellen Miller, and her son Jeff put the show in the top ten all three years, but things were beginning to unravel. Tommy Rettig played Jeff Miller. Though small in stature, fifteen-year-old Tommy was no longer a boy, and he was fed up with the restrictions.

Tommy: I couldn't go in the main door of a theater to watch a movie. I couldn't go to public school. I always had people asking me where my collie was. I couldn't escape being Jeff Miller.

Jan Clayton, who played Ellen Miller, wanted to move on, too. She wanted to go home, back to her Broadway roots and her theater pals. Only George Cleveland wanted to stay . . . and Lassie, of course. So, quietly, Maxwell had put the show on the market.

The Wrathers felt *Lassie* had not been marketed appropriately. They offered Maxwell $3.5 million, and retained Lassie's owner and trainer,

Rudd Weatherwax for his $100,000 a year and Lassie at $1500 a week. Maxwell agreed to stay on for the first year and Bonita came on as associate producer. It was a done deal; *Lassie* had new owners. Then the three adults began their search for Tommy Rettig's replacement, a boy the show's 25 million fans would embrace.

That brings us back to that lunch. Bonita lamented her unsuccessful search for a new boy to her pal Ann. She said she wanted to start with a much younger child, but after meeting two hundred little boys, she felt utterly discouraged. The problem had reached crisis proportion. Bonita described the ideal boy for the role of Timmy. As the legend goes, Ann Dozier responded with something like, "No wonder you can't find him. We have the boy you're looking for in Japan." Off they went to RKO to view the rushes, the footage sent back daily for developing.

Bonita watched, and the more she saw, the more she was convinced Ann was right. She returned to her husband triumphant. She had found the perfect boy. I was under contract to RKO, but of course that would soon no longer pose a problem.

RKO's collapse and eventual sale to television producers Desi Arnaz and Lucille Ball was not an isolated incident in Hollywood. The industry was changing, even if change was slow. Warner Bros had jumped into television as early as 1950, but by 1956 MGM was still on the fence. Most of Hollywood still felt TV was "déclassé."

Bill Beaudine Jr.: Television was looked down upon in those days. If you tried to move up to doing features, they'd say, "But all you've done is television." It was the bottom of the barrel.

Fran: We didn't even have a television. We used to go to a neighbor's house to watch *The Ed Sullivan Show*.

Mom and I returned from Japan with stories to tell and gifts for everyone. After the Christmas holidays, things at home returned to normal. The family breathed a collective sigh of relief, and, for the most part, all was forgiven. This was the turning point, a crack in the surface that could have healed.

Instead, my parents were presented with not one but two offers for me from the new land of television.

Mom: We're home thinking his career is over when we get a call inviting us to Beverly Hills to talk to Bonita. She told me she'd like to have my son for a series on television. I said, "I don't know about such things; you'll have to talk to my husband." This was on a Saturday and they asked if I could bring him tomorrow. But B.A. was in Texas on business for Convair. They said, "Get him on the phone, tell him to fly in tomorrow morning for a meeting and we'll fly him back that afternoon. We'll pick up the costs."

Dad: When she told me, I said, "Is this legitimate? What kind of people are these?" . . . but I thought it was a nice way to come home for the weekend!

Mom: We were young in those days.

Dad: I flew home Saturday night. Meanwhile, Cecile had gotten another offer for Jon to play on the new *Tarzan* TV program. As soon as I got home, she hit me with both of these propositions and asked, "What are we going to do?" Meanwhile, we were to be in Beverly Hills by noon, so we had to get this rationalized. We analyzed it a bit.

I don't know where Lola Moore was during all this or why she wasn't at any of these meetings. Mom had never even seen *Lassie* when this offer came, except in the movies, which she loved; so she told Dad the TV show must be good, too. And that Bonita Granville was a quality actress. "I'm told [Jack Wrather] owns the Disneyland Hotel. This is good," she told Dad.

Mom: Sol Lesser was going to do *Tarzan* with Gordon Scott. The little boy in *Tarzan* doesn't wear much clothes, and I'd had so much trouble with William's asthma. I thought that could be unhealthy, but we couldn't make up our minds because there was a lot of money behind Sol Lesser too. We didn't know what to do. Sol said to take his lawyer to the meeting. I asked if the Wrathers would mind. Sol said, "They're in business; they know."

That was putting it mildly. Jack Wrather had the Midas touch. In 1955, Walt Disney negotiated with him to build and operate a hotel for Disneyland. Wrather included in his contract the use of the name Disneyland Hotel on any hotel in the state until 2054. The following year he would purchase *Sgt. Preston of the Yukon* and Muzak. He developed hotels in Las Vegas and Palm Springs and eventually owned the Balboa Bay Club and Chris Craft Boats. He founded L.A.'s PBS station, KCET. He spent $25 million restoring the *Queen Mary* and saved the *Spruce Goose* airplane from demolition in 1981 as a favor to his friend Howard Hughes. Later, as a close friend of Ronald Reagan, he was one of the first people to encourage Reagan to run for public office in California and served as a member of Reagan's "Kitchen Cabinet." Jack and Bonita Granville Wrather saw the future of television in entertainment and they saw me as part of it. They were in business, all right.

Mom: They had a big building in Beverly Hills. Of course, they had a whole batch of lawyers there, but the main one was Monty Livingston. In his office, I'd never seen so many books in my life . . . red books . . . expensive books, gorgeous. But I get to walk in with my husband and a lawyer that I didn't have to pay. I kept my mouth shut and they did the talking. Just before they signed, I said, "Everybody tells me that in a series, you ask for foreign rights." They said, "Oh, we won't be translating the show in other lands. They didn't do it with Tommy Rettig and we won't either." They wanted us to sign in . . . what was that word? *Perpetuity.* So, we signed. The first year, they sold it to twenty-five foreign countries, right away, quick. The Wrathers were wonderful, wonderful people. They were so good to us, and I'm sure she felt badly about this afterward because she was such a good mother and a good friend. But we never discussed it. I never mentioned it ever.

Bonita Granville Wrather.

Dad: Cecile also asked if Jon could make a movie during hiatus; so, they put that in the contract, but the budget of the movie must be at least a quarter million dollars. We were overwhelmed, and then I had to get on a plane and go back to Texas. It was a business meeting and it was logical, so we just did it. Jon was obligated for seven years, but the Wrathers could terminate the contract at the end of each year.

Mom: I didn't get shook up about it. I thought it was a nice little show and I loved that dog, but it was nothing special to me. We didn't know the magnitude of it.

The ultimate decision, actually, lay with the dog. The first time I saw Lassie, I ran and threw my arms around him. Rudd Weatherwax watched carefully. "Go ahead, kiss his face, Lassie. Give him a kiss." Lassie obeyed and I laughed, delighted. Rudd laughed too. For me, it was love at first sight for Lassie . . . and for Rudd. I spent a long weekend at the ranch with them. Afterward, Lassie gave the bark of approval, two paws up for the new kid.

Part Two: The Lassie Years

"Every boy needs a dog and every dog needs a boy."

—RUDD WEATHERWAX

At the Brown Derby with TV executives.

William: You can't make Hollywood hire you. You are at its beck and call. A lot of it had to do with Jon being in the right place at the right time. *Escapade in Japan* was what got him the *Lassie* series. My mom didn't have control over that. They just happened to be in the right place at the right time.

It sure was the right place that summer of 1957. Seemed like everything was happening at once. Not only did the Wrathers set up an endless stream of interviews and photo shoots for publications like *TV Guide* and *Life* magazine, I also had to pose for studio publicity shots with Lassie, dozens of them.

Unidentified newspaper clipping: Between lunges, swoops, slides and dives which punctuate his conversation, Jon will tell you he likes rice and fish, eating with chop sticks, fishing, Abbott & Costello movies, Superman, the Lone Ranger ("We saw Superman in Japan and when he's there, he talks Japanese!"). He also likes candy, Christmas, climbing trees and a little girl in Japan. When asked who his parents are, he was likely to answer, "Jane Wyman and Bing Crosby."

Bonita took a personal interest in me. After all, she not only brought me to the show, she named me. My character's name was Timmy, which was her own mother's nickname, although she spelled it "Timmie."

Lloyd Nelson: Bonita and Jack had close hands-on to the production. Jack didn't have much to do with it. It was Bonita's baby, and I think he bought it for her because she wanted to stay in the business. She was good at it, and they threw her a bone every once in a while and let her work as an actress. That went on fine.

Mom: A big Texas oilman moved to Hollywood. He married a beautiful starlet named Bonita Granville. He didn't want her to be working all the time so he said, "Pick a TV series that you like. No matter what it is, I'll buy it for you." She liked *Lassie.*

The Original Cast

Not one of us realized it was literally the first day of the rest of my life, not Bonita or Mom and most certainly not me. June 1957 This was just another job. All I knew for sure was how long it took to get there and back in those days before freeways. Pomona was more than an hour from KTTV Studios in Hollywood. We had to be on the road by 6 a.m. Fran and William were still sleeping. I was too most days; I'd sleep in the car. I had breakfast at the studio.

Stage 1 looked like any other soundstage I'd been on. I'd seen the show and recognized the barnyard set and the Miller house. Tommy Rettig and Jan Clayton were warm and welcoming. Now I realize they wanted out and I was their ticket . . . all but Gramps, George Cleveland. He wanted to stay, but sadly, he would be the first to go.

Tommy Rettig had been working since he was two years old. His mom, Ricki, was one of those awful stage mothers you hear about—aggressive, manipulative, controlling. Rudd's son, Bob, was the same age as Tommy. He and Tommy were great friends and often spent weekends at the ranch together.

> *Bob Weatherwax:* He had no life. Tommy said the only life he ever had was when he came to my house. His mother couldn't refuse because my father had Lassie. I'd take Tommy out and do real guy things with him, things he was never allowed to do. He always thanked me for that.

Back when Bob Maxwell and Rudd were searching for the perfect boy to play Jeff Miller, they got a tip from Frank, Rudd's brother, a dog trainer who worked with Tommy on the Dr. Seuss film *The 5000 Fingers of Dr. T.* He reported that Tommy was a good actor and great with animals—the magic phrase for Rudd. Tommy's costarring role in *River of No Return* with Marilyn Monroe and Robert Mitchum got Maxwell's attention. Eventually, the choice came down to two boys, Tommy and Lee Aaker, one of the hardest working kids in showbiz in both film and TV. Each boy spent several days with Rudd and Lassie, just as I would.

Lee Aaker later landed the role of Rusty on *Rin Tin Tin.*

Lee Aaker: I went out to Rudd's ranch with Tommy. I'd met him on a movie called *The Raid* with Van Heflin and Anne Bancroft. He was a year or so older and we got along fine. I'd just come back from Mexico where I'd done *Hondo* with John Wayne and I was pretty beat up, down to skin and bones—not taking anything away from Tommy, because he earned it. He was great in all the stuff he did. They wanted to compare us working with the dog, the chemistry or whatever, at least that was my perception . . . and Tommy was picked to play Jeff Miller on *Lassie.*

But now, after three years and 102 episodes, recognized wherever he went as the "Lassie boy," Tommy was more than ready to let it go. He was still small—five-foot-four—but Tommy was too old for the role. Both he and the producers were in agreement about that.

Tommy: I had been working in show business almost without a break since I was five years old. I wanted to go to a regular school. I was beginning to discover cars and girls.

Darlene Rettig Insley: He felt like he couldn't pick up girls as the boy on *Lassie.* He wanted to go from there to being a teen idol. He didn't want to be the kid on *Lassie.* He was starting to be type-cast.

Lloyd: Tommy was a nice boy, definitely on the way to teenage rebellion, but a nice kid. Donald, who played Porky, was a little obstinate and the two of them together could do some damage as far as production goes. For instance, they had a scene where they had to ride bikes, an exterior somewhere and they rode 'em out of the scene. "Cut! OK, come on back." Well, they walked back and left the bikes. "The bikes are the property department. Let them get them." Little things like that where we wanted to give them a paddling, but they were too old.

Too old—that was the significant phrase.

Jan Clayton played the perfect post-war 1950s mom: strong and independent, while soft and caring and 100 percent reliable. She and Tommy shared a true bond of love and would for the rest of their lives. Warm and affectionate, with a wonderful smile, tiny like my

real mom, she loved to hug and I loved to get hugs. Best known for her work on Broadway, in 1945 Jan received rave reviews in Rodgers and Hammerstein's *Carousel* opposite John Raitt. She had recently divorced her second husband, Robert Lerner, brother of Broadway composer Alan Jay Lerner, but she had suffered a much more devastating loss the year before. Her teenage daughter, Sondra, was killed in a one-car accident returning from a baby-sitting job. Since then, she'd wanted to return to her roots in the theater. The crew adored her. She was generous and professional six days a week, nine months a year, but her heart was no longer in it. She began quietly drinking at home, the start of a ten-year battle with the bottle which she would win. She spoke inspirationally about it many times in later years.

Jan: "My drinking got worse after my daughter died. Before that I was a social drinker."

I adopted George Cleveland instantly. He was exactly what you saw on TV—the wise and affectionate patriarch. A Hollywood veteran, he'd been in almost 150 movies in his fifty-year career. He loved Jan and Tommy, and that clearly translated onto the small screen.

George Cleveland: I treat Jeff exactly as I treat my own grandchildren—like my grandfather treated me. Discipline is a means of helping children to grow up. . . . The spoiled child is going to find rough sledding when he grows up.

After a few shows, Bob Maxwell realized Jeff needed a best friend with two feet. Fifteen hundred kids tried out for the role of Porky Brockway before Donald Keeler was cast. His real name was Joey D. Vieira, but 1950s television removed any trace of ethnicity. He took the last name of his aunt, Broadway and Hollywood star Ruby Keeler. Donald was a great addition to the cast and a lifelong friend to Tommy. The show really was what you saw: a happy family.

Donald and I pose on set.

Tommy: I think we were all so comfortable because the characters we were playing were very much like we really were. . . . Jan Clayton was a second mom to me. . . . George Cleveland was very much like Gramps. Joey and I were a great deal like Porky and Jeff. It was a warm, comfortable place.

Life on the Farm

After three years, by the time I got there, the set worked like a well-oiled machine. I slipped right into their routine. We filmed twelve to fifteen pages of script a day, six days a week—five for me. An average day was ten hours: one hour of transportation, an hour for lunch, an hour of recreation broken up throughout the day, four hours of work, and three hours of schooling also broken up—unless it was summer, then no school at all.

I was nine years Tommy's junior, not old enough to "hang out" with him.

It took three and half days to film each half-hour episode. We might be shooting scenes from different scripts on the same day, especially if we were on location. If we'd traveled to Franklin Canyon Reservoir or all the way out to Vasquez Rocks, the producer had to get his money's worth. It made sense in dollars, but was pretty confusing for me in the beginning. Sometimes I had no idea why I said something until I saw it weeks or months later on TV: "Oh! That's why we did that!" I just memorized what they told me to for that day. Mom read me the script every night and I learned the whole thing, my lines and everybody else's.

I kept that schedule five days a week, nine months out of the year to produce about thirty-seven or thirty-nine half-hour episodes. And on weekends and during the three-month hiatus, I had appearances, parades, children's hospitals, and more all over the United States. Lassie and I hit the major cities together.

The law stated that every minor needed a guardian on the set. Mom got a weekly paycheck as mine, but not every mom was suited for it.

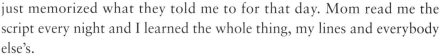

Stan Livingston: My mom was there the first year, but three, four months into it, she couldn't take it . . . plus she needed to be home for Barry. They hired Tommy Cole's mom for me. [Tommy was an original Mousketeer.] She was great. The whole time I was on *My Three Sons*, she was my guardian. She was somebody really objective who could see what was happening on the set as opposed to a parent, especially my mom. If something went wrong, my mom was a terror. She had that same assessment of herself—that she might say or do the wrong thing—so it was better she wasn't there.

Talk to the Animals

Tommy found the father figure he needed so desperately in Rudd. I adored Rudd, too. I never knew my grandfathers, and he fit the bill perfectly. I know he liked me, too, but where Lassie was concerned, he set the tone right away. He made a deal with me. If I didn't bug Lassie, didn't sit on him or pull his tail, he'd give me a Lassie puppy. He made a game of it. I earned points for good deeds on the set and when I had 100 points, I'd get the puppy. It was all I thought about. I'd climb to 38 points, then slip back 2 points by accidentally stepping on Lassie's foot.

Bob Weatherwax: Dad wanted to keep Lassie looking natural, which meant not looking at the trainer. He didn't want Lassie doing "tricks" or to appear "cute," nothing corny or unbelievable. Lassie would actually portray that character and change moods. If it was a sad scene, Lassie should come in slow, head down. He should feel that mood. That's all done with voice inflection.

The verbal commands were the hardest to get used to. We had to learn to say our lines with pauses long enough for Rudd or his assistant Sam Williamson to speak a command, which the editors would later cut out. If Lassie needed to look up, they were up on ladders behind the cast to deliver the command.

Note Rudd (with Sam behind) above the director.

Bob Weatherwax: Dad was really good at that. He could figure out where to whip that bark in right between the dialogue. "What do you think, Lassie?" and he would bark, or "Let's go here" and Lassie would bark and then they would go. His voice would come in right between the lines. So they'd just edit it out.

Frank Inn was around, too, with every other kind of animal we used. He'd been working with Rudd since the MGM days, and on *Lassie* before I got there. His career would span more than fifty years

and his animal stars included Cleo, a bassett hound who costarred with Jackie Cooper in TV's *The People's Choice*, Tramp from *My Three Sons*, Arnold Ziffel, the pig from *Green Acres*, many of Elly May's exotic "critters" on *The Beverly Hillbillies* and film star Benji.

Frank Inn: I furnished all the other animals on *Lassie*: the wolves, the coyotes, the foxes, the birds of prey, I think I worked a bear, too—whatever they used. I had about every kind of animal there was. Rudd always called me because I was his friend. I was holding his hand the day he died. The things I've learned working with Rudd and Lassie, Tommy and Jon gave me the knowledge that made me able to carry on. It was such a beautiful thing that it's hard to describe.

Passing the Torch

The original plan was to introduce me and complete the transition in three consecutive episodes. In the first, I play an orphan running away from my aged auntie and uncle so as not to be a burden. I hide in the Miller barn where—big surprise—Lassie finds me and alerts the family. By the end of the first show, Ellen has convinced my worried guardians to let me spend the summer with the Millers and Lassie.

Three shows came and went . . . and three more . . . and six more and no transition. The producers were happy. Sponsor Campbell Soup was happy. Everyone was hoping Jan and Tommy would change their minds and stay. Ellen Miller could adopt Timmy . . . until they discovered a single woman could not adopt a child in any state in the country in 1957. They suggested a love interest, marriage, and then adoption, but Jan wouldn't agree to any lengthy scenario. Maybe the characters could leave individually: Gramps breaks a hip and has to convalesce in a hospital. Jeff leaves for school. Ellen can't run the farm alone and must sell. While the producers went back and forth about it, tragedy struck and made the decision for them. Seventy-one-year-old George Cleveland suffered a heart attack while playing golf and died July 15, 1957.

We hadn't noticed the signs, but it had been obvious something wasn't right. George and I had a great relationship. A week earlier, I'd played a practical joke on him. In our scene, he was supposed to put sugar in his ice tea, but I'd secretly dumped a glob of ice cream in the sugar bowl. When he discovered my prank, he got so angry, he walked off the set for fifteen minutes. Mom wanted to spank me good, but Rudd talked her out of it. He did take away six points from my total, though, the most I ever lost at one time. It just wasn't like George not to laugh. Now I realize he was ill. Production shut down completely while the producers decided what to do.

Change Is Gonna Come

I didn't get time off. The Wrathers used the break to intro-duce me to the New York press at a big ice cream party for

> July 1957

them and their kids at the Plaza Hotel. (They'd do the same thing for the Hollywood press at the Beverly Hills Hotel in August.) That same week, I was interviewed by more than fifty publications, was on two radio programs, visited the UN for UNICEF, saw the Smithsonian and the Statue of Liberty, and made a speech about Japan to the student body of a Brooklyn junior high school. I was also the guest of honor at a brunch at the Hampshire House for fourteen clothing manufacturers. As a result, a complete line of boy's wear—shirts, pants, sweaters, socks, sneakers, ties, and more—would soon be in stores bearing the tag: Jon Provost, Timmy of the *Lassie* Series. Of course, this was long before the days when performers got a piece of the action. My parents knew nothing of that. I wasn't complaining. My allowance had increased from 25 cents to 60 cents.

Mom took advantage of this time to make some decisions of her own. The forty-mile drive each way was taking a toll. It was dark when I left for work and dark when I got home. I'd barely seen the sun in weeks and the ten-hour days were wearing Mom out. After some discussion, she and Dad decided we should rent an apartment near the studio.

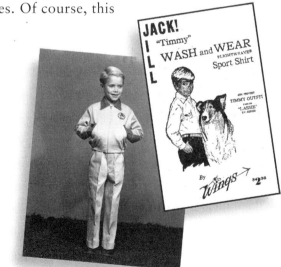

Mom and I would stay there Monday through Thursday and come home for weekends. Fran and William, in Arkansas for the summer, would be told when they came home. Meanwhile, Mom set about finding a lady to take care of them after school and to cook supper for the family.

Mom: I hired a senior citizen. I didn't want a young nanny around B.A. I was smart that way because Jon and I were away a lot. But I always had nice women from church or the neighborhood who were usually thrilled to death to make a little extra money.

William: We had different people . . . when we lived in Pasadena, it was some German couple who lived in an apartment over the garage. . . . It seemed like there were a lot of different people coming and going over the years who came in and took care of us.

Mom quickly found an apartment within blocks of the studio, and the Wrathers and CBS took care of everything. When production started up again in September, we left Dad, William, and Fran and went to Hollywood.

August 29, 1957

Our group was in a good mood. The movie was well received. We drove to the party on the Sunset Strip near Crescent Heights in—what else?—a Japanese restaurant. The Imperial Gardens was throwing a "sukiyaki shindig" on Bill Dozier's tab. Los Angeles columnist Kendis

Special advance screening of *Escapade* and press party.

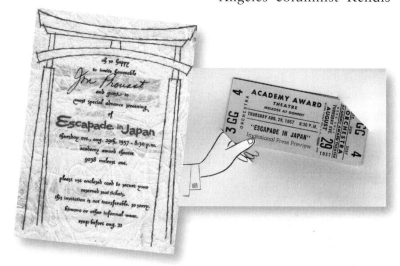

Rochlen, known as the "Brenda Starr" of the *Los Angeles Mirror* newsroom, reported the event this way:

> [The party] set at least one record for Hollywood—all the women were dressed alike. The men too, for that matter. All the guests donned identical Happi coats as they entered. It was interesting to watch one curvaceous starlet trying to arrange the wrap-around Japanese jacket so that it wouldn't cover up too much of her cleavage.
>
> But the person who got the most attention from the photogs was an excited young actor all of 7 years old. Jon Provost, the youngster who turns in such a great performance in the picture, turned in an amusing performance at the party. While his elders were occupied with such thirst quenchers as Sake Martinis and Nippon beer, Jon was occupied with his own project. He quietly had himself a ball mixing up the shoes of the guests who had elected to follow Japanese etiquette and remove their footwear at the entrance to the dining area.
>
> This accomplished, Jon then proceeded to practice a familiar Hollywood rite—he table-hopped. Or rather, he table-skipped. This kid's no fool. He didn't miss the Bill Doziers, director Arthur Lubin or UI bigwig Dave Lipton.
>
> I asked the 7-year-old how he liked all the fuss that was made over him as he was leaving the Academy Theater after the preview. Jon shrugged this off like a professional. "I'm an actor," he told me. "It didn't bother me."
>
> "Did you think you were good in the picture?"
>
> "Yep, and I'm working tomorrow, too. Are you?"
>
> As I said, this kid can hold his own. As movie moppets go—and there are times when we wish they would, Jon is unusual. He's poised, but not precocious. And considering he was up long past his curfew, he behaved himself very well.

Sounds like I had the run of the place. Being the only child in a very adult situation, I always created games—some say mischief—that could be played alone.

Louella Parsons: It's the consensus that Jon is one of the best child stars since Shirley Temple.

Beverly Hills Citizen News: Little blonde Jon Provost is a smash hit as is his Japanese pal, Roger Nakagawa. It should be shown to as many men, women and children as possible all over this globe for it proves that understanding and love between people is not only possible but probable under natural conditions if children get to know one another.

Hollywood Reporter: Two kids swipe the picture as smoothly as a couple of Bowery Boys filching an apple from the corner fruit stand . . . excellent performances, charming, heartwarming.

Los Angeles Examiner: . . . delightfully refreshing, one of the most unusual movies ever made.

Arthur Lubin: Jon Provost is alert, intelligent. He crawls right into your heart and he's all boy. He's the first potentially great child star that's come along since the days of Shirley Temple, Jackie Coogan and Jackie Cooper.

The Transition

September 8, 1957 Timmy Martin is introduced on *Lassie*.

Paul Petersen: I remember the transition from Tommy to Jon as being really quite a big deal.

Every magazine from *Life* to *Good Housekeeping* carried the story of my debut. Shielded from any pressure or simply unaware of it, if all this was a big deal, I didn't notice. But fans of the Millers knew this signaled the end. Most were aware of George Cleveland's passing and were waiting to see how it would be handled. And they wanted to size up the new kid, the usurper to Tommy's throne.

Erskine Johnson, syndicated columnist: Hollywood's littlest little actor appears destined to become one of television's biggest new stars. His name is Jon Provost and he's just seven years old. He has an unruly mop of blond hair, the face of an angel, a devastating deep-dimpled smile and saucer eyes so hauntingly wistful they may become permanently embedded on TV screens.

I'd shot twelve episodes with Tommy, which bought Bob Maxwell some time to try to convince the network to do a story based in truth: Gramps died. Bob felt a big responsibility about what he put on the screen. He loved to hear that an episode of *Lassie* had sparked a family discussion and regularly consulted child psychologists about ideal content.

Bob Maxwell: One of the things we found out is that a child should have an honest-to-goodness cry once in a while. It's easy to make a child laugh: all you have to do is throw a pie in someone's face. It's much more difficult to make them cry. But if they cry, they remember it.

No major character on a family series had ever died. Again, Maxwell turned to psychologists and religious figures who advised him to be simple but frank. They cautioned against euphemisms like Gramps had "gone to sleep" or millions of kids would be terrified to go to bed. Maxwell wrote and rewrote, and each version was flatly rejected by CBS, Campbell Soup, or both. Finally, six weeks later, after he'd agreed to remove all words like "death" and "die," he got script approval.

Thanks for the Dog, Jeff

The Transition begins at the Miller farm after Gramps's funeral. Timmy overhears Ellen and Jeff talking about selling the farm to a nice couple, the Martins, and moving to the city. Timmy won't be able to go with them. Afraid he'll be sent back to his relatives, Timmy runs away. Paul Martin finds him with Lassie's help and saves him from drowning. In the end, they buy the farm and keep Timmy. And, as the Millers leave the farm for good, Jeff gives Lassie to Timmy.

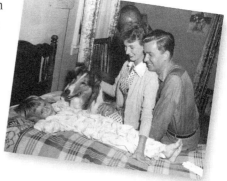

My new family, Ruth and Paul Martin, were played by Cloris Leachman and Jon Shepodd. We soon began calling him Big Jon on the set to tell us apart. He'd done stage work and some film and television, mostly comedy. This was definitely his big break, and he was thrilled to be part of this successful show.

Big Jon: I have always been called Jonathan, but CBS thought it sounded too English, so they shortened it. Cloris Leachman and I had gone to school together at Northwestern, but we had not seen each other for a while.

Cloris was a beauty contest winner with a strong background in theater and early television. She was full of energy, but not at all maternal off screen like Jan had been. And technically, she never did sign her contract. She held the producers at arm's length. I think everyone felt the distance. In this first show, people wrote it off as nerves.

During my seven years on the show, I did a lot of my own stunts; as I got older, I begged to do them. But in this first season, the producers chose not to risk my life in the drowning scene. Instead, they risked the life of "water baby" Stanley Livingston, years away from his role as Chip on *My Three Sons*. At seven, he was a big fan of the show and idolized Tommy and Joey.

Stan: We had been told this was his last episode, that he and Porky would be leaving. All I kept thinking about was that I wanted to get their picture and their autograph. They both gave me a picture that day. I remember Tommy being very, very nice . . . he seemed adult already.

[It was] probably one of my earliest jobs in the industry. I went to swim school in Hollywood, and the lady who owned it was very publicity minded . . . a whole side of her pool was glass so the press could photograph us underwater riding toy bicycles and tractors. We were in a bunch of different magazines and a "You Asked for It" segment.

I looked like Jon. I was about his height, exact same hair color, so from a distance I could look like him if I was struggling under water. In the audition, I swam for them in a pool with my clothes on, pretending I was drowning, and got the job. But we shot it in a small lake, and that scared me a little. When I actually got thrown in the water and started splashing around, they told me to go down and come back up. The water was terrific from the top, about three feet of water sitting on about two feet of silt . . . real soft mud, like goop. When there is mud, there is suction. I was trying to keep my feet out of it, but they said go down. I stepped in it and thought, "I'm not coming back up." I could just get my mouth to the top to get air, but started swallowing water and panicked. I think somebody finally jumped in and pulled me out the last time I went down. Afterwards everyone said, "You looked like you were really drowning," and I'm thinking, "Yeah."

Lloyd: We did a nice farewell show. I helped Tommy with the transition, saying, "Remember, this is the episode they're going to remember you from, so hit it hard; do it right because it's going to be your next job." He always appreciated that.

Joey Vieira: My life was a little different than Tommy's. Tommy was on to bigger and better things: driving, girlfriends, and all that at sixteen. I was very fortunate; I never skipped a beat. I kept working and did so for another few years. I wasn't excited to leave. It was fun. Those were all nice people, and I got along well with everybody. When it ended, there wasn't sadness; I just turned the page.

Tommy and I would come to be real friends as adults, forever linked as the *Lassie* boys. I didn't have a clue yet what that meant; Tommy knew all too well.

Paul Petersen: We hated our image. It wasn't all of us. It wasn't even fair. For both of us, you've got to remember, we are stuck with these goody-two-shoes images which, believe me, did not fit. Here's Tom and Paul representing everything classically American. It was worse for poor Tom than for me because he never grew. He was immediately recognized, never allowed to be himself. . . . I spoke with him many times about this: When he passed that part down to Jon, he did it with a heavy hand. He looked at that little boy and that innocent face and thought, "Kid, you don't know what you're in for." That most certainly was his attitude. How grateful he was to have finally gotten out.

Tommy: I think my favorite episode would be leaving the show. I wanted so desperately to get out at that point. It was a pure pleasure to be able to give Jon Lassie and walk away and be something of a normal teenager. . . . My last day on the set was the happiest day of my life.

In the last scene, the cast assembles at the kitchen door to say their goodbyes. Lassie hesitates when Jeff calls her and, instinctively, he cuts

to the heart of it: he loves Lassie, but Timmy needs her. Besides, Lassie is no city dog, and Jeff is moving to the city. She needs to run free in the country. In an enormous, selfless gesture, Jeff gives Lassie to Timmy. As the Millers drive away, Timmy hugs Lassie and calls out, "Thanks for the dog, Jeff!" Or so I thought. Watching the show recently, I discovered that Timmy merely says, "Thanks, Jeff." But, as Tom and I grew to be friends over the years, whenever I saw him or we spoke by phone, I always ended the conversation with that line: *Thanks for the dog, Jeff.* It was a favorite custom we both waited for at the end of every talk. That's why I know those are the last words I ever said to him.

The Timmy Years

Lloyd: I worked with Jon from his first day on the set to his last. He was the smallest, cutest, blondest boy I had ever seen. Tommy was a giant compared to him! At least Jon knew the crew, but he had a whole new mommy and daddy now. I don't think he had a new dog yet, but that came in pretty soon. He was a little pro, and if it bothered him, it didn't show.

I was used to people coming and going, to calling a variety of people Mom and Dad. Ellen and Jeff were gone; Ruth and Paul Martin came in. My job went on regardless. I just kept doing what I was told. At least the crew stayed the same, because I'd made friends with a lot of them. I worked more closely with Rudd and Sam and loved both of them, especially Rudd. Sometimes I went home for the weekend with him. Sometimes William came too.

William: Rudd was a character. His ranch had all these other animals and a little lake. It was neat getting away from the city and the streets and the congestion, being able to walk around with our guns and shoot at things.

Bob: My father liked Jon. He liked to do that so that the dog would get a rapport with the boy, the actor. My father was a funny man. He came up from a hard life; he couldn't express himself. And a lot of that toughness in him was expressed through that dog. I think my father could express it more with children and dogs than he could with people. Children and dogs are "unconditional." You don't have to worry about what they are plotting to do.

Bob Weatherwax.

Rudd had two sons from different marriages: Jackie, who was twenty-nine at the time, and Bob, sixteen. Bob went into the service shortly after I joined the show and didn't return until 1963. Jackie worked full-time, but he had a drinking problem. It made him undependable. It would also kill him early on.

Wally Nogle, the sound man, let me curl up in his lap, put the headphones on, and listen to all kinds of stuff. Harold Murphy, or just Murphy as we called him, handled props and special effects; there was always something fun going on with him. Don Schoenfeld, the makeup man, spent a lot of time with me; he really watched out for me—partly his job, partly his nature. He treated me like one of his own. I got really close to the dialog coach, Lloyd Nelson, especially after Mom wasn't allowed to read me my lines anymore beause noticed that Timmy was speaking with her Southern accent.

Rudd Weatherwax.

Lloyd had been hired as a guest actor on *Lassie* fresh out of the Pasadena Playhouse. His scene was with Jeff and Porky, so Lloyd, feeling insecure, grabbed the boys and rehearsed the heck out of them. The shoot went so smoothly, they invited Lloyd back for the next week and it turned out to be the whole series.

Lloyd: We were buddies, so he had someone to play with when he had a recess break and I didn't rehearse him. We got the work done and the welfare worker got the school in. He couldn't read at first. I had to teach him the lines. I'd tell him what the story was and he'd read Timmy's part, not the whole script; I'd tell him all the other parts and then I'd coach him a little bit like, "you're scared in this scene" or "in this scene you just said goodbye to your best friend." I'd give him the emotion and he'd come through like a champ. He was a smart little guy.

Lloyd Nelson.

I was smart and memorizing lines was a breeze—one or two run-throughs and I had it. For a while that hid the bigger problem, but now it was apparent. I couldn't read. I could barely print "Your Pals, Timmy and Lassie" on the studio portrait they sent to the fans who wrote to the show. I could only read a handful of words. I clearly remember looking  at the word *off* and seeing *oof*. At first, Mom thought it was a result of me being pulled in and out of school; and just nine months earlier, I had been in Japan. During the break in production when George Cleveland passed away, the Wrathers sent me to a specialist, a strange man named Dr. Volf.

Convinced I had a psychological learning block, Dr. Volf held tuning forks to my ears and had me listen through earphones to recordings of high pitched, electronic screeches, which were supposed to rewire my learning block.

Paul Petersen: The quackery of the practitioners that surround Hollywood are beyond belief. Studio doctors are up for sale. They would do anything: abortions, hearing tests, speech therapy, supply pills.

Years later, Volf was charged with practicing medicine without a license. My actual problem, dyslexia, wasn't discovered for many years; but as Lloyd said, we found ways to deal with it. Besides, within a few short weeks, we had much bigger problems on the set.

Behind the Scenes

Lloyd: Then we had Cloris and Big Jon come in. He was a good actor. We were the same age and got along great. I got along with Cloris too, but she was a complete change of pace from Jan. What the company objected to most was that she never signed a contract. She kept telling them she was still reading it. The sponsor was Campbell Soup and when they asked her which kind she liked best, she said, "I don't care for any of it; I make my own." That didn't go over too well.

The producers felt Cloris's cool attitude translated onto the screen, even while she and Big Jon tried to heat things up. They'd made an agreement—a conscious decision—to bring some physical affection to

Ruth and Paul. Just four years earlier, Lucy and Desi went through a pregnancy and birth on TV and could not use the word *pregnant*. All TV couples had twin beds with a nightstand in between, and anything resembling passion was a strict no-no. Big Jon and Cloris pushed the boundaries, holding hands, hugging, pecks on the lips. But it was not enough to warm up the producers, and a decision was made to add a Gramps-type character for that purpose.

Within a month, they hired George Chandler to play Uncle Petrie. What a career he'd had, starting in vaudeville where he billed himself as "The Musical Nut." I got a big kick out of that. He started in films in the late 1920s and had worked with Jean Harlow, Carole Lombard, Tyrone Power—actors Lloyd was teaching me about. I liked him. He was full of stories and had lots of patience for a little boy.

> *Lloyd*: George Chandler was a doll, a character actor from way back. He was always having the crew for a swim and a barbeque up at the house. He was just like a next-door neighbor.

Maybe Cloris saw George as a threat. She was fighting for more screen time as it was, and another adult meant less for her to do. Whatever the reason, their disagreements ended up in the gossip columns, which reported a feud on the set. Meanwhile, the TV audience hadn't seen anything yet. The transition episode hadn't even aired. Cloris and Big Jon hadn't been introduced to the public. The audience liked me with the original cast, but would they accept me without them? The press was starting to build as the air date for the transition episode got closer. The Wrathers and Bob Maxwell sat tight.

> *Big Jon*: For me, it was a warm, family place to be. There was no distance. George Chandler was an irascible man, but he was not unpleasant. He always worked hard and always did his job extremely well. Lloyd loved to write poetry, a really nice human being, very steady and very real. I liked him a lot. Everybody was absolutely fine, even those who came in and out, like the vet, Arthur Space . . . these men were all

Arthur Space
played Lassie's
vet, Frank
Weaver, from
1954 to 1964.

part and parcel of an on-going story and they knew it and they were very, very reliable.

Sondra Space Thiederman: Dad had an extremely strong work ethic and he was deeply devoted to details and to punctuality, to knowing your lines and hitting your marks and doing it right and there was nothing casual about it.

Susie Space Swan: It was so hard. He painted houses, he dug ditches . . . and he just survived. His hustle to be one of the 2 percet of working actors . . . it was really tough and the example was tough. I'm very proud of the whole era.

Mr. Space was part of Lassie's ongoing story, but more than that, he was part of the fabric of early Hollywood, part of a small army of hard-working pros. And he and I had more in common that I ever realized.

Sondra Space Thiederman: Our father was a loner, very uncomfortable socially. We believe he was dyslexic. He hated cold readings at auditions, had hated school, felt completely inferior. That's why he did not cultivate relationships in Hollywood that would have allowed him to have a still richer career. Daddy had a deep, natural talent. It's a shame that a thing like dyslexia could interfere with the ability to show that to other people.

Walking the Walk

At one of my first personal appearances after the show aired, I walked into an enormous auditorium and all these people roared and applauded for me. I turned to Mom and said, "But they don't even know me." I just didn't get it . . . but I would.

Paul Petersen: In our era we did thirty-nine episodes a year as opposed to today's twenty to twenty-four. People just don't understand—not only the work requirements, which, on a child, are very confining, but the impact! There were only three networks. When people sat down to watch Lassie, one third of America was watching. That's thirty-some million people—not like today when you have a hit show with eight million people watching. And it was Lassie, for God's sake. People may say they didn't watch, but the fact is if you had kids in your house, then *Lassie* was on your television schedule. That was the deal.

Fran: The family started becoming different after the *Lassie* series, because everybody knew Jon everywhere we went. And it was hard with Mom gone all week. Dad was really there for us. He was a strong father figure in Mom's absence.

I was used to staying different places with Mom, apart from the family. For me, this was normal. The apartment was much more convenient and not extravagant at all, even though the studio was paying. Mom got only what we needed and nothing more. The building was old and had that "grandma" smell. That's all there was around the studios, inexpensive housing put up in a hurry in the '20s for the hordes of people who moved to Hollywood to get into the movies. Our apartment was small, no television; there must have been a radio, but I don't remember. I got home and still had enough time to play with some great kids I'd met, Jeanne and Bryan Russell. Then I'd have dinner, study my lines, and go to sleep. Sometimes William and Fran would visit. We had a bed in the wall for them, a Murphy bed, and Fran had never seen anything like that before.

William: I was a little resentful, but I don't know if I took it out on Jon as much as I did on my parents. I'd come in and stay with them in Hollywood. The traffic noise and trucks whining as they went down the freeway was constant day and night at the apartment. Jon had to be at the studio at 7:00 and we'd have to get up early and go. Normally, I went to spend some days in the city with them or do a little scene and get some work out of it. It was fun at times. There were some perks . . . like the gypsy wagon. The studio gave it to him and it made a nice little playhouse.

On the wagon.

The gypsy wagon was less than half the size of a real covered wagon, but large enough to be pulled by a horse on the show. We all loved climbing all over it. That they gave it away after using it only once symbolizes the transitory nature of television at that time. There was no permanence about it, no thought to saving things. Johnny Carson began his reign on the *Tonight Show* in 1962, and a few years later those first shows were taped over at the network because the tape itself was considered more valuable than the shows. We never dreamed the day would come when *Lassie* would be seen in 120 countries. Right now, I was doing a nice show with good friends and a great dog . . . and I got a free gypsy wagon. Life was pretty good.

Dad seemed to take this lifestyle as it came with no arguments or signs of frustration. In fact, he didn't seem to react much at all to the new situation. He hadn't even bought a television set. Mom went out and bought a secondhand one with her paycheck.

Mom: It wouldn't fit in my Simca, so the salesman tied it on the back. I was afraid it'd tip the whole thing over, but we made it home. I pulled into the back with the chickens and the horse and the goat and my husband sees this big box, but he doesn't know what it is. Naturally, he asks and I don't say a word. I let the kids holler, "Daddy, Momma bought a TV!" He said, "What do you want with a TV?" I said, "We want to watch *Lassie*! Don't you know our son is on TV every Sunday night?" Before that, we had to go next door to my neighbor's.

The Russells on Meeting Jon

Jeanne Russell: We lived on a street right in back of the studio called Fernwood (which Norman Lear later named a series after). In those days, there were no big parking lots, so the studio personnel parked on the street. One day there was a knock on the door. A production secretary from the *Lassie* set said they needed a small child to do some pick-up shots. They had spotted Bryan on the street. Would he be interested in doing it? My father was a singer and my mother a musician, so they knocked on the right door. My parents and grandmother took Bryan over to the set. All he had to do was hold up a can of Campbell's soup. They needed a little hand and didn't want to pull Jon out of school.

As the magical mysterious physical break in Hollywood went down, Cecile started talking to my grandmother on the set and those two clicked; they were like kindred souls. My grandmother was very much into health foods. In the '50s, she was culturing her own yogurt and pressing her own carrot juice. And as a French war bride who moved to Alabama, she also cooked Southern, so they clicked instantly. My grandmother said, "When Jon has a break, why don't you come over to our place? Jon can get out of the set atmosphere. I'll feed him some good food; he can play with the kids." When that started happening, Cecile said that whenever they needed extras, she would make sure we were used. That was how our break took off. It takes someone like that to take you under their wing. She sort of shepherded us into the business . . . and being in show business has defined my whole life. So Cecile's like my show business fairy godmother!

Bryan Russell: What a sweetie Cecile was, and how infatuated with her my grandmother was! She had 101 questions, and Cecile was very approachable. That did more to open the door than anything. My grandma came home and said she'd conversed with this great showbiz mom. In retrospect, that was huge.

Jeanne: I have an overwhelming sense memory of how the set smelled—sort of dank and cavernous mixed with the smell of paint and resin . . . the sweet smell of the makeup . . . the way the paper cups smelled at the water cooler . . . the sound of nails being pounded into fake walls—a hollow, muted sound—and then the buzzer of the shooting bell.

Television was an industry that was shaping our culture. Everyone watched the same television shows. When I met [Jon] I was on the set and I remember being totally numb with awe. I had a real cognition as to who he was as opposed to being just another kid. He would go about his business and I would be sitting in a corner of the set and they would call us on and we'd work, usually a school thing. But I really started to get to know Jon at home. All of a sudden, here was this little god in my house . . . that was almost paralyzing.

Bryan: I wasn't very awed by it, interestingly enough. I was a big fan of the show, but I guess it was the innocence of youth. I didn't

elevate that to celebrity status. I just watched Jon work. I remember the wardrobe: the blue jeans and the red-and-white check shirt. He was just so cool and so professional, so relaxed in that environment, that I just picked up on that vibe, "Oh, this is cool. Here's a kid doin' what he's doin'." It seemed so natural.

Jeanne: Jon had this incredible, normal, boyish energy, ready to break loose, have fun, and just shove off the confines of a soundstage. He was great—really outgoing, funny, feisty. He was a player, not intimidated by anyone and full of self-confidence. He would play with our bikes and scooters with real zeal.

We were also invited to spend weekends at their home in Pomona, and that's when I got to know the rest of the kids. Francile and William were just as cute as Jon. I didn't get to know them well—they were older—but they were very sweet and normal kids. Jon was definitely the heartbeat of the family; everything sort of revolved around that. I sensed jealousy from both of them. . . . We were sort of extended family to Jon and Cecile and we were also becoming part of the show business clan, which they [Francile and William] were not. I guess that further provoked a reaction when we showed up on the weekends in Pomona. It was like, "Who the hell are you and why are you here?" They were always very sweet to me, but it was clearly a part of their family life they didn't participate in. It was a mystery to them.

October 1957

A personal appearance in Philadelphia for Cambell's.

November 1957
5: *All Mine to Give* opens; the Pomona Christmas Parade
17: live TV appearance
23: special guest at Father & Son Breakfast at Lincoln Ave. Community Church in Pomona
25: *Life* magazine photo spread and feature article by Shana Alexander, the magazine's first female staffer and columnist

December 1957
1: "The Transition" airs; Jeff passes the mantle to Timmy; photo with Rose Parade board in preparation for New Year's Day; commercial spot with Lassie for the Community Chest
14: Christmas party at Port Hueneme Naval Air Station

The Jack Benny Show

Mr. Benny loved kids. We laughed together from the start. The show was shot in the San Fernando Valley at the CBS Studio Center. My appearance is at the start of the show during his monologue. Mr. Benny introduces me to the audience as the new kid on *Lassie*. He makes conversation, then pointedly asks, in character, "You must make a lot of money now." The audience roars with laughter, well acquainted with Mr. Benny's persona of stinginess. I tell him my allowance has gone up from a dime to a quarter. "A quarter, huh? Why, that's just what it costs to join my fan club, Jon. Wouldn't you like to be a member?" As I reach into my pocket for a coin, Lassie charges out, takes me by the wrist and pulls me away, leaving Jack, elbow in hand, three-fingers to the chin, to sigh, "Well!"

Musical Chairs

Lassie and I got to ride a float in the Rose Bowl Parade! We had been to the parade a couple of times as a family, so I was pretty excited to be in it. The view from the float was incredible. Two million people jammed the streets below me while 90 million more watched on TV—more than any other event in television history to date. Our float, "Childhood Dreams," took first place. I leaned back on a log holding a fishing pole over a peaceful stream as

January 1, 1958

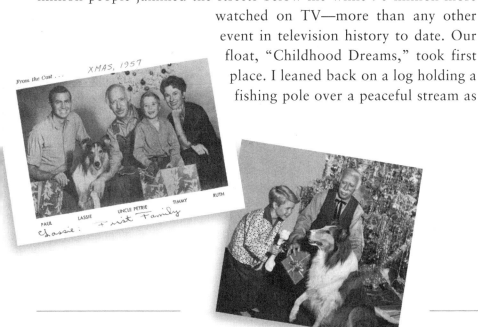

From the Cast . . .

XMAS, 1957

PAUL   LASSIE   UNCLE PETRIE   TIMMY   RUTH

Lassie: First Family

Jack Wrather with his stars: *The Lone Ranger*'s Clayton Moore, *Sgt. Preston of the Yukon*'s Richard Simmons, and Timmy and Lassie.

Lassie sat nearby on a hill of flowers. Frank Weatherwax rode with us, out of view, below. It was too early in the morning for Rudd.

On January 19, Uncle Petrie was introduced in an episode called "The Ring." In the episode, he makes a Lassie ring for Timmy that became a series "premium," an item fans could get by sending in 25 cents plus a label from Swanson TV Dinners. More than 77,000 rings were given away. These days, on eBay, they go for a lot more than a quarter.

Over Christmas break, Mom had juggled the family again, pulling William and Fran out of school in Pomona and enrolling them in the Hollywood Professional School for working children. Founded in 1930, the school boasted an impressive roster of alumni: Mickey Rooney, Judy Garland, Natalie Wood, Betty Grable, Donald O'Connor . . . and now, Fran and William. I thought it was so she could spend more time with them, but they couldn't live with us in the apartment; we were hardly there. Instead, she sent them to live with my agent, Lola Moore. Frankly, I couldn't have told you where Fran and William were. I had enough to keep track of on my own. I just went wherever Mom told me.

Fran: We never saw Mom. She was never around. I think she did it because she couldn't find anyone to look after us after school. Daddy was working and they'd never think of paying someone, so she brought us to Lola. Lola was the sweetest woman ever. She was real good to me. I lived there for a while with William and then a while by myself.

William: Some of it was fun. Once Eisenhower was coming into town for a political convention and we all got to get on a bus and go to the Burbank Airport and meet him. I thought, "How many people get to do this?" Some of it was a chore because I was being made to do it. I went along with taking singing, dance, and different things for a while. It was kind of fun, but I had other interests.

Mom: Jon realized the responsibility he was carrying, and when he was a little older he was up and dressed before I was. This was a job. In the Baptist church, you're called to something. He was just called to do this. He was such a good baby. Fran had colic. Bill had asthma. Jon was so good. He liked everybody. He came out smiling.

Lloyd: Cecile was Jon's mother all the way, blonde and bedimpled. They looked like they belonged together, down to earth, no airs whatsoever. She was very good with him, a pro as far as getting him there on time, going over his lines with him at night, things like that. I know B.A. didn't bother. I think he was very fortunate to have the family he did because he wasn't the star there; he was just another member and that was wonderful. I give her a lot of credit. Jon never had a star complex. He could have ruled the roost, but he didn't; he was just one of the guys.

That's the thing; I wasn't treated any differently at home than my brother or sister. It happened with strangers, on personal appearances, wherever people called me Timmy, not Jon. Then, I was "on." I'd smile, wave, and make speeches even if I didn't feel much like doing it, because it was part of what I did; I didn't question it.

Big Jon: Jon on a daily basis was absolutely a dream; it was a fact. He never was in any way intolerant or temperamental. He was always right there. They had a classroom right there on the set. He went into his cabin, did his studies, came out, did his dialog, and was a perfect little man, extremely professional. When they would take photo ops with him sitting on my shoulders, I absolutely adored it because I thought of him as one of my own. I loved to be around him. He was the character they wanted. He gave them exactly what they wanted. There was never any question of what his contribution was going to be, never!

Lloyd: We pulled gags on each other all the time. We were doing a kitchen scene, eating around a table, typical dialog, and Jon has to pick up a cereal bowl and has a line like, "Can I have some sugar on it?" and instead, I told him the line was "Can I have some ice cream on it?"; and, of course, he said it and it blew the scene; but I laughed and everybody accepted that it was my joke on him. I got him, but I'd get it back tenfold. He'd hide my script—he loved to do that. He drew pictures of me with horns on my head . . . they were good times.

February 1958
15: Fox Theater appearance for *Escapade in Japan* at 3:00 p.m. and 5:00 p.m.

I enjoyed myself most of the time, but it *was* work, and I was a kid. I got tired and cranky and didn't want to do it just like anyone would. And Mom punished me the way kids were punished in the '50s—with a hairbrush or a belt. Afterward, I'd wipe my tears and go out to smile and wave and make speeches.

Lloyd: At KTLA the first year, we were at the cafeteria having a Coke on a break and he didn't want to go back to work. I told him he had to be a little professional now—which meant diddley to a seven-year-old. "I'm not going." "Yes, you are. You have to go back. It's your job." "I will NOT." He played with the Coke, knocked it over, and spilled it. And so right there in the cafeteria, I put him over my knee and gave him a couple of quick swats. He cried, but I carried him back and he went on. The little pro, he went on. And I think he respected me for it because we got along better than ever after that.

Today, of course, no crew member would even think of taking a child actor across their knee, though I'm sure many would love to. This was the '50s. Lloyd spanked me in a commissary full of people and no one ran over to stop him, or to ask if he was my father. They saw the spilled Coke and an unruly child. I was just being a kid. Lloyd knew that. I was never angry with him, and I never pushed him that far again.

Exit, Stage Right

When *Lassie* wrapped for the season, it came as no surprise: the Wrathers and Cloris Leachman parted ways.

Cloris Leachman: When I realized all I'd be doing was baking cookies for seven years, I was out of there.

Unfortunately it cost Big Jon his job, too. The network felt if he remained but had a new wife, it would provoke questions. Better to make a clean sweep and recast both Ruth and Paul Martin.

Big Jon: Cloris had some established friends who kept nagging her to advance, to go on. Geraldine Fitzgerald, Marlon Brando—Marlon lived next door to her—and they thought she was just wasting her time. Eventually, she felt it herself, although we never talked about it. Her leaving really was a surprise to me. I received, or rather my agent received, a call saying my services were no longer needed. It was as simple as that. I was terribly sad because I wanted to stay. As a matter of fact, there was a small rebellion with the crew to change things, but it didn't happen. Cloris went on to better things and I love her dearly. It was an interlude in her life.

Lynne Shepodd: It was my dad's big break. We bought a house in Hollywoodland. He was way disappointed about the censors not allowing a partial change in characters. The show punished Cloris by not running '57–'58 reruns in the United States, but in the process, they also punished my dad. I felt bad for him.

Lloyd: Jon had bought a new house, a great house with an entryway with a cage full of doves, all gone, all gone. So bye-bye Cloris. It was a good job if she didn't have one, but it wasn't a "charactery" thing, and she was a great character actress. It was nothing to show her talent.

There was no love lost on Cloris's side, either. Several years later, she told the *Saturday Evening Post:* "They had to find reasons for us to be morons so the dog could outsmart us. I can't say I miss the dog. We were never that close."

The last of their shows aired June 8, but we'd said our goodbyes months earlier. Bob Maxwell left, too. Only George Chandler and I remained. The Wrathers had to begin again. The first thing they did was to sell Tommy's shows into syndication as *Jeff's Collie* to be broadcast around the world in dozens of languages for . . . well, it's still on the air, so I guess that's "perpetuity."

March 16, 1958

Timmy and Lassie were on the cake at my eighth birthday party. My family and some neighbor kids gathered around and a photographer took pictures. Rudd was there, Lloyd, Big Jon and his family, and Cloris, too. The biggest surprise of the day for me came from Rudd. I had earned my points on the set working with Lassie. Now

Rudd kept his promise and gave me a Lassie puppy.

Lloyd: He named the puppy Rudd. We all loved that.

School Daze

With the show on hiatus in the middle of the school year, I returned to second grade at Kingsley Elementary School, across the street from our house. Public schools weren't prepared to teach kids who come and go, but Kingsley tried, calling me a "guest student." Between *Escapade* and *Lassie*, I'd hardly attended first grade at all. I spent a little more time there in second grade.

Jerri Potterville, classmate: Jon and his family lived across from Kingsley in that big white house on the corner. People still call it the Provost house. We all thought Lassie lived in the house with him. We never believed him when he said she didn't live there. We were always trying to peek in the yard to see if we could see Lassie.

Dan Altenes: Jon enrolled sometime after the start of the regular school year. When he came into our class, Mrs. Vaniman told us not to get too pushy, give him breathing room, but as soon as the first recess bell rang, Jon was surrounded by a crowd of kids that must have numbered at least a hundred. As he moved around the play area, the crowd kept moving with him—a gigantic people pile.

Craig Smith: The teachers and the principal implemented the "snake" to provide a little control. Kids formed a great long line that followed Jon around instead of a big group.

Ed Donahue: Children were not allowed to be within fifty feet of Jon because they would try to pluck out a strand of his hair and pick off something from his clothes. It was ridiculous what other kids would do.

Lonnie Hill: I was a grade ahead. Everyone knew the Provost house. I remember Lassie being there and the media coming around. One summer day, I was riding my bike by his house and a lady from a magazine asked me if I would wrestle with him while her photographer took pictures. We wrestled in Jon's front yard. That was the only real contact I had with him other than seeing him at school with hundreds of kids around him.

On another day with another photographer, I was asked to pose in a bath and I refused. Mom said we could put bubbles in the water, but I would not budge. Something about it didn't feel safe. But the kids at Kingsley? That was completely different. I always felt safe and in control.

Jerri Potterville: Jon was behind me in line. I turned around and he kissed me. After the teacher went outside he threw a pencil at the back of my head. He wasn't that sweet little boy he was on TV! He had the class laughing and ducking flying erasers and pencils. Looking back, I think it was more for Jon to have some contact with "real kids" than learning. I had a big crush on him and I am still teased forty-some years later about my first kiss.

Yes, I was already a fast-moving Hollywood type who obviously had no idea how to behave in a classroom. When I asked Mom why the kids gathered around me, she said, "Because you're Timmy," but I never understood what that meant. Years later, when we lived in Beverly Hills, I set up a stand in the front yard like all kids do, not lemonade, but a shoeshine stand. Grooming was very important in my life and I'd just gotten this cool shoeshine kit. I'd been out there shining the shoes of amused neighbors at a dime a pair for about an hour when my parents figured out what I was up to and put a stop to it. Mom told me I could never do anything like that again "because you're Timmy." That was the reason I couldn't do a lot of things and why I was obliged to do many others. And why I was privileged to do still others. But what it meant—being Timmy—I would not understand for decades to come.

April 1958
Youth in Film award
May 1958
Riverside Sheriff's rodeo

In June, as they did every year, William and Fran left for Arkansas.

Mom: Jon could only go during hiatus maybe for a week.

Dad: But he did go and he made special appearances in the surrounding cities there because everyone knew Jon and he was a famous person.

Mom: They even sent the *Arkansas Gazette* with photographers to shoot him at the farm with the hogs and the animals. We got a whole page in the *Gazette*.

Desilu

Ace Collins, author: Television was no longer a new toy; it was big business and no one seemed to know more about making money in this business than Jack Wrather.

Just in the four years *Lassie* had been on the air, there were millions of more viewers. Mr. Wrather's vision of television's potential was beginning to give him a return on his $3 million investment. During the hiatus, he brought in Bob Golden as producer. Bob was well-connected in Hollywood, and Jack felt he could handle the nuts and bolts of a weekly series along with being a great help finding a new set of parents.

The next big change was the studio, part of the Wrathers' clean sweep. Our new home, Desilu Studios, was my old home, RKO. Both the Hollywood and Culver City facilities were sold for $6.15 million to Desi Arnaz and Lucille Ball, a former RKO contract player like me. Desi reigned at Culver. Lucy ran the show at Gower. One show that shot on both lots was *The Untouchables*, the adventures of 1930s crimebuster Eliot Ness and his men. Abel Fernandez played Agent William Youngfellow.

Abel Fernandez: Camaraderie on the set [was great] because we were all part of a family, the Desilu family. Desi was always walking around with his golf club—talk to everybody, go to every set, see everything— on both lots, everywhere. Lucy was always running around the Gower lot because they had everybody who was under contract over there. Culver lot was more outsiders. We only saw her once or twice while we were there, but Desi we saw all the time.

Bob Weatherwax: That's where I started. On the righthand side was *Ben Casey* and the next two stages were *The Untouchables*. Then we had *My Favorite Martian* down the street. First picture lot I ever worked on.

Abel Fernandez: We had a lot of shows going on over there . . . *My Little Margie,* Annie Sothern's show. All the Desilu lots were busy. Over at Culver, you had Betty Hutton. The pay was lousy and the work was twice as hard—but it was great.

Bill Beaudine, Jr., production manager, Lassie: It was all part of the game for us, part of the work . . . very much a family feeling. In the early days, studios had TV programs. They never said, "Well, there's nothing for you to do. You're laid off." They'd keep their crews. The season would usually start in spring and go through the summer up until the late fall, just before Christmas. Then business would drop down and everybody would be off until the following spring. It was more secure. You became a part of the studio group and you worked for somebody.

Hollywood still had that "hamlet" feel to it as well. It was a neighborhood. Working actors walked from Desilu to nearby Paramount or Raleigh Studios. Restaurants and watering holes sprung up: Nickodell's, Lucey's, O'Blath's. We were just a few blocks from the Brown Derby, NBC and CBS radio, the Hollywood Palladium, the Moulin Rouge, and the brand new Capitol Records building. It was the first circular office building and looked like a stack of records on a phonograph spindle. I'd heard the building would revolve at 33⅓ rpms but was very disappointed to learn that it didn't move at all. Fans often waited outside these restaurants and theaters, autograph books in hand. No photographers or flashing bulbs, no pushy paparazzi—it was orderly, respectful, and fun for everyone. Hollywood still had a lot of charm.

Susie Space Swan: We lived on Glen Tower, then we moved to 2640 Beachwood in a house built in 1910, one of the few built before the Hollywoodland development as a summer house for someone living on Bunker Hill. I was born and raised there and went horseback riding at the stables at the top of Beachwood. Jon Shepodd lived up on Ledgewood, and I'd see him at the market; he'd ask how Dad was. It was a wonderful area. I used to beg Daddy to drive down Beachwood to Primrose; it was so steep, it was such a thrill . . . and the Hollywood sign when it said HOLLYWOODLAND.

Bob Golden felt comfortable on these streets; he knew them. He also knew what a special property the Wrathers had in *Lassie*. Now that we had a new home, he and Bonita began their search for the lady of the house.

The New Guard

Bob Golden: If we were going to fool with *Lassie,* we had better do it right or we were going to hear about it. It wasn't like doing another show.

Lloyd: We were thinking it had run its mile. Tommy's gone. Jon is in, but it's only one year. We have a new cast coming in. We didn't know who was going to play Ruth Martin and we didn't know if we'd come back.

Actress Betty Lynn, who would find fame as Thelma Lou, Barney Fife's patient girlfriend on *The Andy Griffith Show,* auditioned for the role of Ruth Martin.

Betty Lynn: The interview was going nicely until they asked me if I had any children of my own. When I told them I didn't, they immediately backed off. "Oh, how could you play a mother without having a child?" I reminded them that I *was* an actress . . . but it was over from that moment.

Fate works in mysterious ways. Bob Maxwell had offered June Lockhart a chance to audition for the role of Ruth Martin before Cloris got it. The only child of Kathleen and the great Gene Lockhart, June's film debut at twelve was as their daughter, one of the Crachit clan in *A Christmas Carol*. Since then, she'd appeared in films and TV and had conquered Broadway, winning a Tony. At the time of the offer, June lived in New York with husband Dr. John Maloney and two baby girls, Anne and June, so she turned it down. But things had changed. The marriage ended and June and the girls moved west. That spring, as June sat at a stop sign in Hollywood, Bonita Wrather and Bob Golden pulled up in a car alongside her. They exchanged hellos and Bob said, "Hey, how would you like to be Lassie's mom?" June said she thought it sounded good . . . for a year or so. Bonita told her that wouldn't be long enough and off they went.

June: As I drove home I thought about what I had been offered and I said to myself, "What am I being so damn grand about? I have two children to support, the part they want me to play has a lot of dignity, the show is already on the air, I wouldn't have to film a pilot, and they have a sponsor. This is really a great gift that has been offered me. I'd be stupid not to at least look into it."

June was working on both coasts, flying all the time. The idea of staying put in one place with her family was appealing. She called Bob and Bonita and accepted the offer.

Bob Golden found Lassie's new dad in New York on Broadway. After service in WWII, Hugh Reilly found steady employment on the stage, working with the likes of Miss Lillian Gish, Anne Jackson, and his favorite, Tallulah Bankhead. The producers wanted a new face, and though he had done many episodes of *Playhouse 90* and the like, he was far from familiar. Happy with the offer, Hugh relocated to Hollywood with his wife and three sons, one of whom was my age.

Hugh: I knew I'd never be Jimmy Stewart or Clark Gable, but security was important to me.

The last new members of the cast were another boy and his dog, Todd Ferrell as Boomer Bates and his dog Mike. Todd and his younger brother Ray had been in a number of shows together and Ray also played little Bruce Ramsey, son of Betty Ramsey, Lucy Ricardo's neighbor in Connecticut; but he never appeared in the credits—a fate all us kid actors suffered. Ray and Todd lived down the street from an agent out in San Marino, near Pasadena, who talked their mom into letting her represent them—like the knock on Jeanne Russell's door. Todd was on his way to audition for the Mousketeers when he got the part of Boomer.

Todd: I watched the show at home, so I was familiar with it. My lines were simple. I didn't have to worry about memorizing a lot of dialogue, so I felt pretty relaxed. The set was a nice place to work, and, honestly, I don't have a single negative memory.

Lloyd: Todd Ferrell replaced Donald Keeler. He was a nice little boy, but Jon could act circles around him.

Lola Moore asked for "favored nations"—a term that means the three leads would receive the same pay—or so we were told. My parents weren't experienced, and Lola never wanted to upset the apple cart. Forty years later, at an autograph show, a fan showed me his recent purchase: June's original contract. There it was for me to see. While I was paid $350 an episode, she was paid $1,000.

Paul Petersen: Lola remained the number one children's agent for one reason: she never made waves.

> **June 1958**
> 16: Attended the opening of Disneyland

Now that the new cast members were in place, everyone was happy . . . or were they? Reporters asked Rudd how Lassie felt about all these changes. Rudd responded, "Lassie won't have any trouble adjusting to a new cast as long as I'm around to give the commands; but he sure remembers members of the old cast when they stop by for a visit. The dog whines and wags his tail and really makes over them . . . but he is crazy about Jon. He's the first actor Lassie ever took to in a big way. The dog will be happy as long as the boy stays on the show."

June Lockhart: When I first started with Hugh Reilly on the show, we shot five episodes all at once. We did all the kitchen stuff from five episodes at one time. Then we did all the stuff out at the screen door from five episodes. And I was changing dresses of course—not Jon, he used the same clothes. Then we shot all the stuff in the pickup truck from the first five shows. We didn't know the names of the episodes . . . and, of course, Hugh and I are breaking into new characters, and well, it was just preposterous. Everybody on the set was totally confused. The prop men didn't know which props to put out. They didn't know whether it was day or night. Of course, the editor and the script people, trying to keep track of who was wearing what and which episode we were doing. . . . They were the first five shows that I did, and we didn't know what episode we were in, or what the climax was, or where we were going! It was just a mess, and this was the idea of our unit production man, replaced later by Bill Beaudine Jr.—mercifully.

June and I were rehearsing a scene seated in the kitchen. She'd only been part of the cast a few weeks and I decided to put her to the test. While we ran our lines, I began kicking her in the leg under the table. Thinking it was an accident, she moved her leg. I kicked harder and found it again. Still thinking it was an accident, she swiveled her legs away. Then I had to scoot way down in my chair to kick her. Clearly, it was no accident.

June: Yes, he really had to work at it. And, can you imagine, I took it for a long time, because I thought, "I'm the new actress on this show. This show's been on for years, I don't want to . . . but I've got to deal with this dear little boy for a whole lot of time and I guess I can't . . ." I couldn't move any further away or I'd be out of the shot, so that's when I said, "Stop doing that! You and I are going to be together for a long time." And I did it loudly and with a pointed finger and everything, right in his face. His eyes got as big as saucers and he sat up straight in his chair. Well, really, everyone froze because no one had seen anything. And I can see Cecile, coming around the corner of the set, "What happened? What's that about?" All fixed; settle down!

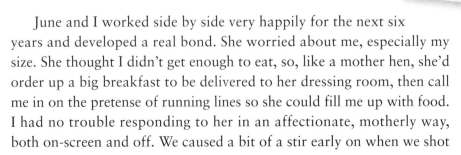

June and I worked side by side very happily for the next six years and developed a real bond. She worried about me, especially my size. She thought I didn't get enough to eat, so, like a mother hen, she'd order up a big breakfast to be delivered to her dressing room, then call me in on the pretense of running lines so she could fill me up with food. I had no trouble responding to her in an affectionate, motherly way, both on-screen and off. We caused a bit of a stir early on when we shot a scene where I kissed her. I kissed June the same way I kissed my own mom—on the lips. Talk about the set coming to a screeching halt. "Whoa! What are you doing?" Maybe it was a Southern thing? Whatever it was, I was never allowed to do it again. Kisses were for cheeks only.

Female presence on the set was in the minority, so it was nice to have another woman join the crew, Grace Kuhn. She'd been working in wardrobe for fifteen years, had worked with June on a film, and, like her, was a divorced mother of two.

Grace Kuhn: The motion picture costumers asked me to go to Western Costumes and stand by while June Lockhart was being fitted for her wardrobe for the *Lassie* show. I said sure. "Oh," June said, "are you going to be on the series?" No, I told her I was just there for the fitting—four or five housedresses, two aprons, and a coat that she wore once or twice. "To tell you the truth, June, I'm going to Hawaii in four days." June said, "I see . . ."

I had just gotten home when the phone rang and it was the union again. They told me Miss Lockhart wanted me to be on the series. I told them I was all ready for a trip to Hawaii. "Too bad," they said. "It's an independent show; you'll get twice the money you get at the studio. Don't throw this away." I figured I could go to Hawaii anytime. I took the job. The money was good and the crew was wonderful.

Lloyd: June would keep us going; she has a great sense of humor. Her mind is going clickety-click all the time. She loves a good joke and humor in any form. Of course, she's a very good actress. And Grace? She was always a pistol.

Grace: June was a great gal, loved working with her. Sometimes she went to the dressing room and napped and it would take us three-quarters of an hour to pull her together again, what with hair and makeup and ironing her dress. One day, she saw me and the hairdresser playing Scrabble and she asked if she could join us. Eureka! That was it. We got June hooked on Scrabble and saved all sorts of time. The director called us the Scrabdabblers. I told him, "If it weren't for us playing Scrabble, the show would be held up another forty-five minutes." He said, "Go play Scrabble!"

Hugh Reilly was genuinely beloved on the set as well, but he hung back a bit more, didn't seek the light as much as June. A strong family man with a stay-at-home sensibility, steady and reliable, he made a perfect Paul Martin.

June: He was easygoing, laid-back, and a very professional colleague. We shared a lot of chuckles.

Hugh: Timmy got into trouble on every show. Junie and I joked that her standard line was "Timmy fell down a well" and mine was "I'll get the pickup."

Ann Aschaver, fan: For every experience in life there's a "y'seetimmy" . . . you know, at the end of every episode, Paul Martin sat down with his son and said, "Y'see, Timmy . . ." and explained what the lesson was. And that's the way life is. There's always a "y'seetimmy.'"

Lloyd: They worked them both awfully hard. When Jon would go home, it'd be up to June and Hugh and George Chandler to do their scenes without Jon. The producers could work them as long as they wanted to. Hugh was a little stiff at first, but he learned the trade, to hit his mark and find the key light; that was about all he was ever asked to do. There was one sequence when June, as the mother, was buying a new hat and she was sitting in this little millinery shop and it was late. She put this little bonnet on her head and June had to look at herself in the mirror. She burst out crying. She was just so exhausted, she couldn't take it anymore. She needed to go home and get some rest, but they wouldn't let her. She dried the tears and went on with the scene and was back the next day at dawn; talk about a real pro. . . .

That's one of the reasons I always wore the same outfit, the jeans and the red-and-white check shirt.

June: It was the same tablecloth shirt so that they could use the stock footage of him riding the bicycle if they were short. It was always available to them to have shots of him going down the road on the bicycle at a distance, and you couldn't tell whether he was eight, ten, or twelve, because he always had that shirt on.

July 1958
22: Press opening: Pacific Ocean Park (a CBS investment) on the Santa Monica Pier
August 1958
Photo op with Noreen Corcoran from *Bachelor Father* for Youth Month
Photo shoots for the Jon Provost clothing line owned by the Wrathers

The same wardrobe made it easier for everyone. No matter what scene from which show we were shooting, I almost always had the right outfit on. (There were occasional stories when I wore a suit.) My jeans and high-top sneakers were "store-bought," with all identifying labels removed. The studio made all my shirts.

Reading, Writing, 'Rithmetic

In September, the new season of *Lassie* began, with June and Hugh as Ruth and Paul Martin, and no one really noticed the change. I am told they did not receive one letter about it. The focus was on the boy and his dog. Bonita and Bob Golden heaved a huge sigh of relief and moved forward.

September also meant it was time for me to return to school. My teacher from the year before was gone. My new teacher was Catherine Deeney.

Catherine Deeney: I had just completed fifteen years at Paramount. I was the resident teacher there, and we had full cooperation of the studio because they knew that the board of education would have pulled those kids right out. So I had no problems at all; but I did have to watch and keep very alert about Jonny's time and be sure that we went to lunch on time and that he had a full hour for lunch—even though he never ate very much—he was such a little guy. And he would play with the dogs or play with Todd.

Todd: We played on the set quietly, and several weekends Jon came home with us. We just did regular family things and had a good time.

Lloyd Nelson: They would put Jon in places I wouldn't approve of. I was close to Jon, he was my son on the set; I was protective, and all I had to do was get Catherine and it was, "No, no, no, we're not going to do that." We knew the people, the cast and the crew, and so we buffered for Cecile and we'd try to do it subtly. First we'd go to the director and if that didn't work, we'd go to the welfare worker and between her and myself, we'd get the kid out of the river.

Grace: Jon's mother—I only knew her socially on the set—was very sweet and very, I think . . . she wanted to be very social. She was a very pretty little thing. I thought Jon was darling, a dear little boy. It was a very closed set with guests only once every two or three weeks. Everyone went back to their dressing rooms to study lines or—for Jon—to school. There was no place to gather, no time to socialize, only at the party the producers threw once a year at the end of the season with the Wrathers and all the big shots.

Mom was always on the set with me. She was never one to be idle and found all kinds of ways to fill the long days at the studio: knitting, reading the trade papers, later making fresh carrot juice for people (Vince Edwards loved it!). Especially in my early years there, Mom kept an eye out for everything. This was all new for her, too.

June: Well, there's so much that he wasn't around for. He was off in school or we would whisk him away to protect him from it. One afternoon, he was sitting in a chair or on a couch in another set, not on the set on which we were working. This enormous light came down with a terrible crash and he was next to it. He was not hurt, but he was frightened out of his wits and crying hysterically. We all ran to him, but no one could find Cecile anywhere. Finally someone found her and brought her over. "What's all the fuss? Is he dead?" I'll never forget it. She meant it as a joke, but Jonny was so upset . . . he just flew to her.

Catherine Deeney: I remember Cecile very well. She was always on the set, always knew where Jon was. She was very cooperative and never disagreed with any of the rules that I set. She was also very watchful because . . . well, this is hard to say, but a child star is property, and often a studio will forget the human side, the feelings. Shirley Temple was a property. Her pictures kept the studio open, but she was their property. Jonny fit that theory. Yes, the dogs were important, but

Mom and Catherine Deeney.

that child was very important. . . . Rudd really loved Jon and he loved that dog. The dog was insured for over a million dollars. Jon wasn't.

In the whole seven years, I missed only one day due to illness. Everybody on the set got inoculated. Maybe it was an animal we had used that had something, but we all had to get a shot. Within minutes, I got so sick; I just went OUT! Mom took me back to the apartment and the doctor came. I was fine to work the next day. The rules were a child could work with a temperature of 100.5 or less. But if it was the last shot of the day or something they had to get and my temperature was borderline, they always decided I could work. I remember consciously thinking "the show must go on." Miss Deeney worked hard on my behalf. The first cause she undertook was getting me a proper classroom.

Catherine Deeney: When I first got there, I complained because we only had a lean-to, and it was frightful. Bonita Granville agreed and had this lovely schoolroom built for us— a teacher's desk and two student desks. She was lovely, very lovely. She'd been a working child, so these things were important to her. She was great, an ally, but I had a very powerful board of education behind me and I knew that whatever decision I made, they would see that it was carried out; so, she was very cooperative.

Bill Beaudine Jr.: The Wrathers were marvelous. Bonita Wrather was a hands-on producer. She was there, but she didn't spend a lot of time on the set. I think she felt that that would be more of a disturbance. . . . She never had any problems. We all respected her.

Bonita (unidentified newspaper clipping): My other duties as associate producer include supervising the selection of June Lockhart's wardrobe, help in casting, work with the story editor, sit in on film cuttings, attend production meetings, and do publicity tours and interviews. It's a full-time job as you can see.

Catherine Deeney: I taught Jon and Todd. The extra children had their own teacher. They were on a different schedule and would have been far too distracting. I was only concerned with making sure Jon got his three hours. Sometimes we had some tough directors, and with them, it was a struggle.

Todd: I always thought they built the schoolhouse so we could make noise inside without bothering anyone on the outside. I liked the one-on-one educational experience and was not behind at all when I went back to regular school.

I was required to have three hours a day of school in study periods of no fewer than twenty minutes during my eight-hour day. I was limited to four hours in front of the camera, five in the summer when there was no school. Because my time in front of the camera was precious, I had two stand-ins who, while I studied, took my place while the crew lit and prepared the scene. A stand-in is supposed to have the same coloring and be approximately the same size. If they chose another child for me, they would have had to work within the same restrictions. The Wrathers compromised; they found adults my size . . . little people. Nels Nelson was a wonderful guy and great friend to me all my years on the show.

Catherine Deeney: I watched those hours, very definitely, because the company often wanted a little bit more time than I thought was right. The child was entitled to three hours of school a day. If they came in after fifteen minutes and wanted Jon then I told them, "This doesn't count." I had many conversations with them. It was a very hard job and they wanted every minute with that child that they could get.

Lloyd: If it weren't for Catherine fighting those battles, Jon would have been shorted on study time.

Catherine Deeney: I think that's true. I found the company to be not too cooperative. They did get a nice reminder from the board of education, I remember that. And I did have to speak up and remind them of what the child needed. That is what I was hired to do. Of those twenty-minute sessions, it took ten minutes for Jon to settle down. That's why the Board of Education said nothing under twenty minutes would count. I had to re-arrange my teaching schedule to make that twenty minutes work. I had to take the child from being Timmy with the dogs and get down to an arithmetic paper in front of him. It wasn't always easy.

We never heard the word *dyslexia* in 1959. Jon was a bright child, but he had trouble with his letters. If I'd ask him to tell me a little story, five sentences or so, he could tell it very well, but he had trouble writing it down. I couldn't assign homework, because he had lines to learn. We never gave assignments to a child in production. On his break time, we played games if that was what he wanted to do—tic-tac-toe or what have you. It had to be a very quiet game. If he wanted to be with the dogs, that was fine. Of course, Jon couldn't get dirty or mussed up, but he knew that.

Paul Petersen: In the era that Jon and I began in this business, it was just the tag end of the major motion picture studio, all of which had an education department and a qualified, really competent person running that department. Kids were supposed to be excelling at school or not get a work permit. But, by the time we started to work, that system had collapsed and every studio teacher was sort of on her own. They either fought for you or they didn't. I kept hearing about Jon having difficulty reading. I had this conversation with Lee Aaker, "How on earth can he do it? How can you be an actor and not be able to read?" Because, of course, you are reading constantly.

Lee Aaker was in the same boat. It's only now, when we compare notes as adults, we discover how many of us were left to sink or swim.

Lee Aaker: Even though I wasn't under contract to Columbia, I went to school there my junior year. *The Donna Reed Show* shot there and I went to school with Paul Petersen and Shelley Fabares. Paul and I became very close. The teacher, Lillian Barkley, just plain pushed me through school there. I didn't do anything. I don't think I even took a test. I joked around with Paul. He was very intelligent. He could read one book and know the next one before you gave it to him. But I don't remember doing anything.

My senior year in public high school was hell. I failed senior English and didn't graduate. Paul came to my house to go to my graduation and I was stone drunk. I blew it off. The studio teacher signed a paper that said I passed senior English and the school gave me my diploma. She gave me a book, came back, and asked if I read it. I said yes and she passed me. I was grateful. I don't think my ego would have allowed me to take my senior year over.

Anne Lockhart: Mom was on weekly series television from the time I was four until I was sixteen. She was never available to help with my homework. I missed a lot. I learned to get real self-sufficient real early. It wasn't perfect, there were a lot of problems, but I was never beaten with a coat hanger. Whenever I'd go to visit [the *Lassie* set], when I was working as an extra, which wasn't very often, I'd get to go to school with Jon. He had his own teacher, and I thought the schoolhouse was the hippest thing I'd ever seen.

Billy Hughes, child actor: I would go to public school, then have a tutor on the set, then go back to public school, which I hated. I was little in stature, and I was always getting shoved and pushed around, the butt of some guy who wanted to make an issue out of being on TV. I was always anxious for the next job so I could get back on the set again.

Jeanne Russell: I was a C student all the way. My short term memory for lines was my strongest muscle, and I used that in school. At one point they weren't going to renew my work permit because I couldn't multiply, and the crew had to drill me on my multiplication tables. Jay [North] was also terrified in school because his education was so terrible—he literally could not do any arithmetic, could barely read.

Mike McGreevey, child actor/producer: I knew Catherine Deeney. People like that really understood what it was about to be a child actor. Boy, she whipped a few of 'em into shape by the time I came along. The kids on *Leave It to Beaver* had the same teacher the entire series— so they had that continuity and they also had each other. When I was at Universal on the *Riverboat* series, my teacher really turned me into a good student.

Sometimes you only remember shooting the scenes and being in school . . . those were the two things you did all day. You didn't hang out on the set; you didn't become friends with people on the set. And that's a shame because that's a big part later, as an adult. That's part of the fun of filmmaking, that socialization that goes on, that feeling of family.

Flip Mark: I went to Professional Children's School and I did correspondence. In New York, you didn't have to have a teacher on the set. I didn't have a teacher for the four months I was in Europe. PCS would send me my stuff, I would send it back, and they would grade it and then send me new assignments. Now they do assignments online.

Patty McCormack: I went to public school . . . it was easier in Hollywood than it was in New York because they didn't think school was any big shakes in Hollywood.

Catherine Deeney: I left at the end of the season when the board reassigned me. If the end of the season was during the school year, Jon went back to regular school. I'm sure it would have offered Jon more stability if I had returned the next season, but the studio couldn't keep me on salary during hiatus and I was reassigned. I was the board's number one teacher back then. The system works completely differently today.

Did I feel like Jon missed out on things? Now you're getting into delicate territory. I had two children of my own, and they did not work. Jon didn't live like other kids. You have to realize there were pluses and minuses. He earned money and ensured himself of a good education in the future.

September 1958 Living with Lola Moore was no longer an option, so while Fran and William were in Arkansas over the summer, Mom and Dad made some decisions for them. William was enrolled as a live-in student at the Brown Military Academy in Glendora, and Francile was enrolled in Parnell Girls School in Whittier where she could take her second Arabian horse. Fran could come home weekends; William couldn't.

Dad: This was a very fine experience for Bill and Fran. And the whole family came home for the weekends.

William: In the beginning, I resented it. I didn't want to be there. It was kind of scary. I didn't like it, but I learned very quickly that there was nothing I could do about it. I couldn't change the situation. I just learned to adapt to it. The way to do it in the military academy is to get some rank. Instead of being at the bottom of the group, you are somewhere in the middle and it's good after a while.

Fran: I did not want to go away to boarding school. I was scared to death, being taken away from my father, my family, my brothers. Oh, I think we both cried an awful lot; we were very disturbed by the fact that our family was being broken up.

William: Sometimes I wouldn't see my parents for a couple of weeks. If you didn't pass inspection or certain other things, you didn't get to go home or see your parents. It was very strict. I think I was there for about a year, year and a half. . . . I think my dad wanted Mom to do what she wanted and he also wanted to support Jon.

I see it as supporting Mom. I know Dad was proud. He chronicled all my films and accomplishments on regularly updated résumés, but he never came to the set. As a matter of fact, in my seven years on *Lassie,* he only visited the set twice. He never got involved. He would only wave his hand and say, "That's your mother's area, not mine. I have no interest in all that show business nonsense." But wasn't that nonsense me?

The Lighter Side of Boys and Dogs

Halloween fell on a Friday. Don Schoenfeld and the whole gang helped me play a great holiday prank on Bonita and Bob Golden. For the last shot of the day, with June and Hugh in the kitchen, I burst in the screen door, red-and-white check shirt, jeans, everything as usual, except I was all bloody and scarred, skin peeling off my face and hair burnt. "Timmy's on fire! What happened, girl?" Everybody made it seem as though it was for real; then after a moment, they all laughed, big joke—ha, ha, ha. We left it in the dailies for Bob and Bonita to find on Monday and I went trick or treating in Pomona as "burnt Timmy." That was really fun for me. I spent a lot of time with Don learning about makeup; so much that later, he gave me my own makeup kit—a big tackle box with all the works.

Todd: I really liked the behind-the-scenes crew, especially our camera-man, Ken Peach. He took me fishing a couple of times. Jon was usually working, so to pass time on the set, I read comics or played with base-ball cards. I liked the times we went on location best.

Location was great! I was indoors all day at the studio except when I walked to the commissary or the bathroom, both a good distance from Stage 7. On location, we were outside; we could get dirty and we could eat all day! No one cooked back on the set; there was no kitchen to heat things up, so all the food served throughout the day was cold—breakfast, lunch, and dinner—unless we went to the commissary. On location, there was a food truck, much like a catering truck today. They served hot foods: egg sandwiches in the morning, soup, burgers. Todd and I didn't care where we were going; anywhere on location was great with us.

The other thing Todd really loved was "his" dog, Mike, a feisty Jack Russell of

Rudd's. Rudd didn't let them spend too much time together to maintain their "working relationship."

Todd: I liked Mike because he was a scruffy little dog who got much less attention than Lassie; so I kind of thought of Mike as the "underdog"—ha ha. Also, there were several collies and only one Mike, so in my child's mind, I thought Mike must be a very smart dog. I still have a framed picture of him on the wall.

There *was* only one Lassie at a time, but in the days before blow dryers, it could take an entire day to dry a collie. If Lassie had to swim, Rudd used a different dog, usually Laddie. And a third collie was used for long shots of Lassie running. Makes perfect sense—why tire the real Lassie running across fields? They saved my energy and time in much the same way.

A few more things about Lassie: they were all male— which makes Lassie television's first female impersonator. Males are larger and more heroic-looking. Besides, when a female collie comes into season, she loses a significant amount of her coat. Maybe it was a guy thing, but Rudd preferred males. He thought females were more difficult to train. Rudd had made a big mistake the first time around, letting Tommy and Lassie Jr. get too close, even allowing Tommy to take him home on weekends. The dog and boy were truly devoted, so much so that Lassie began to question Rudd's commands, checking with Tommy to make sure they were OK with him. Rudd had to separate them, and it was painful for everyone. He wasn't going to make that mistake with me or with Todd; this was another reason he gave me my own collie. Lassie himself would only take commands from Rudd.

One thing I really learned from Rudd was respect for animals. His whole process of training was different; it was a love-guided training. He respected his Lassies just as he respected people. It set the tone for the whole set, and I will always take that with me.

Later, when I was an adult, June shared with me a holiday song the cast and crew sang at the Christmas parties on the set: "Deck the halls with boughs of holly, fa la la la la, la la la la; Hide the balls on that old collie . . ." Every once in a while, we had to stop a scene and do just that, though I wouldn't understand exactly what was going on for a few more years yet.

Bob Weatherwax: They ran a poll once to see who made the most mistakes in the show and it came out that Lassie made the fewest and Jon was second. Really, I remember my father telling me that. It was the actors who made the most retakes.

I recall one and only one mistake Lassie made in my presence. He was supposed to save me from drowning in a pond. Nels Nelson, my stand-in, was called in to do the scene. I went behind a rock and Nels came out the other side and jumped off the cliff. I was standing out of camera range behind the boulder when Rudd gave the command, "Save him, Lassie, save him!" Fortunately Nels was not really in trouble because Lassie ran to me, grabbed me by the seat of my pants as I hid behind the rock, and dragged me out in front of the camera.

Tommy: I'm not so sure people accept Lassie's apparent perception on the show as being reality any more than they accept a mouse can talk when they're entertained by Mickey Mouse. In return for suspending that belief in reality, you go into a wonderful fantasyland by choice, which feels good to be in. It's wonderful to be able to see that. It doesn't hurt anyone to be able to look back and see that there was a time when things were a little more peaceful, a little more quiet, a little more decent, and a little safer for all of us.

About this time, Rudd suffered a terrible blow. He lost his beloved Pal, the very first Lassie, the MGM star who'd worked with Roddy McDowall and Elizabeth Taylor. Pal had starred in the pilot for *Lassie* with Tommy, too. By the time I met him, Pal was seventeen, blind, and deaf, but he had the run of the ranch. Rudd loved that dog as much as a person, and his passing broke Rudd's heart.

Lloyd: Rudd wrapped up Pal in an old, red shag rug and buried him out in the country on his ranch. That death broke him up more than any of the others.

The next month, Mom spotted a house for sale about a block from the studio on Melrose at Lucerne—four bedrooms, two stories. She convinced Dad to buy it. We could vacate the apartment, take in boarders, and Mom had the idea that she just might start her own child actor's studio.

November 1958

> *Jeanne Russell:* My mother and Cecile were going to open a school together, and they were actually going to teach other show business children—coach them in singing and dancing and the whole bit.

> *Darlene Rettig Insley:* I remember Cecile was thinking about starting an agency. She wanted me to act and she wanted to handle me. Cecile said she was going to put Francile in the industry and that they were writing a series for her. There weren't a lot of female agents; that was new, just coming in. She was spunky.

Sometime after this, Mom began to suffer from what she called "female problems," which eventually led to a hysterectomy. That forced Mom to let go of her plan. But she still had me . . . and her hopes for Francile.

The Holiday Spirit

Lassie and I participated in the Santa Claus Lane Parade on Hollywood Boulevard. The parade was always held the Sunday following Thanksgiving. Sparkling decorations hung across Hollywood Boulevard as simple floats, high school marching bands, animals, and fancy cars carrying waving celebrities passed throngs of people who gathered all along the route. My first time seeing it was from the inside. Mom and I went to a big tent where all the celebrities were before the parade. One by one, they'd come get you and load you into a new convertible or a fancy antique auto and off you'd go. I would later be in hundreds of parades, but this one always held a special significance for me; maybe it was the camaraderie beforehand, hanging out with my

November 30, 1958

Lassie and I met Jayne Mansfield and her daughter at the parade.

peers. It was one of the few times we were all gathered together. As the years went by and I came to know and work with them, I looked forward every year to kicking off the holiday season over hot chocolate before the Hollywood Christmas parade. I was deeply saddened to see the tradition end in 2006 after seventy-five years. The floats got huge, sponsored by corporations instead of local businesses. The celebrities were vying to be interviewed to promote their latest property. It got harder and harder to sell the TV rights. Times change.

> Paul Petersen: That's one of my first memories of Jon, because we all rode in that silly parade and loved it! We used to meet at the car dealership at the end of Hollywood Boulevard, at Hollywood and Gower, where we assembled before the parade. That is really the first time that Jon and Cecile and my mom and I sat down and talked . . . just over hot chocolate or something they gave us before the parade. I was interested in how he was doing on the show because I knew Tommy Rettig. We shared the same sponsor, Campbell Soup, so we had a lot of points of contact. If I remember correctly, the conversation before the parade centered around the funny gift baskets Campbell Soup would send out to the stars. They gave us each a huge wicker basket full of all the stuff they couldn't sell: mock turtle soup, dented cans—it was a joke.

December 1958
Trip to Sacramento with George Chandler for Campbell Soup
14: Grand Marshall with Lassie for the Santa Annual Frolic Parade, Santa Ana Jr. Chamber of Commerce—they had the largest crowd in their history

The Wrathers made up for Campbell's cheapness. They gave Todd a watch, inscribed on the back, which he still has. They gave my parents two sets of special Lassie drinking glasses—which I still have in the original boxes. And they turned me loose on an FAO Schwartz toy catalogue with a $250 limit, which was a fortune in those days. I got presents for Fran and William and for some neighborhood friends, too.

December 21, 1958 Our first Christmas episode aired. We ended up doing four Christmas stories. I love to watch them now, and I can't imagine why Bob Maxwell never did a Christmas episode with Tommy. Shooting them was tough—there you are in July and August sweltering in a coat and hat and gloves on a ninety-degree day. But this first Christmas episode was all shot indoors on soundstages. In this episode, the Martin family and Lassie are shopping for gifts in Calverton. When we went "into town," we went next door on the set of *The Untouchables*. Most Lassie fans never knew that Calverton and Capital City were the Chicago stomping grounds of Al Capone and Eliot Ness! Lassie sees a little girl—Lloyd Nelson's daughter—running into the path of an on-coming truck. She shoves the girl out of the way but is struck by the truck herself. The story of the courageous dog makes the papers and radio. Arthur Space does all he can, but he is unable to perform the surgery Lassie needs. The only doctor who can do it is unreachable. I am glued to Lassie's side and praying for a miracle—and I get it. The doctor hears of Lassie's plight on the radio, travels to the Martin farm, and operates on Lassie on Christmas Eve. Boomer and Mike and all the neighbor children and their pets gather in front of our house.

> *Lloyd*: I remember the director because he was older and mean and wanted it his way. My daughter, Melody, was only three or four at the time. When Lassie was hit by the truck, she was supposed to cry, and she didn't understand. The director, George Archainbaud, said, "Pinch her! Hit her a little bit." I blew my top and so did the welfare worker.

Mr. Archainbaud was old school. He'd started working in films in 1917 when they ground out two-reelers on a tight schedule and a tighter budget. He was not quite seventy and maybe, like George Cleveland, he wasn't feeling great, because he died about six months after we shot the episode.

In the end, of course, Lassie is saved. Melody and her mom offer to pay the doctor, but he refuses a fee—a real Christmas miracle! In a very rare moment, the show ends on a close up of Lassie and me looking directly into the camera. With fake snow falling and a choir singing, June looks up at Hugh, "Merry Christmas, Paul." "Merry Christmas, Ruth." There is a longing look between them, but no kiss. Uncle Petrie looks at me, "Merry Christmas, Timmy." I put my arms around Lassie, her head still bandaged from surgery. "Merry Christmas, Lassie and (to camera) a very merry Christmas to all of you." Bark! Bark! Bark!! Not a dry eye in the house.

I made a guest appearance on the *Tennessee Ernie Ford Show.* The name of the show was really *The Ford Show,* referring to the sponsor, Ford Motor Company, not to the colorful, folksy singer and comedian, Tennessee Ernie Ford, whose home-spun catchphrase was "Bless your pea-pickin' hearts!" He sang some Country & Western and lots of gospel, and he was backed up by a singing group called the Top Twenty. Each week, a celebrity guest appeared in skits or sang with him. He started in 1956, and his first Christmas show guest was Lee Aaker. This was live television. They made what's called a kinescope of the show as it happened live. The 1956 show was so well-received that for the 1957 Christmas show they did the exact same show live with Lee Aaker without a change. For 1958, I guess they thought they better do something different, but they stuck with a "boy and his dog" theme by using me and Lassie.

The show opened with a light "snow" falling on Ernie and the Top Twenty "riding" in three open sleighs while singing carols as white-capped mountains and scenes of winter wonders flashed behind them on the blue screen. Danny Nero's mom was one of the Top Twenty, and as on *Lassie,* they used the kids of the cast and crew too, so Danny was on the Christmas show with me.

> Danny Nero: The blue screen process was invented in 1958. The opening shot with the blue screen sleigh ride was state-of-the-art at the time.

Ernie walks a few paces toward his "home" and shares his philosophy and many laughs with the audience while he chops wood to bring inside. That's when Lassie and I pass by, bundled up and carrying a hobo's kit—a long stick with a bandana bundle tied to the end. Naturally, Ernie stops me and asks where I'm going on Christmas and why I'm not with my family. I "bah, humbug" the whole thing, explaining that my parents don't love me because they didn't give me what I wanted.

"Well, what did you ask for?" Ernie inquires.

"A 12-gauge shotgun and a baby sister . . . and I didn't get neither one. . . . OK, I'm too young for a shotgun, but what's holding up my baby sister?"

Poor Ernie tries to tiptoe around having to explain about baby sisters. No matter, I'm having none of it. Lassie and I are going to go "drifting," maybe to Mexico to stay with friends of Lassie's, Mr. and Mrs. Gonzales—two Chihuahuas. For the trip, I've packed the "bare necessities": my pet frog, a peanut butter sandwich, and a paper clip.

"What's the paper clip for?" Ernie asks, handing me another laugh.

"To clip the frog's lips together . . . so he won't eat the sandwich!"

Of course, Ernie convinces me to come inside by the fire where the Top Twenty and all their kids are gathered. He tells me the story of Christmas, and I learn about the true spirit of the day, that it's not all about getting presents. He sings some gospel and I fall asleep in his arms . . . so sweetly simple.

> **December 1958**
> 30: *The Quigley Count of Theater Operators* and *Film Daily Roundup* voted me "Best Juvenile Performance" for *Escapade in Japan*
>
> **January 1959**
> Celebrated Rudd's first birthday with neighborhood party

Danny Nero: I was all of six and couldn't look less interested in what was going on! Mom remembers the stage managers were too busy to give any direction to us. Mom, a pretty blonde, takes me by the hand to shake hands with Jon. And Jon! He had all of this dialogue with Ernie and he didn't miss a beat. He was really terrific. And this was live television!

Anne Lockhart: My earliest memories are of watching my mother on television when we lived in New York. I absorbed the concept very early that this was what Mommy did, but when she came home, it was different; she wasn't doing that. I knew she wasn't Jon's mother, that she was my mother. There was no jealousy whatsoever, because I knew it was just her job, but in a strange way, I also felt related, very connected to him. . . . Mom spoke about Jon at home very affectionately, repeatedly coming home over the years and telling a story about what had happened at work that day, what a remarkably good actor he was, how true and honest his work was.

I only had a problem watching my mom on television one time in a show. I think it was from [her] first season and actually, it's one of her favorites. She gets a flat tire on that old pickup truck—remember that thing?—driving through the woods. She gets out to change the tire and the tire rolls away. She goes chasing after it and gets her foot caught in a bear trap, and there's a cougar above her on a rock, growling at her. She says to Lassie, "Go get the c-clamp;" and the dog rushes away and comes back with something and she says, "No, that's the cheese slicer." She tells that story and it's terribly funny. When this show aired, I believe I was no more than four. She had gone out to dinner that night and I was home with my sister and our nanny, and I flipped. I was crying and so upset that this evil lion was going to eat my mother, to the point where the nanny had to call Mom to come home. That is the only memory I have of the line between reality and television being blurred for me.

Reality and television came together for me that winter when the Lone Ranger—Clayton Moore—and his horse, Silver, were special guests on *Lassie* in an episode called "Peace Patrol." The Peace Patrol was a real organization that encouraged children to support their country by saving U.S. Savings Stamps and trading them for Savings Bonds. Jack Wrather saw a great opportunity here. This had to be one of the first times a character from one show played himself on another show. I couldn't have guested on his show because it took place in the Old West, but the character of the Lone Ranger is timeless. It wasn't at all out of place to see him on *Lassie*. He was only on the set for a few hours, but it was really neat to meet him and to sit on Silver. Before the

Masked Man left, he gave me one of his silver bullets. That and the mask and a hearty "Heigh Ho, Silver! Away!" was what the Lone Ranger was all about. I treasured that silver bullet for many years before I eventually gave it away. Sure wish I'd held onto it.

I worked with some other memorable performers that season as well: future *Gilligan's Island* professor Russell Johnson, Rand Brooks, Kathleen Freeman, J. Pat O'Malley, and Charles Herbert, my "brother" in *He Laughed Last*. Ted Knight, unforgettable as Ted Baxter, the buffoonish news anchor on *The Mary Tyler Moore Show,* began his show business career as a ventriloquist. He played one on our show in "The Puppet," in which he somehow manages to convince Lassie that Suzy, the talking sock puppet, is a real dog.

February 1959
The New York Film Critics named Jon the top kid movie actor of 1958.

In February 1959, my second season on the show came to an end. I said goodbye to Lloyd and the guys, June and Hugh. Miss Deeney went her way, leaving behind a proper classroom for me. Producers let go of some of the cast, too. Uncle Petrie had been brought in to smooth Cloris's rough edges. With June and Hugh, that was no longer necessary, and fans wanted more contact between father and son, so George Chandler was dropped from the cast. Todd was also dropped. Producers said they wanted a friend who could "teach Timmy something," but in the end his character was never replaced.

Todd: My family had, by then, moved to Garden Grove, where I was a bit of a celebrity. Following *Lassie,* I made a movie, *The Great American Pastime,* with Tom Ewell, and my name was in the paper. People started knocking on my front door for autographs. Mom was very nice about things; she even did a fundraiser for a neighborhood boy. Eventually, she got tired of driving Ray and me in for auditions. I was tired of it anyway and just wanted to be a "normal kid" growing up in the orange groves in Garden Grove.

Todd graduated from USC in 1970, about the same time he "got healthy" and dropped seventy-five pounds, which he's kept off all these years. Ann, his wife of thirty-plus years, and their two children say he's very quiet and doesn't like the spotlight at all, but they all recently got a smile out of a new neighbor's tribute. The Ferrells moved to a small, fairly remote town. "Someone put a sign up in front of our new house that reads: Ferrell Residence, Home of Boomer Bates."

March 1959
21: Patsy Awards at Art Linkletter's Playhouse

March 29, 1959

The Beverly Hills Easter Parade was the brainstorm of Beverly Hills business man Warren Ackerman and is significant to me for one reason or two people. This is the day I met Jay North and Laurie Ackerman, both of whom became lifelong friends.

Jay North: They used to do an Easter parade down Santa Monica Boulevard; that was the very first time. I watched him on *Lassie* and I was a very big fan. I introduced myself to Jon and he just looked at me at first. He didn't know what to say to me and I thought that was kind of interesting and strange. He just sort of stood back and stared at me. I don't know if he was aware of who I was or that I was a fellow child star . . . I think he just didn't know what to say.

Laurie Ackerman: My father was very active in the Beverly Hills Chamber of Commerce and Cecile was very accommodating about Jon appearing in the Easter luncheon and parade. Jay North introduced us and, after we'd talked for a while, Cecile came over and said, "She seems like a nice little girl. Give her our phone number."

April 1959
1: The California Federation of Women's Clubs awarded their Television Award as Outstanding Young Actor to Jon for his portrayal of Timmy.
5: June Lockhart and her fiancé John Lindsay slipped quietly off to San Francisco to marry at the home of a friend.
May 1959
1: May Day festival in Cucamonga
9: Served as Grand Marshal in the Youth Baseball Parade in Riverside
10: St. Paul's Cathedral to greet moms and kids and discuss long-range prevention of crime and delinquency

Dad: In the spring of 1959, we waited patiently for the Wrathers to say yes to another year. The program was now very successful both nationally and internationally in twenty-seven countries. They had all these projections for salary increases for the next four years, and Cecile and I reasoned that the *Lassie* producers would indeed pick up the yearly options for the remaining four years of the seven-year contract. If we really believed this, then we could consider changing our lifestyle and getting the family back together. I had been with Convair over six years now and really enjoyed my work, but if Cecile and Jon were going to continue to work in Hollywood, then perhaps I should find a job somewhere in the big city. I knew a lot of the people at AiResearch, and by golly, they made me a nice offer. I terminated Convair on May 31, 1959, and started at AiResearch on June 8. The Convair gang surely gave me a nice farewell party. Now we needed to find a house. So again, I showed Cecile a map. Here's AiResearch, here's the studio. You find us a house somewhere in between.

William: The whole family had to adapt in different ways. Going away to school was only temporary, just until my parents decided what to do. They were trying to adapt to the change.

Dad: They seemed to accept it very well. There was never any indication of jealousy. We were just a normal family; nobody was hot-headed or excited and everybody just took things in stride, and that's what I've tried to teach them. When we sent them to boarding school, they went along with it. She took her horse and William . . . learned discipline. I'm a conservative. I don't do things wildly. So Fran and William accepted this as a normal activity.

Back to "Normal"

Disneyland had opened in 1955. But in June 1959 I got to be part of Disney's live television special covering the dedication

June 15, 1959

of the Matterhorn, the Monorail, and the Submarine Voyage. The coveted "E" ticket was also introduced. Everybody and their cousin was on this one, including Vice President Nixon and his whole family, Art Linkletter, the Ozzie Nelson family, the Disney Gang—Annette, Tim Considine, Fred MacMurray, Kevin Corcoran, Tommy Kirk, and, of course, Walt himself. Plus Clint Eastwood, Dennis Hopper, Jeffery Hunter, ZaSu Pitts, Bob Cummings, Edgar Bergen, gossip maven Hedda Hopper, Nels Nelson, and many more. I sat on Vice President Nixon's lap at the parade led by the "Music Man" himself, Meredith Willson!

What a kick-off to summer! Then, as usual, Fran and William went

to Grandma's and I went back to work, which was decidedly *not* "the happiest place on earth."

Rudd was still grieving over Pal, and we all worked hard to cheer him up. Then he was hit with another devastating blow. Lassie Jr., his pride and joy, was diagnosed with cancer. He'd been losing strength in recent months and now had to be retired permanently. Poor Rudd went into a deep depression. None of us could reach him. The producers panicked. This was something no one could have foreseen. Rudd didn't have a fully trained Lassie pup with the right look—the classic nose and thin white blaze up the forehead. Lassie also needed a full white collar and four white feet. Sometimes Rudd got lucky and got just what he needed in one litter; sometimes it took multiple breedings to get just the right combination. Then came intense training and socialization. The next Lassie, Baby, was too young yet. Rudd was forced to use a temporary dog, one of Lassie Jr.'s sons.

On the new dog's very first day, June and I were in the kitchen for a dolly shot—where the camera, mounted on a wheeled platform, moves on tracks, in this case, forward toward the screen door. A light was attached to the top of the camera. During the shot, the camera rolled off the tracks and the lamp on top came crashing down right beside the dog, who bolted off the set. It took hours to calm him down. Spook, as he was nicknamed, was never the same. Every time we had a scene in the kitchen, he whined and shook. The accident ruined him for work. I liked Spook, but since I knew that he was temporary, the bond between us never developed.

My First Wheels

From Stage 7, the nearest bathroom was the equivalent of two city blocks away; at least it felt that way to me. Every time I needed to go, the cast and crew had to wait out the long walk there and back. Time is money, and I wasted plenty of both with each trip. The Wrathers came up with a clever solution. Lucille Ball got around the studio in a yellow golf cart with a white fringed top. One day, I came to work and sitting there in front of my dressing room was this cute yellow miniature golf cart just for me—kid-size. It had three wheels, one in front, two in back . . . and one "big wheel" in the driver's seat. I was positively thrilled. Desilu had no back lot, no Western town, no New York streets. It was mostly soundstages with wide alleys between them. I could get up a good speed and take the corners so fast that my cart would tip to one side. On two wheels, I'd drag the metal edge of the cart along the asphalt, dodging trucks and workers, sparks flying. After a few near misses, studio employees cited me as a threat to them, as well as to myself. They wanted to take the cart away. But the Wrathers gave me one last chance. I quickly learned to adhere to the rules of the road— unless no one was looking.

Lloyd: Jon's cart? He was the Indianapolis 500!

Bill Beaudine

Bill Beaudine Jr., production manager: They brought me from *The Gale Storm Show* over to *Lassie* and I was there until '72–'73. Bonita and Bob Golden oversaw the writing of the scripts and the script conferences and made their changes. Then I took it, scheduled it, budgeted it and they went out and made them. I wasn't usually on the set. I was in charge of taking care of all the logistics, getting the equipment, hiring the crews and overseeing, helping directors, what locations to use. I was the one that suggested they use my dad. He'd done *Rin Tin Tin, Naked City*. He'd done a lot of low-budget features where the schedule was tight and the budget was tight, and that's what television budgets were. You had to do it pretty simply in the time that was allowed and he accepted that. Through the years, Dad did over eighty shows.

Whitey Hughes, stunt man: I worked for Mr. Beaudine Sr. at Disney; he had done a lot of work there . . . *Spin and Marty* . . . very talented, great with kids and animals; that was his specialty, I guess you might say. He could get things out of animals and kids that a lot of directors couldn't.

At six-foot-one, Mr. Beaudine towered over me like a grizzly bear . . . and was about as warm. At sixty-eight, he'd worked in the business fifty years already, starting as a prop boy and extra in 1909 and moving up

the ladder as a writer and director, working with silent-screen greats like Mack Sennett, Mary Pickford, Tom Mix, Mabel Normand, and D. W. Griffith. Mr. Beaudine's silent-screen two-reelers and, later, his Poverty Row, low-budget serials like *The Bowery Boys* were the perfect training ground for early television. All told, he worked on more than 500 films and 350 television episodes. He was used to grinding out low-budget films on a tight schedule. Everybody called him "One Shot"; he got everything the first time, shot only what was necessary, and felt most problems could be fixed in editing. He did not put up with any "tom-foolery." He wanted things his way, which almost always included me wearing a hat, usually a silly straw Tom Sawyer kind of thing. I hated it. He liked it. I wore it.

> *June:* Sometimes after a day with him, I didn't even remember my own name. I'm "the girl" or, if he's in a good mood, I'm "Ginsburg" or "Sam." He called everybody "Sam," even his wife; but I was the only "Ginsburg"!

Mr. Beaudine called Lassie "the meat-hound." Boy, Rudd hated that, but there was nothing he could do about it. The more he protested, the more Mr. Beaudine enjoyed doing it.

And, in a holdover from his silent film days, Mr. Beaudine spoke out loud to the actors in between their lines. "Now look at the dog . . . now speak to him." (Fortunately, we were already used to that with Rudd directing Lassie.) He'd stand, constantly twisting and smoothing his handlebar mustache—waxed to stick out—bellowing orders at actors, never calling people by their real names. Men like Bill Beaudine were the last of a dying breed in Hollywood. I marvel now at the breadth of his experience, but at the time, I only saw a cantankerous old man.

Bob Weatherwax: Beaudine was an S.O.B. He was old and set in his ways. The bathrooms were a good distance away, and he rarely wanted to take the time. Instead, he urinated inside the barn. Then when we'd go to shoot in there with hot lights, it was horrible. He didn't care.

Outside Looking In

Flip Mark: This was the first thing that I had seen that was really "Hollywood." New York was different. It was all cameras and moving around; it wasn't so set up. In New York, it's rehearsal, block it, and then do it live. This was the first time I had seen how disjointed it was from what you see on TV. I hadn't worked in that environment. It wasn't unsettling, just new. It was very orderly. My electricity was being on the set. There wasn't the pressure of it going on the air live in a week, so I felt a little more relaxed.

Flip's Episodes:
"The Whopper"
"Alias Jack and Joe"
"The Champ"
"The Alligator"
"The Wallaby"

Mike McGreevey: William Beaudine was the director, a pretty gruff old guy. I was frightened by Rudd; he was pretty gruff, too. There was a lot of tension on the set because the dog wasn't working properly. I felt sorry for the dog, because the week before they'd had an accident and the dog was spooked. Maybe that's why Rudd was so uptight. I got the sense that the dog was probably the most important person on the set. That would have gotten to me after a while.

My real memory of that show—other than the fact I had to learn how to milk a cow—was the feeling on the set. All these adults were dependent upon a dog and a child. They had tailored the set to be very laid back and quiet and very directed toward making a child feel comfortable. I remember wishing every set was like this.

Mike's Episodes:
"Growing Pains"
"Bessie"
"Land Grabber"

It was his home, his domain. He was king of the castle, showing me all over in his golf cart. It was the season he got it. He was a very good host. I look back and realize he must have been so happy to have someone near his age on the set.

We went out for two days on location in Laguna and Jon got sunburned. They were all so upset, fussing over him and putting cream on him, and Jon didn't know why it was such a big deal. I don't think he had a total concept of how important he was to the whole thing. He knew he was being fussed over; every kid knows that. Ron Howard said that to me. I don't think Jon knew how important he was to the production. He was isolated.

Keith Thibodeaux, Little Ricky Ricardo: We filmed the *I Love Lucy* show at Desilu Cahuenga which was also where *The Andy Griffith Show, The Dick Van Dyke Show,* and *The Danny Thomas Show* shot. I loved Lassie and my dad would take me over there to see the dog. Jon was usually working when I came on the set so it was limited.

I always felt like Jon was really alienated from kids. That's my observation, even as a kid: when I think about Jon, I think of him as being solitary; and that's not good for a kid. I don't mean he kept to himself . . . I mean that's what I saw when I looked a little deeper than what was on the surface. I would have liked to have gotten to know him better, but it just wasn't to be. We were on a treadmill.

Lloyd: Jon was a great performer. Oh my God, he could make you laugh in one sentence and the next minute you were crying. He was wonderful, absolutely wonderful. He was natural, wasn't nervous, didn't get edgy. He did a good job, but Jon never had any time to himself. One time we were shooting a scene in his bedroom. So, we tucked him into bed and by the time we were finished, he was sound asleep. We just covered him up and left him there. He was so tired. Everybody was pulling at him, left and right: welfare worker, the director, of course, me. . . .

Anne Lockhart: I was aware of the responsibility and the load he had to carry. During the hiatus period when my mom was off, the time would seem so incredibly short to me, and I remember thinking about him and how difficult it must be to have such a little bit of vacation all year long, to have to be working and in school every single day. I remember being amazed that he didn't have the time to do the things that normal kids did. And during those hiatuses, they often put him to work traveling for Campbell Soup or something. It was grueling. As much as I knew from the age of four that I wanted to do the same thing, to be in this profession, I knew I wouldn't want to do that.

Don Schoenfeld: It's a lousy life for a young person, boy or girl. All his friends were adults, so the crew tried to do things for him to make it more normal . . . like taking him home, watching what he ate and how he was dressed, the whole bit. Was he dressed warm and comfortable? We watched Jon like he was one of our kids. That was all that we cared about.

June: Of course we liked Cecile. She was a dear, but we were all aware of her limitations. She certainly was not always there as guardian when she should have perhaps been. But she did the best she could. And I mean that in the kindest of ways, truly . . . she hadn't had the opportunity to have a good education. All of that sort of flopped over when this groundswell of attention happened to him. And we all adored Jon so much and were just so anxious that he be well looked after.

Lloyd: We were family. Jon adopted me and it was great. He was not aware that other children did not have adult friends. That's very profound. Of course, I knew he was missing something, but I don't think he knew it at the time. One day, we were going down the street and all of a sudden some little boy runs out and hits Jon, I mean just slaps him on the back or shoulder. He recognized him and shouted, "You shouldn't be here; you're on TV." He couldn't really go anywhere with kids. He couldn't relax; and yet, he was unaffected.

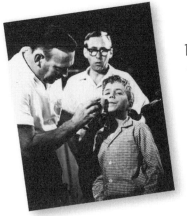

Don Schoenfeld: We used to take him home every now and then to play with my boys. He went to my youngest son's Bar Mitzvah and when he saw all the presents, he said he wanted a Bar Mitzvah, too. It would take an exceptional mother to raise them properly, and he didn't have one. She was a typical studio mother; she pushed Jon all the time. She was more interested in pushing the kid and getting publicity than the kid himself. Honestly, anything, anything for publicity.

Don, Lloyd and me.

Pioneering or Domineering

Fran: Mom tried to get me into show business after Jon. You know, it was the Lennon Sisters. I think that's what my mother thought she was going to have—the Provost Children. We were all going to be stars. Of course, William didn't succeed and neither did I.

I tried to stick with it longer than William did—a lot longer. But I was camera shy. I had a hard time talking. Jon didn't know better; he was two years old, two and half when he started. I was already eight, ten, twelve. It wasn't something I wanted.

She lived her life through Jon. I don't blame Mom, and I could never blame Jon. She had a dream, a little farm girl's dream, and Jon made it come true. I think it just took over her life.

Jeanne Russell: Cecile and my grandmother and my mom, they were women from the South. My grandmother's progressive spirit is what drove her from France to America. Once here, she observed how America worked. She wanted her children to be accomplished and a desirable part of the community. She realized that is how you moved up the caste system in our society. I just always sensed that Cecile understood that, too.

Cecile had this driving work ethic, and this was like the brass ring, an opportunity to really make something of your life. It was a tremendous compliment to have your family members desired by the hottest, fastest growing industry around. I think both of our families pursued this out of love for the entire family and wanting to bring everyone up.

There was cost, but there was also benefit to the career. Both of our families had the sense to parlay that type of an opportunity into a career-making break.

This was coming out of the war years. Television was in its infancy, and show business is seductive. It was flattering and fun and the ride of a lifetime. I think, like anything, when you have perspective, you say, "Oh, putting this much into it in this area is not wise," but there weren't a lot of examples before this; this was pioneer days. I think it would have taken a fool, given the opportunity that Cecile had, not to have taken advantage of it.

Limits and Off Limits

Lloyd: At Desilu/RKO, I took him on the stage where Ginger Rogers and Fred Astaire danced, and I don't know if he was too young to relate to that, but we had little history lessons all over the lot. Barbara Stanwyck was there and Ann Sothern. I tried hard to instill in Jon a sense of the history that was there around him, to take pride in his profession.

I enjoyed those excursions. I loved exploring the lot. My cart had become my ticket to freedom. Sometimes I needed to ditch the set altogether, to escape the rules of being quiet, staying clean, and all the pressure. Whenever I had fifteen or twenty minutes free or had a bag lunch on the set, I jumped on my cart and covered ground. For twenty minutes at a stretch, the studio became my personal playground. I'd scoot across the lot, peeking into soundstages and buildings, poking behind scenery. Late one afternoon, on the west side of the lot, I found a steep driveway leading to a cavernous space underground, underneath a soundstage. Nobody had to tell me I wasn't allowed down there. It was one of those great places a kid knows is off limits. I had to be extra careful not to be seen because—with that red-and-white check shirt—everybody knew me a hundred yards out. I got run off the first two times I tried to go in. But I knew my way around pretty well. I learned to stay one step ahead and was never caught again.

I called it the catacombs. Damp and cold and very scary, it was even more exciting because the place was forbidden. Once my eyes adjusted to the dim light, I could see that the space was gigantic. I crept forward, keeping an eye out for rats or any other creatures that might have been lurking in the corners. I passed storage areas—dozens and dozens of them—all tightly fenced in and locked up—holding full-sized props from forty years of filmmaking. There was the entire front of a house, a covered wagon and teepees, parts of sets, hundreds of cans of film. My imagination lit up. Each prop sparked a story. In my mind, I went to another world where I bravely won battles and rescued villages. When I was there, I could lose all track of time.

After I had memorized every inch of the catacombs, I searched for some new excitement. I discovered a two-story storage building that, for me, held treasures more valuable than gold. The rooms were dark and dusty. Cobwebs covered the long shelves that stretched from floor to ceiling. And each shelf was filled with race cars, bridges, houses, tanks—the miniature props from RKO's long history. It was an instant little boy's fantasy world. I tried to figure out which movies they were from. Some I recognized, others I didn't. I even found the plane I crashed in in *Back from Eternity*. The ships were my favorites, all kinds of ships, from schooners to ocean liners to submarines or WWII boats with guns. Sometimes I found the same ship in different scale or in various stages of destruction. Some were new, others had holes blown in them and were partially burned. I knew better than to touch them, but I didn't need to. Just seeing them was enough. In seconds, I was diving in the subs, firing torpedoes, and blowing up the enemy.

Whenever I could, I'd sneak back to the storage building—digging in old corners and looking for new ones. One lunch hour, I made it to the second floor and my greatest find of all.

I could not believe my eyes. Even from across the room, I recognized him. Everything else in the building faded in his presence. Slowly, I moved forward. There was an old chair. I dragged it over to the corner so I could reach the second shelf. I climbed up, taking care not to bump into the dusty shelves—I was in costume and couldn't get dirty. Besides, they'd ask me where I got so dirty and I didn't want to give away my secret place. And then, there I was, eye to eye with King Kong. He was about sixteen inches high. I knew the movies well enough to know that Kong wasn't the giant creature he appeared to be onscreen. Hey, even

Lassie was a boy. Moths had gotten to his fur. He needed to be patched in places and looked like he'd battled one too many stegosauruses. But it was King Kong, all right. Actually, there were a couple of him—two were busts, and two were full figures. Nearby stood the other prehistoric creatures Kong had conquered: the python, the pterodactyl, and the triceratops. No question, this was one thing I had to touch. Slowly and carefully, I lifted his arms. He was fantastic. It was possibly the greatest thing I'd ever seen in my whole life. In the future, if there was a kid guesting on the show and I wanted to impress him or her, this is where I brought them . . . and it never failed. And as I recall those moments when I shared this treasure, they were special for another reason. At that moment, I wasn't Timmy. I was Jon. I was the one who knew where King Kong was.

Finding Kong, "the eighth wonder of the world," was the coup of all time, without a doubt, one of the greatest moments in my young life. These times, these games, my imagination were special to me. I got away from work, from a world of adults constantly telling me what to do, what to wear, what to say, and how to say it. I managed to stick to almost all the rules and still find a way to play, even if it was mostly in my mind.

On the set, I found ways to amuse myself in a solitary way. I enjoyed the work. It was always fun, but even the best job has its moments. Shooting could sometimes get pretty dull, standing still while the same scene was shot over and over from different angles. To break the boredom, I made up a game. The scene had to match from every angle. If there were flowers on the table in the long shot, they had to be there in the closeup, too. I would move props around from take to take to see if anyone noticed . . . or to see if I would notice weeks later when I watched it on TV at home. If a glass of milk was full in the long shot, I'd drink half of it real fast before the camera moved in close. It was a real kick for me when I got away with it.

If I had free time on the set, I always checked in with my good pal, Harold Murphy, the props and special effects man. He went by Murph or Murphy, not Harold. I really enjoyed the episodes that had to do with any kind of special effects. Whenever he was getting ready to do something—blow something up or catch something on fire—I was con-

stantly at his side like a little puppy dog and he would have to say, "Now come on, Jon. Stay away. This is dangerous; these can really hurt. These can blow up." I was just like any little kid around fireworks. I loved that kind of stuff. A day with special effects was my favorite kind of day.

And we all loved the latest addition to the cast. The producers still felt the need for an older male figure on the show, but not on the farm; one who lived nearby as a neighbor would be perfect. They cast silent film comedian Andy Clyde, a funny little wiry guy, to play the character of Mr. Cully. He and Bill Beaudine had worked together in 1922 for Mack Sennett.

Lloyd: Andy Clyde, oh, what a delightful man he was. He was just a wonderful person.

Andy really was irresistible. I couldn't help but smile just seeing him. While he was on *Lassie*, he was also a regular on *The Real McCoys* playing a friendly neighbor to the irascible Oscar-winning Walter Brennan. Everybody lit up whenever he was around.

My third season of *Lassie* premiered in September 1959. No fans had written in when June and Hugh replaced Cloris and Big Jon the year before, but thousands now wrote to ask about Spook. "Where did the real Lassie go?" Nothing was ever officially explained. They didn't want to say that Lassie could get sick or die, so they said nothing and eventually it all went away.

September 13, 1959 The episode called "Old Henry" aired, and another premium was offered. In this story, Paul gives Timmy his first wallet with a picture of Lassie on the front. A commercial at the end of the show explained to kids how they could get their own Lassie Wallet—for just five different labels from Campbell's soups. After six months, when the offer was closed, Campbell's had sold 1,343,509 wallets and over 6.7 million cans of soup.

Beverly Hills

Dad: Cecile worked hard on the search for a new home and came up with a perfect little place, an attractive Spanish-style, four-bedroom house in Beverly Hills on South Peck Drive. I found out later Beverly Hills was a prestigious city and we were living among the big shots, but that didn't have any influence on my decision. It was four or five miles from the studio and six or seven miles from my work, just perfect, so we bought it and moved in in September. I renovated our new home including a complete kitchen modernization.

Bryan with Walt Disney; Jeanne as Margaret.

Fran and William went to Beverly Hills High School, Fran as a freshman and William, a junior. I was enrolled in Beverly Hills Catholic School, but I would not attend until spring when the show ended. I can only guess that my Baptist mother and my Episcopalian father chose a Catholic school for me because I would be allowed to start late in the school year. It didn't matter to me. I was so relieved. I'd let go of the Pomona house a long time ago. I hardly spent any time there anymore. And my closest friends in Hollywood, the Russells, were working all the time. Jeanne now played Margaret on *Dennis the Menace* and Bryan was on TV: *Lawman, Death Valley Days, Wanted: Dead or Alive.* I was tired of the apartment and the isolation from my family. For me, the move to Beverly Hills meant we could all be together again.

Rosemary Hilb Shaw, neighbor: Compared to other neighborhoods, it was very affluent, but for a Beverly Hills neighborhood, it was just a normal neighborhood—kids playing in the front yards, playing baseball across the street, that sort of thing. We did end up moving to the north side [of Wilshire Boulevard], which was a little more affluent. The kids didn't play out in front; they played in the back.

Fran: Beverly Hills was small in 1959, very charming, not Beverly Hills today, that's for sure. There were even vacant lots for sale on Beverly Drive. It was more like a little village, and everybody knew everybody. He could not go anywhere without being recognized. Wherever we

Campbell's sent me and Lassie to New York City.

went, everybody would say, "There's Jon Provost." Come on, I felt really special. My brother made me "special." What was there not to like? Finally, I was someone different. "That's Jon Provost's sister." I was really proud of that. We had a collie dog, Rudd, and I'd walk him down Peck and all of a sudden I'd hear whistles. "Hey, Lassie!" And I was Lassie's sister, Jon Provost's sister.

William: One of the things that used to irritate me a lot—it still happens now, but I've gotten used to it—is being called Lassie's brother. My mom would even introduce me that way sometimes. I guess she thought it was cute. I didn't. What used to really irritate me was the fact that a lot of times one son, Jon, and Fran, the sister, would be mentioned, but I wouldn't. I was the other son. It was like, "Meet my son Jon who was on *Lassie* and Fran is his sister." And I wouldn't be introduced. After a while, I got used to it. Then it became a joke. I guess that's why both Fran and I tried to distance ourselves. It was embarrassing at times when my mom would be out eating dinner and she'd lean over to another table and say, "You know who my son is?" I'd be going, "Yeah, William Provost," but it would be Jon.

In October 1959 I was on a TV special called *Lincoln Mercury Startime*. It had an amazing ensemble. The stars included: Nixon and his mother, Ed Wynn, Ann Blyth, Vincent Price, Teddy Rooney, and Angela Cartwright of *The Danny Thomas Show*. Lassie was there, too. Angela and Teddy played Becky Thatcher and Huck Finn to my Tom Sawyer in a modern version of Mark Twain's tale.

Controversy

Around this time, June caused an accidental commotion in the press when a reporter included that she downed half a jigger of scotch during the interview. She admitted to occasionally enjoying a scotch, a practical joke, and swearing on occasion.

June: Well, you never saw such a fuss when the article appeared. A delegation of "suits" flew out from the sponsor's headquarters in Camden,

New Jersey. I had to attend a meeting with nine men at which this breach in the image of Lassie's mother was deplored.

June agreed never again to do anything in public that would go against Ruth Martin's image: no drinking, no smoking, no cleavage, no controversial stands for as long as she was on the show. Hugh Reilly was also forbidden to take any other role that would undermine Paul Martin's wholesome image. Todd Ferrell's contract had had stipulations, too. He couldn't play a juvenile delinquent or someone who was cruel to animals as long as he played Boomer. Apparently the thought was that audiences were so unsophisticated they wouldn't be able to disassociate Ruth Martin from June Lockhart. Maybe they were right, but contractual requirements like these went a long way in type-casting actors, a curse many were never able to overcome.

The most controversial episode—at least behind the scenes—was "The Mascot." In the past, the producers had pursued story lines that included Hispanics, Asians, and Native Americans. But sponsor Campbell Soup held out against using African Americans in a script for fear of a boycott of their product in the Southern states. This was just months before the first lunch counter sit-in at the Greensboro, North Carolina, Woolworth's. Racial tensions were heating up and Campbell's worried about airing this episode, which cast baseball great Roy Campanella, a black man, as a role model. Campy, as he was known to his many fans, played for the Brooklyn Dodgers and was considered one of the greatest catchers ever to play the game. In January of 1958, his car hit a patch of ice. After the crash, Campy, thirty-six at the time, was paralyzed from the chest down. He worked hard physically and emotionally to come back, displaying great courage. Now, just a year and a half after the accident, he felt strong enough to appear on the show. If ever there was a role model, it was Campy. Bob Golden pushed and the episode aired—with great success.

Everybody's favorite, Hollingsworth Morse, directed the episode. Holly mixed well with everybody—actors, crew, kids, animals, whatever. He'd directed *Sky King* for three years and almost fifty episodes of *The Lone Ranger.* He'd been with *Lassie* since the beginning and would direct fifty episodes of our show, too. This particular episode required a skilled touch. Mr. Campanella hadn't done much work in front of the camera, and nothing in 1959 was wheelchair-friendly. Holly was the perfect guy for the job.

Campy was something else. He fought bitterness and depression, wrote a book about his experiences, and ended up mentoring young players and working with the Dodgers well into his seventies. During his few days with us on the set, he was warm, approachable, and very inspiring both on camera and off. I am honored to have worked with him.

I watched this episode as an adult, while I was going through a challenging time with my own kids. In it, Timmy overhears one boy's threats to another on his baseball team and then is threatened himself. Timmy struggles with turning in the bully, but he fears reprisal. Eventually, he takes his problem to his dad. I know a lot of parents who would have told their child they did the right thing coming to them and they would handle it from here, relieving the child of further responsibility; but not Paul Martin. He said Timmy knew what was right and what he alone had to do. Timmy had a sleepless night, but the next day, he handled his own problem. It was some great tough love and exactly the right advice—then and now. I mentioned it to June the next time I saw her, how surprised I was that such timeless parenting came from men in the 1950s. "And from men in prison," June said. "Excuse me?" I responded. She explained that Bob Golden hired many writers who'd been blacklisted during Senator Joe McCarthy's witch hunt for Communists in Hollywood in the early 1950s. Hundreds were prevented from working and a few served time in prison for their beliefs—or for being in the wrong place at the wrong time. Robert Lees was one of our writers who invoked his Fifth Amendment privilege at the HUAC trials and was quickly blacklisted. He wrote under the name of J. E. Selby and used a front—a stand-in—to deliver the scripts he wrote for *Lassie* as well as *Land of the Giants* and *Green Hornet.* I am proud of this show for so many reasons; now I have one more reason.

Tommy and Darlene

Nine days after Tommy Rettig's eighteenth birthday, he married his girlfriend, Darlene, in a private ceremony in Fawnskin, California, at the home of Darlene's aunt and uncle.

Paul Petersen: In short order Tommy whisked off his fifteen-year-old girlfriend and turned her into his wife. It bordered on a scandal.

December 1959
Directors Guild Christmas party with George Chandler
19: Christmas party in San Diego at Port Heuneme
Tommy Rettig weds Darlene Portwood

Tommy was cruising Sunset Boulevard with a couple of buddies in his new Chevy convertible when he saw Darlene and a friend sitting on a bus bench on La Brea. Petite with a tiny waist and lots of curves, Darlene was a little doll. She and her friend recognized Tommy and drove around with them for hours. When Darlene sang along to a jingle on the radio, Tommy was blown away by her voice. He drove her home to his mom's at two o'clock in the morning so she could hear her. Naive and inexperienced, Darlene was swept off her feet. Tommy's mother Ricki continued the seduction by waving a singing career in front of her.

Darlene: She was a manager of singers like Jackie DeShannon, and she became my manager. We used to go on personal appearances. When we got paid, she'd say, "They really don't want to pay you. You just sign the check and give it back to them because it's payola." We didn't know squat and signed the checks. Come to find out many years later, she was cashing them.

Jon and Francile came in with their mom to meet Ricki. Cecile was there trying to get Fran into the business. They were like scared little rabbits, following whatever his mother said to do because that was the right thing. "Stand up straight because this person is very important and do this because of that. . . ." Ricki and Cecile would engage in a game of one-upmanship, a bunch of phony bull between them. That was the first time I felt sorry for Tom. Ricki would always groan and say Cecile was such a stage mother and I'd think, "Are you kidding?"

Long in the Tooth

Because we shot scenes from different episodes at the same time, everything needed to match, including my teeth; I had to have all of them. Anytime baby teeth toward the front of my mouth were loose, I was whisked off to a Beverly Hills dentist as arranged by the Wrathers. The loose tooth was pulled and a bridge was made with a false tooth or teeth to fill in the gap. When one of my front teeth was loose, they decided to pull both at the same time . . . that wasn't a fun day. I can picture it like it was yesterday. The dentist used a hammer and pliers, banging away and twisting the tooth. I'd been given Novocain, but the sound of the hammer and the twisting, it was absolutely horrific.

One day, Lloyd and I were at Paramount Studios for lunch—their commissary was much better than Desilu's—and we ran into Bob Hope. He said he wanted to meet me and pulled me up onto his lap. All kinds of people were standing around watching us. Apparently this guy was a big deal. Mr. Hope said, "Make me laugh, kid." It got real quiet and everyone stared at me. I opened my mouth—and I dropped my choppers. Mr. Hope cracked up, then shouted, "Somebody get a camera!" We recreated the moment for posterity.

Posing with Hollywood legends: Bob Hope, Ernie Kovacs, Cesar Romero, Buster Keaton.

Boos and Booze

George Pittman, on-set teacher: Jon is a very serious child and surprisingly shy. I am very strict with him. He makes A's and B's, but he would get away with anything he could.

If that sounds a bit harsh to you, it did to Mom, too. There was something . . . odd about Mr. Pittman. He was different in a way that made Mom uneasy. She just didn't trust him. After a while, she began timing my study sessions in the schoolroom and discovered Mr. Pittman was shorting me an hour a day of school. Five minutes here, ten minutes there and the producers got an extra hour with me in front of the camera while I got only two of my three hours of daily lessons. The rumor was Pittman was getting a financial bonus for falsifying my school records. Mom had him fired, but the bottom line is someone in a position of power was "encouraging" the teacher to cheat me of what little education I was receiving. And my bosses and crew genuinely cared for me.

Mom saved the day, but she couldn't be everywhere. Usually, there were no problems for me, especially when I was with adults; I knew what they expected from me. It was kids my own age I wasn't sure about. Fortunately, my instinct saved me on more than one occasion. One day around this time, I was playing in my dressing room with another boy who was a guest on the show. He initiated playing "doctor," and I innocently pursued this path of "I'll show you mine if you show me yours." This was all new for me. He led the way and we giggled and pointed, and it was all perfectly normal. Then the boy said he wanted to show me something else and told me to turn around. When I did, he tried to hold me and rub against me. The giggling stopped and something felt . . . wrong. Not so wrong that I shouted for help or even told anyone, but wrong enough that I pushed him off me and never forgot it. Now, as an adult, I realize this poor boy was acting out something that was being done to him. It was a cry for help, but I didn't recognize it then. I only knew to move away from it.

Things ran smoothly on the set, though Rudd still battled depression from Pal's loss and Lassie Jr.'s ongoing battle with cancer. A tough, old-school type of guy, Rudd and some of his crew pals had been known to knock back a few drinks, and their lunches at Nickodell's, around the corner on Melrose, were infamous. Believe it or not, they took me sometimes. Mom never went with me. When Rudd took me to Nickodell's, it was just us guys . . . none of whom really watched out for me. Once I was running full speed around a corner and just missed slamming into a large waitress armed with two fully loaded trays. She hit me with a one-two verbal punch instead and I never ran in a restaurant again.

Lloyd: The guys drank their lunch, but that was never anything to worry about. They didn't have much time to do serious drinking.

Darlene: Even drinking, Rudd had more sense than anybody.

Bob Weatherwax: Oh, yeah. I went there, too, but I didn't participate in what they did. It was usually the sound man, Wally Nogle. He was a good friend of my father. It was a group of the guys that worked together . . . all old buddies at that point in time. They would go to lunch and have those "two martini" lunches. Well, you could do those things, but they got their job done. I remember, we had a director, Chris Nyby, and we knew we were finished for that day because all of a sudden the prop department would bring him out his drink. Then we knew we were down to our last shot. It was what they called "the martini shot."

Cecile: Rudd was a real drinking man, a real drinking man. I went with Jon and saw these things, but I didn't say anything. Jon had a good job and Rudd was a good guy. He drank on the set, but he turned out a good day's work and earned his money. He genuinely cared for Jon.

As an adult, I smoked Luckies for years. I wonder if that was subconscious. I never noticed any effects from the drinking, only that after lunch, everybody drank orange juice.

Grace: After lunch, that's when I'd go trolling—that's what I'd say to June and we'd laugh. The crew was all men. June and Ruby [June's hairdresser] and I stayed in June's dressing room. After lunch, I'd grab a cigarette and go once around the stage visiting all the guys. There was a room at the back of the stage for Rudd and his boys, his assistant Sam. After the scene was over, they'd go back in that room and drink.

Paul Petersen: If Rudd was there, he was drinking. There was the old

Hollywood way which accepted the golf cart that had a mobile bar and everybody participated. *The Donna Reed Show* wasn't exempt. We had liquid lunches. Carl Betz, my TV dad, took me for my first drink when I was fifteen . . . and they winked and served me because I was with him. I thought it was great. I remember doing *F-Troop* when the bar was on the back of the golf cart. I got to work with David Janssen because I could keep him sober two hours longer than any other actor. That was the era. Look at Robert Young, a classic story. Here's a guy who is playing America's father on *Father Knows Best* who admits that he was a practicing alcoholic while he was doing the show.

Stan Livingston: *I Love Lucy* was my favorite show and Bill Frawley was my favorite character. When we found out he was coming on *My Three Sons,* I thought, "This is so cool, Fred Mertz is going to be my grandfather!" He pretty much was. I thought he was the coolest person on the show. Nobody else would curse; he would curse really creatively. Nobody could control him. He was just a terror when he wanted to be one. He'd break everybody up during the scene because he wouldn't say the line, he'd say something else he felt like saying. Then every time we'd get to that spot, everybody would start laughing and we'd have to shoot it over and over.

Bill drank at lunch. He'd sit there and wouldn't want to leave. He'd have cronies show up at Nickodell's. We always sat in the same booth and I'd be sitting right beside them. Finally, it would be time to go back, and he wouldn't want to leave. I was the only one he'd listen to, so they'd send me to try to get him back. He'd be loaded by then, four or five drinks at lunch. He offered me a drink once. I didn't want to hurt his feelings so I drank it. I remember it was horrible. I think somebody yelled at him about it.

Lloyd: Rudd and Sam were both pretty good drinkers. He always had a station wagon and Lassie'd ride in back with the stunt double dog. One time when we drove out to Roland B. Ranch, Rudd opened the door and he and Sam both fell out on the ground, blasted to the gills. But they had amazing recuperative powers and they'd get the job done and do it well. It was more of a comedy routine than upsetting the company. The studio had no idea.

Rudd delivered, and everyone accepted his behavior. He was going through a tough time. Every so often I went home with Rudd for the weekend. It was a long drive out to Newhall, and Rudd usually stopped at the Rag Doll Bar way out in North Hollywood, across from the Palomino, a well-known cowboy bar. Lassie and I waited in the car while he had one or two more for the road. Then the three of us would travel the rest of the way to the ranch.

One such night at the ranch, after I'd gone to bed, I was awakened by the sound of shotgun blasts followed immediately by breaking glass. BOOM! CRASH!! BOOM! CRASH!! Rudd and his third wife, Betty, got into a hell of an argument, which Rudd ended by blowing out the living room windows with a shotgun. I told Mom about it on Monday, and all she said was, "You know those crazy Hollywood types." I know it sounds pretty extreme now, but I never felt scared or in danger. I knew Rudd would never hurt me, and he never did. I loved him like my own blood, and it was a tremendous moment for me to be able to place my own son in his arms decades later.

Lions and Tigers and Chimps, Oh My!

Lassie was a one-take actor, but other animals frequently caused havoc on the set or on location. Many afternoons were spent chasing runaway pigs or raccoons and once, before my time, a lion got loose on the soundstage. Jack Weatherwax slammed the stage door seconds before the animal bounded out onto Sunset Boulevard.

> *Flip:* I did several episodes, but the one I remember most is the one with that stupid wallaby. We were way out in the Valley on location and that wallaby got away. We were all chasing it. They finally caught it almost twenty miles away.

We worked with several chimps over the years. For one episode, we'd worked for a few days with an older male chimp and had one more day to go with him. The chimp's trainer looked like what you'd get if you called Central Casting for a big game hunter: jodhpurs and boots, a bush jacket, and a pith helmet. He had a firearm strapped to his side. Lloyd and I got a big kick out of this guy looking like he was prepared to face the king of the jungle and here he was with a chimp in a pair of overalls. As I was leaving the studio for the day, I walked by the chimp and reached out to rub his head, sort of a "see you tomorrow" gesture. Instead, the chimp grabbed my thumb, stuffed it in his mouth and started chewing. Blood was spurting and I was screaming, and the chimp took off with my thumb and me in tow. Everyone is running and yelling and the chimp is dragging me back and forth. The trainer is screaming at him, "Stop! Stop!!" Finally, he grabbed his gun, loaded with blanks, and fired into the air. The chimp was so startled, he let go of me. Someone wrapped my hand in a towel and rushed me to the studio infirmary. They cleaned it up and got me to the emergency room, where they sewed me up and saved my thumb. Next day, I gritted my teeth and finished the shoot with my attacker. The show must go on.

School

Lassie finished for the season, leaving ten or twelve weeks in the school year. Right after spring break, I started at Beverly Hills Catholic School on Linden Drive, south of Wilshire. All classes were coed and taught by nuns, which was a whole new experience for me. If ever I felt like a fish out of water it was now—I didn't know anyone. At least we all had to wear the same thing.

March 1960

Billy Hinsche of Dino, Desi and Billy: I was in the fourth grade, about nine. Jon's a year older. Loads of children from famous people went to our school. In my class alone, we had Hal Roach's daughter Kathy; Jeanne Crane's daughter Jeanine; Dino Martin Jr.; Lisa Farrow, whose parents were John Farrow and Maureen O'Sullivan; Steve Carey, MacDonald Carey's son, so that was pretty commonplace. But Jon was different, because he was a bona fide star in his own right. When you're that young, I don't think you're really aware of the magnitude of your friends' parents' stardom. That's stuff you don't really think about. I am sure that everyone in that school watched *Lassie*. Jon was special, and it was a bit of a stir when we heard he would be coming to school. As opposed to children of famous people, he *was* the famous people.

I was looking forward to meeting him. I was very anxious to get to know him a little bit and be in his midst. I liked him as an actor, and I thought that he had the coolest job in the world. He was very blond, and unfortunately, he got a lot of taunting from the older guys. I felt sorry for him in that regard. He would get into fistfights with guys. Oh yeah, he was a scrapper, and I've got to commend him for that because I wouldn't have wanted to be in his shoes. It was horrible the way that some of the older guys treated him. Plus it was such an easy fight because he was so little. He would turn beet red and just be flailing away and got sent to the principal's office a number of times for fights. He had a rough time there.

Stan Livingston: Jon and I would run into each other and talk about school. We didn't like it. It was just my awkwardness, not knowing how to handle it—going back to school and having to face all these kids wanting to ask you a zillion questions or wanting to beat you up; that was the other side of it. I wanted a private tutor to help me finish out the rest of the year, but my parents were smart enough to know you had to have some kind of social life, to meet kids my own age. Looking back on it, I can see how a tutor could really mess you up. If you had the wrong type of parents, you could come out of there feeling so special and privileged, you'd just be obnoxious. To just deal with it was better than being segregated—even if I got my ass kicked.

I suppose Stan's right, but BHCS was never easy. While I was on hiatus, I finally had time to check out our new neighborhood. Maybe I'd have an easier time there. Right away, I met the Conflenti family across the street. Frank and Adrianne, Lucille and Marty Jr. were really nice kids, and they had a pool where Fran, William, and I were all welcome.

Ron Greene with Adrianne, Lucille and Marty Conflenti.

Frank Conflenti: Jon was just the kid next door that was on TV. I really enjoyed his parents. I would just walk over and visit with them. Jon's mother would make me lunch and we'd sit and talk. I am sure Cecile is the reason that my mother got my brother and me set up with an agent.

Bill was always tearing out in that Mustang. Bill was a good-looking kid too! His sister was drop-dead gorgeous! Bill and Fran were all about the party. Jon didn't get as much in that way because he had to be so public at an early age.

The Conflentis' is where I met another neighborhood friend, Ron Greene. Ron had a brother William's age, and we all became great pals. Ron and I got on our bikes after school and he showed me the ins and outs of the territory and introduced me to another friend of his, Mike Shepherd. Mike lived with his mom a few miles away. The three of us would become thick as thieves.

Jay North

Jay North: Being around Jon was one of the positive aspects of my experience in the business, and I'm thankful that I did have my experience—even though it was horrifying for me—I got to meet Jon and have him as a lifelong friend. I didn't have any siblings and looked at Jon as a brother figure and bonded with him in that way—bowling, miniature golfing. We spent time on weekends doing things I imagined brothers would do together.

April 1960
12: Attended Patsy Awards
16: CBS Employees Club Easter party for 50 foster children with Lassie and Jay North

Jay was a good guy—Jaybird, I called him. We were paired for years at publicity events: we both looked the same age (I'm a year and a half older); we were both blond—poor Jay had to have his brown hair bleached regularly; we were both the youngest stars of our own shows; and both of us were great friends with Jeanne Russell. But Jay and I were very different, and our experience in Hollywood was very different too. Jay never knew his father. His mom, Dorothy, was a single working mother. She showed up for the more public events. Jay was left in the care of an aunt and uncle who were very cruel, very cold. And though we never knew it then, Jay told me later that when he got dirty or flubbed his lines, they would hit him in places where the bruises wouldn't show. He was so intimidated.

Jeanne: Jon and I were once at the water cooler together on the *Lassie* set. He was telling me a story when they called him back to work. "I'll be there in a minute!" he shouted back, confident, not cocky. He finished his story and then went to work. Whenever Jay was called to the set, no matter what he was doing, he dropped it immediately and rushed over, apologizing all the way. When the camera rolled, he put on that big grin. Jon was feisty as the dickens off camera and he turned on the big innocent eyes as Timmy. I mean, that's who you remember right? He was a lot calmer as Timmy, but more importantly, he was a consummate professional. In fact, that professionalism has defined my relationship with Jon and with Jay. We were friends, but there was always that underlying thing of us being professionals. We were being trained to do the same thing. It was like we were soldiers in the trenches together rather than just buddies who hung out on the back stairs.

Jay: I felt closest to Jon; we just developed an instant rapport. I couldn't relate to other kids outside the business. I didn't know how to relate to them. I felt this closeness to Jon because we were going through the same life experience, and I felt safe around him. I was exposed to the ridicule of other kids who were jealous and resentful of my success and didn't know how to relate to me. I always felt comfortable and protected with Jon. We were both working professionals. We were not adults, and yet we were not children either; we were caught in this limbo stage. I was able to play little league on weekends, and I did have some normal friends. But Jon was my peer.

I felt really close to Cecile. She would be at the parades and the parties. B.A. just didn't seem to be there. He was MIA, so to speak. I'd see him at the house in Beverly Hills, but I didn't know how to relate to him. Jon, myself, Cecile, and Dorothy, we were a foursome. My mom and Cecile were really very friendly, no professional jealousy between them, though I sensed that on other sets from other parents. Cecile was such a sweet lady and very protective of me as well as Jon. I always felt that she was my second mother, always felt so comfortable around her and B.A. I never got to know William or Francile well; they were older.

Jay and I did start to spend some time together, and naturally, after one event, he asked if I could spend the night at his aunt and uncle's. We played, made Jiffy Pop, whatever little boys do on a sleepover. Sunday morning, we made breakfast and finally settled in front of the TV for cartoons in the master bedroom. I don't remember Jay's aunt that morning, but his uncle was in bed with coffee and the Sunday paper spread all around. "Hey boys, want to read the comics?" "Sure!" We jumped up on the bed and reached for the funny papers. Jay's uncle lifted up the blanket, "Come on, get inside where it's warm." Under the covers, he was naked, holding himself. I fell back off the bed. I'd never seen anyone do anything like that before or even heard of it, but instinctively I knew to run. I mumbled something like "No, thank you" and avoided him for the rest of my visit. That night, I told my mom that I didn't want to spend the night at Jay's house again. She just said OK; she never asked why and I never told her.

> **April 1960**
> 29: Photo op at the Marine Air Reserve Training Detachment, Memphis, TN
> 30: *TV Guide* Party in Houston; June, Lassie, and I are on cover

Personal Appearances

Dad: One day when I came home from work, Cecile told me that Jon had been invited to be a celebrity guest at some old auto race, but she turned it down. I asked her what kind of old auto race and she said somewhere in Indiana. "What?!" I said. "Do you mean the INDIANAPOLIS 500?" She said, "Yes, I think that's what they told me." Boy, oh boy, she really had to undo that one the next day; and, of course, Jon and I went and had a marvelous time. They liked Jon so well that he was invited back for the next two. Cecile and Jon went in 1961 and Bill and I went with Jon in 1962. What a wonderful experience, and we were entertained royally—thanks to Jon.

May 30, 1960

The weather for the race was bright and clear that Memorial Day. So many people had gathered all along the road leading up to the stadium. Dad and I loved it. Lassie never went to Indy; the cars were too loud for him. The most fun for me was taking an Indy 500 parade lap in

a special car. Cesar Romero rode with me. Dad sat in the front with the driver. Cesar and I waved from the back seat as we drove slowly around the track. People were cheering and waving flags and everyone shouted what they always shout when they see me—to this very day, "Where's Lassie?" Cesar leaned over, "Tell them she's in the trunk." I used that line for years.

It really was a great time. I love race cars and we got to get up close and personal with them, in the pits. I even got to sit behind the wheel of one. I helped crown the Queen of the "500" Festival, and Dad and I attended the Governor's Ball. Every time I traveled to a new city, we always made time to visit some local children's hospitals, which was something I really enjoyed.

Mom: That's what's so special about Jon. These poor little bodies, deformed and twisted . . . and he'd just go up and start talking. Nothing fazed him. He just accepted it.

June 1960
Pilgrimage Theater for the L.A. Christian Education Program

Someone once said my mom would have taken me to the opening of an envelope. She did accept most invitations that came along . . . which is no doubt how I ended up the Grand Marshall of the Costa Mesa Fish Fry and Parade. I was still at an age where I didn't question any of these events. Mom simply told me the plan for the day and I went. We went down the day before and, at some point, I was alone in the motel room when the phone rang. It was a group of kids who'd tracked me down.

Cherrie Dolloff: My brothers and I found out Jon was staying at the Coral Reef Motel. We called and they put us through to his room. We were all trying to get together to play, but none of us had any transportation, so we were not able to. We were disappointed and ended up chatting on the phone for a while instead.

William: He grew up doing what he was told to do and didn't know any better because this was his whole life. He'd come home, have to learn his lines for the next day, go back to work. On weekends, it was personal appearances, parades, what have you, or going out of town for some festivities. He probably wondered, "How come Fran and William don't do this?" We would go along once in a while, but not all the time. For a while, I'd rather stay home with my friends or go do something else. We could do that, but he couldn't. I do remember there were times where he wanted to do certain things, but he didn't have the choice. He had to do it.

I wasn't the only one feeling isolated and alone. Fran and William were pretty much on their own. We all thought or at least hoped that things might change when we lived under the same roof again, but it didn't happen. Mom was still with me on the set all day and at any and all appearances on weekends; but, in an attempt to cover all the bases, she made sure they never came home to an empty house.

William: When we moved to Beverly Hills, my mom was always at the studio with Jon during the day. She had a little old lady named Heloise taking care of the house, so there was an adult there for Fran and me when we came home from school. She was a real character. She drank some of my dad's liquor, and we had to start marking the bottle to see how much she drank.

Fran: William had stopped going, but I still visited the set sometimes. Lloyd Nelson, I loved him, and of course, Rudd and Jackie and Sam always had big hugs and kisses for me. I think the crew knew that I was lonely. They had worked so many times with so many child actors that they saw what happened to the siblings. And they read my mother really well.

In June I attended the 12th Annual Emmy Awards at NBC's Burbank Studio. This was the first Emmy show to be broadcast in color, so there was a lot of excitement about it. We were all personally excited for June Lockhart, who was nominated for Best Actress in a Leading Role. (Jane Wyatt, the mom on *Father Knows Best*, ended up winning it for the third time.) I was a presenter, teamed up with Danny Thomas, who possessed what we called in the business a big schnozzola. He took one look at me, pointed to my face and said, "You call that a nose?"

June 20, 1960

The Emmys and Hollywood made history that night. For Outstanding Performance in a Variety or Musical Program or Series, the

August 1960

7: Tommy Eugene Rettig, Tommy and Darlene's first child, is born.

award went to Harry Belafonte for his television special *Tonight with Harry Belafonte*, making him the first African American to win an Emmy.

About this time, Bonita sponsored my mother into the Motion Picture Mothers Club. My mother loved clubs, and she belonged to many throughout her life. But this became THE club for Mom. I don't think she ever loved anything more.

> Mom: Bonita Granville's mother belonged; her name was Timmie. She said, "Cecile, now you're the mother of a star and you will love this club." And boy, did I fall in love with it, and they fell in love with me. I was on the board of directors from the beginning. This opened up a new life for me and I enjoyed every minute.

The organization was founded in 1930 as a small social group. Many mothers of child actors had moved to Los Angeles from all over the country and even other countries, and they welcomed the friendships. Quickly, they incorporated, with membership limited to one hundred and charity within the industry as its chief purpose. In 1942, the Motion Picture and Television Country Home and Hospital was founded and became the main beneficiary of the efforts of the moms.

> Cecile: When I went into the Motion Picture Mothers, Cesar Romero's mother was still living, Gary Cooper's, Judy Garland's, Natalie Wood's . . . all these wonderful people. I never believed I'd be in the same room with them. I became a president, but most of those had died before then. I was a very active member for more than forty years.

Working Kids

Midway through the season, Spook's replacement was finally ready. Baby joined the cast, and he was gorgeous, with eyes so expressive he melted hearts from across the room. But Baby was much more than just a pretty face. He could do things that just blew me away. Once, I was up at Rudd's ranch for a weekend. He and Lassie and I were fishing in a pond about a quarter mile from the house. Rudd discovered he was out of cigarettes. He told Baby to go back to the house and get some more cigarettes and off he went. I figured this was going to be like the "c-clamp" episode: Who knows what he'll come back with? But sure enough, ten minutes later Baby came ambling back with a new pack of cigarettes in his mouth. That's smart.

Bob Weatherwax: Baby could do anything I told him except read or talk. I could tell him to fetch magazines, to call my dad, and many similar commands.

After Lucille Ball and Desi Arnaz divorced in 1960, they attempted to continue running Desilu together, but it was quickly apparent that that would not work. Desilu had already begun producing *The Lucy Show*, so it was decided that Lucy should be the one to assume full ownership—making her the first woman to head a major studio and one of the most powerful women in Hollywood.

Stan: Right after I started *My Three Sons*, Lucy got this cream white Continental convertible. I thought it was just the coolest car. I was looking at her car one day and she came out and said, "Oh, you like that car?" I said, "Yeah!" "You wanna ride?" She came out of her office, which was in the middle of the studio. I pointed and told her I had to go back down there, so she rode me back to Studio 11 in her car. She was real nice, and when I'd see her, she'd always come up and talk to me. I was a big fan of hers.

Jon was already in his third or fourth year of *Lassie* and we would run into each other on the lot. The adults had all these golf carts to ride around in and Jon had a miniature one, and I thought that was the coolest thing. He let me try it, but I never did get one. At least I had my bike.

We had blocks of time where they didn't need us. We'd take off on our bikes and go to different departments, knock on the door and say, "Hey, what do you do here?" I remember this one really cool place where they had clay. It was for people who would sculpt things for sets. I'd always go there and get a big block of clay to bring back and do stuff with it. We'd just explore these different places. We found a prop room. What lured me in was a King Kong right in the doorway, about 6 or 7 feet high; I think it was on wheels.

How crazy that a kid who lived on a farm in the country wasn't sup-

posed to get dirty. [Jon was] more restricted, and perhaps more pampered in a way. It comes with the turf. We were like the second bananas on our show, where Jon really was the star . . . and the dog. I think the way people related to him was different too. He wasn't allowed to do certain things. Our producers wanted us to look like real kids. If we came in with a scrape, they said great. Don [Grady] and Tim [Considine] were like older brothers to me. That was before Barry was on the show. They used to torture me with older brother type things. We were always playing basketball or baseball, and we'd see Jon and tell him to come over and he didn't show up or couldn't. At that age, we thought he was too stuck up or aloof. We just thought he was on a different level and chose not to integrate himself with other kids. We always had kids on our show, and we'd always sucker them into baseball, basketball, skateboarding—whatever we could drag them into. But we could never get Jon down there.

I got a double whammy: I didn't know how to do those things *and* the Wrathers wouldn't let me do them. There were no moments with Dad showing me how to hold a bat, no playing catch with William; he and I ran lines together instead.

The other side was that they had the impression I was aloof. Later, as a teen, one of the fan magazines wrote that about me and I was really stung by it. Although compared to today's tabloid climate, I guess I got off lucky.

Bryan Russell: Jay was pretty active in little league, and so was Kurt Russell, but I wasn't. My little league experience was my acting. I always loved baseball and wound up coaching little league with both my son and daughter. I got to relive a little of what I missed through my kids' experiences—with a youthful exuberance because we *are* experiencing it for the first time.

Billy Hughes: The poor boy [Jon] was horribly sheltered in that he was never allowed to do anything because he was always on the set. It must have gotten really old. Every boy wants to go out and play baseball. You need a break. And it did become real work week after week after week.

Roger Maris and Mickey Mantle with Bryan in *Safe at Home.*

Billy Hughes guested on *Lassie* that year with the great character actress Ellen Corby as his "ma." Right away, he was different. He had more of the Southern ways that were so familiar to me after all my visits to Arkansas. Turns out his family hailed from there and from Oklahoma. They were driven west during the Dust Bowl. He was more like a country kid than a city kid.

Billy Hughes: I was raised by my grandmother. She was an uneducated woman in the sense of academia, but she was a very wise and prudent lady and she took on this challenge of raising me and my brother Krauss, who was also in the business. She and her family were from Tennessee and Arkansas, so technically, I was a country kid.

I thought Lassie was a wonderful, wonderful series and Jon was an exceptionally good child actor. I know he was well pampered by the cast and crew because he was the star of the show, and I felt he should be treated like that. It was like all eyes were constantly on Jon to make sure he was protected, to make sure his makeup was always just right, his hair was always just right, his clothing was always right. His tutor made sure he got his training. I never was jealous; I thought it was entirely appropriate, that this was the way actors should be treated, especially stars like Jon. I thought it was really neat. He was whisked away after the scene to his tutor with people admonishing him the whole way, "Don't get dirty; don't muss your hair." I thought this was the "star treatment." I see now how restrictive it was, but at the time I was in such awe and felt so privileged, I didn't notice.

> **December 1960**
> 17: Christmas party on *USS Norton Sound* in Port Hueneme

Billy was wonderful on the show, playing part of a backwoods family in an episode called "Cracker Jack." It was so well received that they wrote a sequel to it that became one of our four Christmas episodes. I remember Billy warmly: he was "country," not at all like most of the kids that worked on the show; and he did more than one episode, but we had no time to bond. He was in and out of my world in three days and the next new face was there. That's how it was for me. New faces everywhere I went. My childhood was chaotic.

That Christmas day, my third Christmas episode, "The Christmas

Story," aired. In the show, Timmy befriends a boy and girl who turn out to be living in an abandoned shack with little food. Efforts to help are rebuffed by the father. At first, it appears he's wanted by the law, but he only fears they will take his children away because he has no means of support. Timmy and Lassie help the family enjoy a happy Christmas. Paul Martin finds the dad a job. Ruth bakes. Timmy wears a hilarious Santa suit that is way too big for him and collects donations for them. Fake snow falls in Franklin Canyon. Once again, all's right in the world. Merry Christmas, everybody!

January 1, 1961 We were in the Rose Bowl Parade again. We spent New Year's Eve with some family in Pasadena connected to the parade so that we wouldn't have any trouble reaching our float by 7:00 a.m. on the corner of South Orange Grove and Bellefontaine in Pasadena. Hundreds of people were already lining the parade route, camped out for the night. We got to see the floats the night before. People worked on them all through the night, and the smell of all the flowers was almost suffocating. My float, "Hearts and Flowers," was sponsored by FTD Florists, and my "riding partner" was Angela Cartwright from *The Danny Thomas Show*.

I knew her a little from appearances with her and her older sister, Veronica, who had just been cast in Bonita's role in a *These Three* remake called *The Children's Hour* with Audrey Hepburn and Shirley MacLaine. Float judging began promptly at 7 o'clock. We made our way in the dark, bundled up against the cold, to arrive on time. I checked out the float top to bottom, including the vehicle that drove it. There was just the smallest opening to see the road. Angela, Lassie, and I got to our spots on the float and strapped ourselves into the special hidden seats built for us to lean on for support.

Angela Cartwright: All I remember is that I was sitting on a heart of flowers. To tell you the truth, I feel like my life WAS a parade when I was young . . . there were so many.

It was a long, cold couple of hours from the start point to the end of the parade. From our vantage point, the parade route looked like it went on forever, with thousands of people stretched out before us. The Rose Parade is unlike any other, just the sheer magnitude of it. People yelled out to me all along the route.

Karen McCoy Montecillo: The float stopped right in front of me, and everyone was yelling at him to throw a flower to them. He kept saying he wasn't supposed to. I yelled at him to please throw me a flower and he leaned over and picked an orchid off the float and threw it to me. This jerk boy grabbed it and shoved me back down on the curb. With that, Jon stood up and yelled down to him, "No! It's for her." He finally gave it to me and I still have that flower pressed in an old family Bible. I remember the incident as if it was yesterday, but I know it wasn't. Ahh! The memories!

> **January 1961**
> 2: Beverly Hills Hotel reception after the Super Bowl for Hubert Humphrey and other officials from Minnesota

Fran

After the holidays, things settled down again at home . . . sort of. Fran and Mom had problems.

Fran: She worked us hard. I think my father would have made a list of chores, but it would have been fair chores in order to earn an allowance: raking leaves, taking out the trash, washing the dinner dishes. But Mom's chores for us were: all the dusting, all the ironing, polishing all the silver . . . I was so embarrassed. Some of my friends knew I couldn't go out until I had cleaned the house. I was my mother's Cinderella.

If Mom really did knock five years off her age, making me a "change of life" baby, then she was well into her "change of life" by this point, which only exacerbated things. Fran could not get Mom's attention by simply being a good girl, so she tried to get her attention being an actress. Though her heart wasn't in it, she gave it her all, but Mom wasn't giving out "A"s for effort. Frustrated, Fran began to rebel.

Fran: One of the perks of having a famous brother was that I got some great dates. I went to something with Don Grady—arranged through my mother—and every girl there just drooled! And Jody McCrea, Joel's son, took me to a real big premiere. I must have been all of fifteen years old. That's the funny thing. My mother let me go out with those people. When I was fourteen years old, I could get in a car with a guy if he was somebody from Hollywood—Jackie Wrather, Kenny Osmond. . . . It wasn't so much "dating" dating, because I was very young, but they were allowed to pick me up and take me places.

In tenth grade, I was dating a guy Mom didn't approve of. She said he was a bad influence. He really wasn't, but Mom just decided she didn't like him. She had "higher expectations" for me. She warned me to stop seeing him, and when I didn't, she pulled me out of Beverly in the middle of the year and put me in Notre Dame, an all-girls school. I couldn't drive yet and that was the end of that. But it also took me away from all my friends, my classes. . . .

March 1960
Beverly Hills Scouts cookie drive launch at City Hall
18: Sports and Travel Show to raise funds for a teen center

Tony Dow, Cara Williams, Shelley Fabares, Paul Petersen, and Jeanne Russell.

Mom had been pulling William and Fran up by the roots and plunking them down somewhere since any of us can remember. Otherwise, I don't know how Fran could have handled it. I was far too young to understand the dynamics going on at the time. I took off with Ron and Mike whenever I had the chance. William tried to stay out of it altogether. He was close to graduating high school, had his close circle of friends, and just tried to fly below the radar.

In February of that year, I auditioned for the movie version of the Broadway musical *The Music Man*.

Jeanne: My mom coached him. I remember them going over the same song over and over again, "Gary, Indiana." It was just comical, because singing wasn't Jon's strong point. Every kid in town auditioned for that. Ronny Howard got it.

March 19, 1961
At dawn, I welcomed the swallows back to Capistrano then drove eighty miles to Santa Monica for the official opening of POP for a parade and my eleventh birthday party.

Lou Tylee, former Junior Cotton King: Memphis was a big cotton town. Every spring, two kids were selected to represent all kids in the Cotton Carnival. I was selected as the Junior King and some girl from

WELCOME BACK SWALLOWS

My eleventh birthday party. *l to r:* Jeanne, Lori Martin, Joey Scott, Ron, me, Flip, Barry Gordon, Charlie Herbert, Teddy Rooney, Jimmy Fields, Roger Mobley; cutting the cake with Ron Howard.

another school selected as Junior Queen. My picture was on the front page of the newspapers. I went to several formal balls where all the southern belles fawned over me. I got to be on the local teen dance party TV show. And, I got to meet Jon—Timmy.

Meeting Timmy was a big highlight for a little sixth grader. We were just boys in front of a bunch of people. I was disappointed Lassie wasn't there; I assumed they were always together. We stood there for a few minutes while all the adults did their important adult stuff. Jon seemed to be operating on automatic pilot. He was polite, but I recall he didn't smile more than just "straight lips." He seemed very much like Timmy from the show—quiet and obedient. He was there to do his job. As for myself, this night was my first date ever. A cute little blonde was up in the stands waiting for me. I just wanted to get all the adult stuff out of the way so I could be with her! I'm guessing Jon had similar thoughts, "Let's get this over and move on to something I want to do."

March 1961

21–23: 2-day trip to North Carolina; day one: lunch with Miss America, a visit to the children's hospital, taping of *Bozo the Clown*, taping of *5 O'clock Fun*, followed by a live press conference; day two: another hospital visit, another live TV appearance, and the opening of a Park 'n Shop

April 1961

Candy for Hope campaign in San Francisco

14: NBC Burbank for the *TV Guide* Awards

Whittier, CA, to launch national bicycle safety program

27: Grand Marshall of the Temple City Children's Parade

29: Memphis Spelling Bee and the Cotton Carnival

Heigh Ho, Heigh Ho . . .

We traveled to the Grand Canyon to shoot our season premiere. This was the farthest we had ever traveled for an

April 28–May 3

episode. We all got in cars and trucks and buses and drove to Arizona. I'd never been to the Grand Canyon, so I was pretty excited. A group of local students from the Grand Canyon School participated in the show. I got to have a snowball fight with some of them, my first. We had enough free time one day for Mom and me to go on one of those mule rides down into the canyon . . . at least I think we did. I rode a donkey in the show, and now I'm not sure which was real. But I'm very clear on the guest actor, Robert Armstrong. The second I saw him, I knew I was looking at none other than Carl Denham, the man who brought Kong to New York. I was thrilled to meet "another" of the stars of the film and told him all about finding King Kong at the studio; he very kindly seemed impressed.

May 1961
St. Mary's Episcopal church with Jeanne Russell
30: Indy 500 with Mom this time
June 1961
8: Grand Marshall for the Annual Days of Verdugos Parade in Glendale, CA
9–10: Portland Junior Rose Parade
18: Pittsburgh Variety Club Telethon

May 25, 1961

Only in L.A. would they have a major celebrity event at the opening of an airport, but that's just what they did for the L.A. New International Airport. We were all in a holding station at Robinson's department store in Beverly Hills. Helicopters picked us up there and flew us to the airport and back because traffic was at a standstill. Crazy! But I finally got to ride in a helicopter.

Summers on location could be brutal. Being stuck outside with temperatures soaring close to 100 degrees—in winter clothes—don't remind me. Up at Vasquez Rocks, Lassie and I looked for buried treasure. Tiburcio Vasquez was a Mexican Robin Hood in the mid-1800s, stealing from the new settlers and giving back to the Mexican ranchers. Legend has it he hid his loot out there, but all we ever found were arrowheads. One hot day in Franklin Canyon, I sneaked up behind different crew members and dumped ice cold water on them. I did this with complete confidence, knowing they couldn't do a thing to get me back. I was working and I couldn't get wet or dirty. OK, I admit it, I was obnoxious. At the end of the day, I was laughing to myself in my trailer about the mischief I created. I got my stuff together to go home, opened the door, and blam!—they were waiting for me. I was knocked back inside by a stream of water from the hose on the portable fire truck, held by every guy I'd soaked that day. They really got me good. They all laughed it up, but no one laughed harder than I did. I loved it.

July 1961
19: Benefit premiere at Fox Wilshire of *Francis of Assisi* for 20th Century Fox
Minneapolis: Aquatenial Association Day Parade—500,000 people came out for it

Anne Lockhart: I visited Mom on the set way out in Rolling Hills, and it was a hot day and windy. My sister and I were standing with Mom's

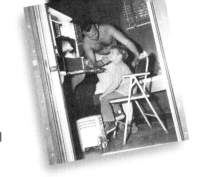

hairdresser, Ruby, when a wind came up and picked up one of those shiny reflectors, carried it through the air and it came down right on the back of my mom's neck and knocked her out cold! Ruby grabbed us and whisked us away. Everyone ran in the direction of my mother and I remember feeling that it was genuine and that everyone really loved each other on that set.

On the set, Rudd rewarded Lassie with treats throughout the day. His wife would boil a beef roast and cut it into little square-inch chunks. It was tasty and, being a kid, burning up energy, I used to eat the stuff all the time. I'd reach into Rudd's pocket or he'd give me some to give to Lassie and I'd end up eating it myself. Toward the end of the day, if he found he was running low, he'd have to cut me off.

Lloyd: Jon liked the dog and the dog liked him. Rudd protected the dog and rightfully so. Jon couldn't play with him because Rudd would say he needed his rest. Lassie rode on a little carpeted platform about six inches off the ground that Rudd pulled from set to set. It was a nice place for the dog to stay clean. Jon used to climb on and cuddle up with Lassie, put his head on Lassie's tummy and they'd both doze off.

Bernie Harrison reported on my visit to Pittsburgh in the *Evening Star* from the dining room at the Mayflower hotel: "Jon Provost, 11, the Timmy of *Lassie*, ate half of his friend's crabmeat cocktail, chatted animatedly with the critics, ordered a hamburger which he didn't eat, told us all the latest 'mommy, mommy' jokes, ordered another crabmeat cocktail 'with all the stuff on it,' autographed a dozen photos, got out on the floor of the dining room to demonstrate Japanese pushups, ordered blueberries for dessert, ate them, smiled wanly, and disappeared. One second he was there; the next, he was gone in that magical manner known to parents."

In New York, Lassie and I appeared on *Captain Kangaroo.* Now I saw what Flip was talking about. The studio was inside

August 1961
31: Antelope Valley Fair and Parade
September 1961
1–4: Pittsburgh
5: Chicago and Washington, DC, to receive the Kennedy Bronze medal
6: Philadelphia
7–10: New York City

a high-rise building. We got in an elevator like we were going to some-body's office, and instead, it was a television studio. I was excited to see the set, Grandfather Clock and all. It was fun to be there, but I didn't see it the way other children saw it. I knew there was no magic behind any of it. I was excited to meet "The Captain" and "Mr. Greenjeans," but they were not some special characters. I met them as my peers. I met all adults that way.

> *Ron Brown, fan:* My mother knew that I always enjoyed seeing Jon on *Lassie.* I found out he was going to appear on *Captain Kangaroo.* This was a problem since I had to be at school. I told her I wished I could see the show. The night before, she told me, "I am going to allow you to leave late for school tomorrow so you can see Timmy." I thought it was quite incredible that my mother would allow me that opportunity. After I arrived at school, the teacher called me to her desk and asked why I was late. I said, "Because I wanted to see Timmy on *Captain Kangaroo.*" Well, she never expected that excuse! I hate to tell you—but she didn't approve.

With Thordis Burkhardt.

I had a new teacher, Thordis Burkhardt, a thin, matronly, Old World–style woman. She was European, Swiss, I think. Her husband, Hans, was Swiss and a modern painter, an abstract expressionist. He was staunchly anti-war and felt that he must sometimes paint ugly, harsh images to illustrate his feelings. We were invited to their home several times, and I will never forget a work of his there—a charcoal drawing of Death stealing a baby from its mother's arms. I still shudder when I think of it. Thordis was strict with me but very nice. Best of all, she would remain my teacher for the remainder of my time on the show.

We had new neighbors in the soundstage next door. The *Ben Casey* show was in full swing with a tall, dark, and handsome leading man, Vince Edwards. Fran thought he was "dreamy," whatever that meant. Mom wandered onto their set one afternoon and made friends. She took her fresh-squeezed carrot juice over there and Mr. Edwards flipped for it. Mom made it for him regularly—and anyone else who wanted some. The lot was like family.

> *Grace:* Vince Edwards used to go to the races. His bookie called every

day and if he lost, he'd get so mad . . . once I saw him tear the phone out of the wall.

Abel Fernandez: We had one shot where we had to run through fire and that day, it happened that Vince, who played Ben Casey, came over to watch. As I was getting ready for the shot, Vince nudged me and said, "Do it, Abe. There's a doctor in the house."

We were shooting two shows at the same time, one at Gower and one at Culver City. We'd shoot daytime at Gower, leave there at 4:00, and go to Culver City and start shooting there. We did that for about six weeks because we were only two weeks ahead of tube so we had to go like crazy—we were all over the place, but it was fun. So anyway, Jon was shooting on another stage. This one day, Jon and his mother came over and Jon's eyes were real big because we were shooting machine guns that day. Everybody was calling out to him, "Hey, Jon, where's Lassie?" It was a joke because everyone called out to us, "Hey, where's Ness?" During the filming, I looked over at Jon and I could see he couldn't see because he's so little and I went and got my chair and I said, "Come on, Jon," and took him over pretty close to the camera and got him seated there. That way was all view and he could see everything. And when he got in the chair, he looked out and said, "Oh, boy!" He was such a good boy, a nice kid. We liked him. He was just the kind we liked. We forgot everything about *Lassie;* he was just our pal. That was it, that's the way Bob Stack and everybody felt. He was just like one of the regulars.

Abe and the guys were great. Mom didn't allow me to watch *The Untouchables* at home; it was the most violent show on TV. So, I loved those days when they'd invite me over for a shoot-out.

During the year, we worked with some great actors: Marie Windsor, Harry Carey Jr., Dick Foran, Jane Darwell, Stacy Keach, William Schallert, Fuzzy Knight, Denver Pyle, Karl Swenson. Lloyd appeared in a few episodes, too. People always ask what my favorite episode is. I guess if I have to pick, it'd be a three-parter we did in 1961 called "The Odyssey."

The story opens with Lassie and Timmy making a "friends forever" pact. He carves their names in a fallen tree and buries mementoes to seal

the deal, declaring it their secret place. Later, at a farmer's market, while playing with another dog, Lassie is accidentally locked in a truck and driven 600 miles before the driver realizes she's in there. Lassie leaps from the truck and begins her long journey home.

For the next two Sundays, Lassie tries to get home and the Martins try everything possible to find her. The future Skipper on *Gilligan's Island,* Alan Hale Jr., befriends Lassie in the woods, feeds her, and tends her wounds. He's very kind, but Lassie has a family and she must get home.

Back at the farm, weeks have passed. Timmy packs up all of Lassie's toys, including a rubber cat squeeze toy. He tells his mom he doesn't think Lassie is ever coming home. He doesn't think she's dead or anything; she's probably living with another really nice family. Even Timmy's mom cries.

Finally, Timmy takes all the toys to his and Lassie's secret place. There are the names carved in the tree. Timmy digs and find the mementoes he and Lassie had placed there together. He throws the rest of Lassie's toys in the hole, all the while wiping away tears. Slowly, he reaches for the shovel to cover the toys when . . . he hears a bark. Timmy freezes. Is he dreaming? Does he dare look? Bark! Bark!! He does look. There, at the top of a hill, she appears. "Lassie!! Lassie!!" Timmy drops the shovel and breaks into a run, arms spread wide. Lassie, barking, runs down the hill toward him. They meet on the hillside in a joyful reunion. . . . just a boy and his dog and their unconditional love for one another . . . one of the greatest love stories ever told.

"The Odyssey" was groundbreaking; this type of multipart adventure had never been attempted in TV drama before. Campbell's, which paid Wrather $7 million a year, fought the idea, believing viewers would not like having to wait to find out what happens, but the Wrathers pushed for it, producing television's first mini-series. We'd do several more in the next two years. In 1962, *Lassie* was the longest running drama on the air, with more adults watching than children.

The last of the Martin Christmas episodes, "Yochim's Christmas," aired. This was Billy Hughes's second episode. He and December 24, 1961 Ellen Corby return, as the Yochims, to the Martin farm on Christmas Eve. Billy Joe is pretty sad. He's lost both his pa and his dog, and he's so far from home that Santa Claus will never be able to find him. On a walk through the woods, he and Timmy and Lassie rescue an elderly man—Lloyd Corrigan, another old-timer from silent films—whose sleigh has tipped over on him. Billy Joe is convinced the man is Santa Claus . . . and in the end, that's just who he turns out to be. The story is sweet, but Christmas in the blistering July heat was torture.

Billy Hughes: It was shot in July, and I still have the *TV Guide* picture showing the set. We shot it up near trees and forest and a little lake. It was 95+ degrees and Jon and I were both dressed in Mackinaws, hats, boots, gloves along with Mr. Corrigan who played Santa Claus, a wonderful actor. They had put foam snow over everything, the trees, the ground, and it looked very real, but the cast and crew are sitting around with no shirts on, baking under umbrellas. It was extremely difficult.

I can remember it being very, very hot and thinking, "My goodness, are we ever going to get through this?" During the breaks, there were people who were concerned that we cooled off and drank plenty of liquids. They let us stand in the shade in all the clothing . . . that was it.

Lloyd: We'd covered the meadow with soapsuds for snow, and Jon was fascinated. We had a suds fight and I got him all wet—I got in trouble for that. Another time, we were on location at some ranch or another and I brought Jon a pea shooter and I damn near lost my job over that one because nobody knew it except Jon and me. He got everybody in the back of the head before the day was over and they made him talk.

Growing Up

A new year and another new red-and-white check shirt, a size larger. I was growing, and my voice was changing; I now had 1962 all my own teeth. Puberty had arrived. Rudd and the guys noticed my extended trips to the bathroom and started giving me "the business." They told me I'd start to grow hair on my palms . . . and when they caught me peeking at my hands, they roared with laughter. The teasing was always good-natured fun; that's what friends did with one another.

Mom: I think he stayed young longer than he would have on the street in public school. The studio and everybody who worked with Jon sheltered him. "You aren't allowed to do this. You can't do that." He wasn't allowed to play with the kids that came in for the schoolroom scenes because maybe he'd catch cold or chicken pox. It would throw all of them out of work if he couldn't be there. It was a big responsibility; they all shared it and didn't allow it.

Lloyd: The adolescent years—Jon showed a little more interest in the opposite sex. When we were alone, I remember teaching him a Cole Porter tune, fooling around learning lines. You couldn't pound the lines into him; you had to break it up with some humor, and I was teaching him, "Birds do it; bees do it; even educated fleas do it, let's do it" . . . and he'd sing, "Let's fall in love." It was kid stuff, but it was great. We had fun. He never asked me about sex or girls.

I really wasn't sure what to ask! Dad never taught me anything about the birds and the bees . . . zip. William and I just didn't have that kind of rapport. All I knew about sex I learned from Ron and Mike, two other twelve-year-olds—the blind leading the hairy-palmed.

Mom's Way

Mom answered all my fan mail. Some came to the studio, some to the Wrathers, some to our house. The Wrathers supplied her with photos, envelopes, and postage and Mom did the rest. She enlisted Fran and William when she could and tried to get me interested, but for the most part, it was Mom. I have to burst some bubbles here, and I apologize for that. I hear from many people who remind me that we corresponded for years. Some say that it meant everything to them that a TV star would take the time to write to "just a regular kid." Others were troubled and received support and sound advice from "me" that influenced the course of their lives. It was never me though—it was always Mom. I was way too busy to write letters, not to mention that reading and writing were never my favorite things. Mom sent these people birthday cards and gifts and remembered them at every holiday. She invited all of them into our home, and many came. Some she corresponded with for decades. A good handful of people I continue to write to today have been writing to me for forty-five years. I see it now as a privilege, but at ten or twelve, I wasn't interested. Mom would tell me that my salary was being paid by all the people who wrote those letters and I should want to help. But reading and writing was work for me, and I already had enough work.

Rudd was going to be on the game show *To Tell the Truth*, which was filmed in New York. You know the one: "Will the real Rudd Weatherwax please stand up?" Naturally, Lassie and I were on, too. First Class airline reservations to Idlewild Airport (later John F. Kennedy Airport) and reservations for a suite at the Plaza Hotel were made for Mom and me. I was never involved in the travel plans, of course, and would not have known what Mom was up to behind the scenes if it weren't for Marvin Silverman.

February 1962

Twelve-year-old Marvin Silverman from Brooklyn was one of those who wrote to me. He received a photo and a handwritten letter. The return address was our home on South Peck Drive.

Marvin: We wrote back and forth and, motivated by the correspondence, I started a little fan club in New York. Then, to my surprise, I remember it was very cold, one of those ice cold days in New York where you could barely walk more than a few feet, and, after school, the mailman brought me a special delivery letter. Jon's mother said they were coming to New York. He had some public relations thing to do for CBS including *To Tell The Truth* and they would like to stay at our house the weekend before. It was just out of the blue. She gave us their phone number and we immediately called and the next thing we knew we were at the airport picking them up. Nothing exciting had happened to me until then.

I went to the airport with my sister, Joyce, and my mother and father. My father was a Polish immigrant who worked at a sewing machine since the time he had come here; and my mother was a housewife. They owned a little four-family house in Brooklyn, two upstairs, two down, people of modest means not used to things like this. The airport was called Idlewild then, a tiny little airport, not congested. In the terminal, you may remember in those days, there was first class section and coach section and they came out of different doors. We were waiting at the first class section and Jon and his mother came out of the coach door! We later found out she exchanged all first class tickets and kept the difference. She absolutely wouldn't fly first class because she didn't want Jon to get a big head.

Jon was worried about walking through the streets. I guess they'd heard stories that New York wasn't safe. He even asked his mother if it was safe to go outside of my house. We lived in a very safe and secure residential area. We tried to do the typical Brooklyn things with them, like taking them to Coney Island for a Nathan's hot dog. It was cold, so it wasn't busy, but some people on the street recognized Jon. He was not crazy about the recognition. Of course, his mom was thrilled. She used to try to get him to put on the TV show shirt. He had it with him for *To Tell the Truth,* but he absolutely refused to put it on otherwise.

In Marvin's backyard.

On Sunday, I had a few friends over to see him. Jon was great; you would never know that he didn't live next door to you all your life and you wouldn't know that Cecile wasn't your mother's best friend. It was absolutely amazing. Then, on Sunday night, the *Lassie* show was on. And that happened to be the week they were showing the first episode of "The Odyssey" where Lassie gets lost. It was a big show that was promoted all over the place because it was a three-part show. He was in my bedroom the whole time listening to music or doing things. He just absolutely refused to watch it, and Cecile said he almost never watched himself.

Monday afternoon, before they left for the Plaza Hotel in New York where Rudd and Lassie would be, I arranged for Jon to be in school with me. He went from class to class with me and then did the school assembly—and remember, this is a New York school, so a junior high would have a couple of thousand kids. The school set up three assemblies for the seventh, eighth, and ninth grades, one after another so everyone in the school could come in and ask him a question. There were 2,500 kids in that school, and he basically spoke to all of them. Kids asked him questions like how he got to our school after being in the woods last night on the TV special. He handled it well.

Once I took him to school, the whole neighborhood knew he was there. When we came home around 4 o'clock, there were hundreds of people crowded right up to the door of our apartment. Cecile was very excited at first and encouraged him to throw autographs out the window, but more people arrived. When it grew to five or six hundred people, we got nervous. At that point, we needed the police and I remember them telling us not to go to the window anymore. They held the people back in a line so we could get them out of the house.

We met them the following day when we went to see Jon on *To Tell the Truth,* we got to come in early and sit in the front row as special guests. As the show opened, he and Lassie were standing on the platform, the "curtain" was raised, the audience went oooooh, and Jon said: "Hi, my name is Jon Provost. I play Timmy on the *Lassie* TV series. This is Lassie. Lassie is trained and owned by Rudd Weatherwax." Then the host read Weatherwax's bio and the game started.

There was not one person in my school after that who didn't know who I was. Every now and then I'll get an email, even now, from people who remember me through Jon and Lassie. Even at the 30th high school reunion, people were talking about that incredible day Jon spoke at school!

Before we left for the remainder of the tour, Mom invited Marvin and Joyce out to visit us that summer. It's interesting that Marvin made note of my reluctance to participate in some of Mom's publicity stunts. This was starting to happen more and more.

William: I think she was just proud of him. She was such an outgoing person that she never saw anything wrong with going up to a stranger and saying, "Hi, my name is Cecile and this is my son, Jon." She felt she was giving them something. She would open up the house to just anybody. She was a very caring person and didn't brush them off like a lot of people did. We had a bunch of crazy people hanging around the house from time to time. A lot of them were very nice. It's amazing how the family stayed in contact with these people all these years.

My twelfth birthday party was at the Luau, a fancy restaurant on Rodeo Drive in Beverly Hills owned by actor Steve Crane, who was formerly married to Lana Turner. Friends of his like Gene Kelly and Ann Miller were often seen there. From the street, it looked like a tropical shack with a tiki décor inside—it was very grown up. The boys at the party wore coats and ties and the girls party dresses. Lassie was on my cake again this year.

Jay, Flip, Charlie, and Susan.

Jeanne: I was glad to be there. We were all dressed up and "working the room." It was kind of like a group personal appearance. It was festive and we were aware that we were celebrities. I remember feeling fat.

Fran's Sweet Sixteen a few weeks later was a special event. Mom volunteered Fran as a page at Daughters of the Confederacy conventions. She'd wear white gloves and run up and down the aisles with messages and things. She hated it, but she did it because it was important to Mom. For her Sweet Sixteen, instead of the dance party she wanted, Mom arranged Fran to make her debut.

Fran: What kind of, excuse me, bullshit is that? Debutante. For a simple little farm girl, she wanted everything so proper. The cotillion. A debutante. Part of the fan mail Mom sent out was about me being a debutante—from Richfield, Virginia, and the Bonnie Blue Flag Chapter of the Daughters of the Confederacy! It was never what I wanted to do. In public, my mother had the perfect family. It was so far from the perfect family.

5 Going on 6

My fifth year ended on a high note, with the show garnering more than 40 percent of the television audience. Campbell's profits soared 70 percent. June and I began doing commercials for them. My salary increased by pre-arranged increment. The Coogan Law required that a portion of my earnings be put in a state-controlled account that could not be touched until I was twenty-one or by court order. The rest of the earnings were given to my parents to cover expenses: wardrobe, publicists, clipping services, agent's fees. California law said you had to have an agent—even though my contract had been worked out without Lola in 1958. She just sat back and collected her 10 percent for seven years. I had very few deductions. Dad told me at one point I was taxed 60 percent of my salary. Whatever was left, my parents put in an account for me. I heard my mother say it a thousand times, "We never spent a dime of Jon's money." My father made a good living and Mom received a salary for being with me. They put what I earned away for me.

Paul Petersen: After I got *The Mickey Mouse Club,* Lola approached Mom because I had to have an agent; so, she got 10 percent for having done nothing. Years later, by the end of my fifth season on *The Donna Reed Show* in '62–'63, I was making $550 a week. I had a song in the top ten, I was a certified "bubble gum" star, and she would not go to Screen Gems to ask for $1000 a week. I fired her and hired an agent who went there and got it for me. Now, was it a difficult negotiation? You bet. Donna Reed even came to me and said goodbye. "Paul, we just can't afford to pay that money." Now mind you, they are paying Carl Betz, who distinctly is second banana on the show, $4000 a week. You think people were tuning in to watch Carl? Of course not. We all know about family shows. People tune in to watch the kid. As luck would have it, I grew up to be something they could promote. This is a consistent pattern—from *Father Knows Best* to the travesty of *Kid Nation* . . . the industry has always underpaid children, and the reason is apparent if you have ever been to a cattle call. When you go in that office, you leave behind your parents. Generally, your mom sits in the outer office looking at fifty other kids and can't tell if there's a difference between them and you; so, the pressure is: if you don't take this job at the money we are offering, we'll get another kid. And it's absolutely true. All the parents are part of the problem. They never, ever hold out for the value of their child to the property. And the producers never establish the worth of the child. They know they can get them for scale. It's scary. Lola was the town's top children's agent because she never asked for more than scale.

Debbie Bond, fan: My father was in the Navy and stationed in Imperial Beach when Jon made an appearance at a movie theater in San Diego. After the movie, he had a question & answer on stage and then we all went outside for autographs. I was a lot smaller than the older kids and had trouble seeing him in the crowd. My sister lifted me onto her shoulders. There was a sailor there that saw my problem. He lifted Jon on his shoulders and walked over to my sister and me. Jon was very gracious. He signed his picture and handed it to me, saying, "I hope you like it." I still have that forty-year-old picture tucked away in my box of memories. I never missed an episode of *Lassie*. Of course, I was in love with Timmy, as were all the girls in my kindergarten class!

April 1962
12: Thalians Premiere Circus Benefit at L.A. Sports Arena
Patsy Awards
20: S. Cal Military Academy Dress Parade, Long Beach
20: Mission Valley Center San Diego
San Diego Navy Air Station with Flip and Charlie
Easter party for Pala Indians
Acted as judge at Hotel del Coronado's Easter Hat Contest
May 1962
Multiple Sclerosis Society of L.A.
Honorary chief on Fire Service Day

May 30, 1962

My third Indy 500 was hot, humid, and overcast. Once was enough for Mom; she stayed home. Dad went again, and William joined us.

Brent Sohn, fan: My family had special passes to tour restricted areas; the Indy 500 control tower was one such area. I saw Jon in the tower walking around like the rest of the race fans. He seemed relaxed, dressed casually in a sports jacket with his blond hair combed back. I remember my first glance at him. I told my parents, "There is Timmy!" I was completely thrilled. He signed my ticket stub for me and was very friendly. I have always been a sentimental person, and as a child I shed many tears watching Lassie and Timmy. Jon was my favorite actor during the early days of my childhood . . . I really enjoy looking back to this special occasion in my life and I will always treasure May 30, 1962, as the day I met Jon (Timmy).

The Fame Bubble

Marvin and Joyce Silverman took Mom up on her invitation and came to visit us for two weeks.

June 1962

> Marvin: It was amazing coming from Brooklyn to Beverly Hills and being in that environment. His dad was an aeronautical engineer and was very low key, very relaxed type of guy. Fran was almost finished with high school and the brother was in college. We were just some other people staying around to them. They were in their own world at that point.

Fran and William had no world of their own. Ever since we came together again as a family, my world had encroached further and further into theirs. Fans called the house or showed up at our door. People drove from other states and left their children with us for days. Mom's Southern hospitality kicked into overdrive. She invited them all in, never turned anyone away. At this point, Fran and William were fighting just to hold onto to their patch of grass. I didn't mind when other people were in the house because it distracted Mom, but the attention, the constant flow of people . . . I had no privacy. None of us did.

Summer meant back to work and Marvin went with me almost every day.

> Marvin: I found it fascinating. For example, the people on the show, particularly June Lockhart, didn't communicate much with Hugh Reilly. Everyone went their separate ways once the scene was over. The people I was used to seeing on TV that were family just disappeared into the dressing rooms. Jon didn't have school in the summer, so he hung out with the adults working on the set. He heard these people, mostly men, talk about stuff. He was exposed to some things at that age most kids weren't—language, subject matter. A midget was his stand in. I got a kick out of that. I had a great time. I saw people and things that you could only dream of. And now, in retrospect, some of the people I got to see and meet are a part of classic TV.
>
> Cecile really went out of her way because we were basically strangers. She made sure we saw all of Southern California. She got us VIP tickets for Disneyland. I guess she knew just who to call there

because we were treated like royalty. Jon was working, and she drove my sister and me all the way out to Anaheim and left us there and then picked us up later in the day. She even drove us to Tijuana and Jon smuggled fire crackers across the border inside of his underwear. I was a nervous wreck when we were coming back across the border.

I guess Marvin learned a lot of new things about me. And he learned a lot from Mom, too. He'd started a fan club for me and was really impressed with Mom's operation.

Marvin: Fan mail was what was done at the dinner table every night. I went with her to the production office. She took a carton of already stamped 9 x 12-inch envelopes and tons of pictures and letters. Every night she would lay all this stuff out on the dinner table and she would ask me and my sister to help.

Afterward, Cecile had to keep reminding Jon to work on his lines for tomorrow. He kept saying, "I'll do it later."—just like a parent telling their kid to do their homework. He sat down to go over about eight or nine pages and in two minutes, he closed it and put it away. I asked him, "Didn't your mother say you have to study your lines?" And he said that he knew it all. I said that it was impossible. He told me to test him and "see if I don't miss any." And he went through it like a flash. That was one of the most amazing things to me.

Jon was such a normal kid in the middle of all of this. You have to attribute that to his mother and the strong family. Also, being a child psychologist now, that was an incredible family. She didn't treat him like he was any different from any other kid. He had his chores. One time he asked to borrow money from me for something that he wanted to buy and I went back and told everyone about it. Here he is working, making more money than most adults.

July 1962 We had some excitement when the Olympic decathlete Rafer Johnson, an African American, appeared on the show. After he won the gold in Rome in 1960, Mr. Johnson turned to sports broadcasting and acting. This time, Campbell's had no objections.

Jay: I'll never forget a shoot we did with Angela Cartwright at the pool of the Beverly Hilton Hotel where we were playfully trying to pull

Angela into the water. We couldn't get messed up. We couldn't be normal kids who jumped in the water. Angela couldn't get her hair wet. We couldn't horse around. It was staged publicity pictures.

Angela: Jon, Jay, and I were often together on publicity photo shoots. Whenever the "kid stars" of the era were photographed . . . there we were. We attended numerous charity events and animal award shows where we often presented awards. They never acted spoiled or obnoxious. Jay was very soft-spoken and Jon so kind.

Paul Petersen: Jon was always groomed and dressed perfectly—as we all were in those days, you know, the little seersucker jacket and tie; we all had to do that. He was a very well-mannered kid. I remembered thinking he had too many restrictions for him as a human being, but then I was chafing under that myself.

William: Jon would get upset every now and then that he would have a personal appearance to do over a weekend after working five days, especially after we moved to Beverly Hills and he was getting older. All the adults pinching his cheek, patting him on the head, rubbing his hair—that gets to be a real pain after a while, too. As he got older, I think he realized it more and more. Once in a while, Fran or I would go along because it sounded like fun, but many times we'd get there and be bored stiff. Eventually, we both stopped going altogether.

Kid stars of CBS; clowning around with Jay and Angela.

Jay: We didn't have the opportunity to just enjoy ourselves and cut loose. We were always in suits and ties like Little Lord Fauntleroys, and all the girls were in party dresses . . . trained puppets who smiled on cue, always the prim and proper little gentlemen and ladies. I don't think any of us really knew what it was like to be connected to our real feelings because we were always expected to be nice, sweet, wonderful little kids who never displayed any temperament, who never got angry, never pinched the girls. We were the studio kids—almost like those kids from "Village of the Damned,"

like we were from another planet. I never felt like we had any connection to real life. I didn't understand how the real world operated. Everything was so perfect on the set and everyone led such a perfect life. Later on, people were not prepared for our imperfections because it went against our perfect image.

Paul Petersen: I was concerned for Jon during his years on *Lassie* because each time I saw him at these various publicity functions, his personality was more and more flat. He was more restrained; he was more in control, more the automaton. When you're living inside of this fame bubble, you don't have secrets and silences. You are given no opportunity to explore other avenues of expression. You are the boy from *Lassie* or I was the boy from *The Donna Reed Show* and that is severely limiting, let me tell you. After a while, you begin to understand that your role in life is the way other people see you, and because we had been raised and trained to please people, we set about doing that at tremendous personal cost.

Patty McCormack: I was a kid actor, and when you're a kid actor you play parts. I was pretending . . . it's not that big a deal. You know what I think is a big deal? Not being free to make mistakes or try on different hats as a kid; in other words, being locked into a certain career may be more difficult than the kind of part you played. At a certain time of life when kids are trying things, experimenting, either we didn't have the encouragement to do that or the knowhow. We weren't taught how to do that. That's a shame and that's the price you pay.

Paul Petersen: But you quickly come to grips with it, because wherever you go in the English-speaking world on your various appearances that the studio sends you on—for no pay, mind you, that's just promotion—you suddenly realize you can't go anywhere without being recognized. And Jon, because of his stature and his recognizability and his place—I mean, it's a loving warm place where people have their Jon Provost memory—he was subjected to constant public scrutiny. If you haven't been famous, you can't really comprehend that. There's no place to escape and every relationship you have is colored by your fame, including the important ones with your parents and your siblings.

Seattle World's Fair

Lassie and I presented a dachshund to the lieutenant governor, then I announced that we were going to walk around so people could get photos with us. With that, hundreds of gleeful children and adults swarmed past the restraining ropes and closed in around us. People on stage grabbed the microphone and begged the crowd to move back, but few did. Finally, Sam and Bob Weatherwax got in and led us out of there. Kids and parents got separated. They were announcing names of lost kids and parents for the next half hour.

> Mom: Elvis Presley was appearing and Timmy and Lassie were appearing. Jon got to take Miss Space Needle or whatever she's called—the princess of the thing—to the Canadian Mounties Tattoo; and the whole stadium is packed and she's with Jon and Elvis didn't get her. He got her the next night, but I wanted her for the Tattoo.

> **September 1962**
> CBS promotional tour
> 9: Detroit
> 10: Syracuse
> 11: Pittsburgh and
>   Columbus
> 12: Cincinnati
> 13: Indianapolis
> 14: Chicago and Seattle
> 15: Seattle World's Fair
>   Lassie Day at the fair
> 17: Seattle's Children's
>   Orthopedic Hospital
> 17: Spokane, appearance to
>   plug *Lassie*
> 18: Yakima
> 19: Portland and San
>   Francisco
> 20: Sacramento
> 21: L.A.

The lucky girl was an eighteen-year-old, Sue Wouters, whose mom was a fair secretary. They went to get a glimpse of the King, and he got an eyeful of pretty, blonde Sue. He sent one of the Memphis Mafia to get her number and called for a date. Elvis and Sue had four dates—in Elvis's suite, because of course he couldn't go out without being mobbed. Sue had some mom, didn't she? Her steady boyfriend, on the other hand, was not so understanding; he broke up with her. Sounds like the story of *Bye Bye Birdie*. Anyway, Elvis left town for a few hours and I swooped in to invite Sue to the Canadian Tattoo. The next day, Elvis saw me and said, "Hey, you got my girl last night . . . but I get her tonight." Somehow, I think Sue had two very different dates.

A short time later, for an appearance in Chicago, Mom was up to her usual antics.

> John Mangoni: I lived in Downers Grove, Illinois. My father was an attorney, my mother a housewife. In sixth grade, one of the projects in school was to write to a famous person. I was always fascinated with *Lassie,* and Timmy was about my age, so I thought I'd write to him. I

wrote to Desilu Studios and said something to the effect of "I like what you do. Please write back." I received a picture of Jon and Lassie with an orange background with his signature imprinted on it. I thought I had his real signature. I wrote back and I got information about a fan club run by Marv Silverman in New York. I wrote to him and got more pictures and developed a pen pal thing with the club president.

Then, to my surprise . . . one day I was playing Monopoly with my best friends and someone knocked on the door—one of my friend's sisters—who said, "Jon Provost and his mom called from California and they want to stop and visit you." I didn't quite believe her, but I went home and Mom said yes, they were coming to Chicago and they wanted us to pick them up at the airport. I thought it was absolutely great.

Being an only child, my parents thought they knew everything I did and were taken aback by all this. My mother was never starstruck and my father wasn't really into movies. This was my thing, and they just stood by and watched. They couldn't believe I pulled this off. At that point, Jon was one of the biggest child stars of all time. I really didn't know how to react to it. I just rolled with it.

LASSIE'S SMALLER—Jon Provost (left), the 14 year old star of the Lassie TV program, was a weekend visitor at the August Mangoni residence, 1148 Oak Hill, north of Downers Grove. He visits with John Mangoni, 14, and the family's chihuahua, Lita. (LIFE Photo)

We picked them up at O'Hare Airport. Here they are coming out of this propeller plane. Jon had a rifle and he was able to carry the gun because they took the pin out before he boarded. I think they were coming from North Carolina. Here is Jon Provost standing in front of me, and I didn't know what to do with him and he didn't know what to do with me. We go home and before I know it, Mom and Dad invited them to stay. Mrs. Provost said she'd love to stay for a few nights. She thought it would be nice to get the news media involved, so she made some calls. Photographers came out to take pictures of us that were in all the local papers. After that, we became pretty friendly with the family.

When you're young and you watch someone on TV, you expect when you meet that person that he will be exactly what you see on TV—Timmy on Lassie—and he wasn't. He had the voice, but that was the only thing that was the same, and that threw me. He didn't seem like a little kid. He was very knowledgeable, very smart. He was very articulate. I remember thinking, "Wow, that's not the little boy I see on

TV." I had to quickly pick up the pace to match that—which was a positive thing for me. I had to get to that level where I could communicate with him and the other people I was going to meet through him like Jay North or Sal Mineo.

Timmy's Great Adventure

During Thanksgiving week of 1962, we went on a location shoot for the episode called "The Journey." We traveled to Sonora, high in the Sierras on the Sonora River. The multi-episode shows had been such a success, Bonita championed this five-part story in which Lassie and I, trapped in the basket of a runaway hot air balloon, struggle to return home from the Canadian wilderness. Of course, while I'm there, I meet up with Dick Simmons—Sgt. Preston of the Royal Canadian Mounted Police on Jack Wrather's other show.

November was already pretty cold in the mountains, especially for us thin-blooded Southern California types. Mom and I were bundled up, especially during the long periods of down time. My study periods were in my dressing room trailer. At least I had the day off of school on Thanksgiving, even if we did have to work that day.

The winding, mountain roads leading to the location were treacherous, with or without the enormous logging trucks that rumbled down them. The driver of our camera truck didn't dare look down as he made his way uphill toward location. He was only a few feet from the edge—a straight drop off the mountain—when a logging truck with a full load roared down the narrow road, straddling the yellow line. It swerved, sideswiping our truck and sending him perilously close to the edge. Only inches saved him and all our equipment, though it probably shaved years off his life.

Locals came to watch the shoot every day. We weren't near any kind of town, just cabins and lots of woods. I'm sure some people drove miles to find us. We were definitely the big news in the area.

Bob Weatherwax: That was the first show I ever did [after the service]. Dad was a tough guy to work for, and he didn't like a lot of mistakes. Dialogue shots where Jon had to act more were single shots. My father, being the head trainer, would do those. I was more involved in having

the dog run over the hill or being the guy he runs to. Eventually, my father started taking naps after lunch and I'd run the show for about two hours. That's when I graduated up.

In Sonora, when Jon was in the balloon, I sat up in that balloon myself with Murphy, the special effects guy, out of sight of camera. They brought Jon down and broke for lunch for Thanksgiving and they forgot about Murphy and me. Somebody yelled, "Lunch!" and they'd wanted to get that Thanksgiving lunch. They left us in the damn balloon, stuck in a tree about ninety-five feet up until we finally got their attention.

Richard Kiel, an actor best known as James Bond's nemesis, Jaws, was with us on location. At the time, he also worked part time as a bouncer at the Rag Doll Bar. Many a night he'd taken care of Rudd there, and the two became friends. When Rudd discovered there was a character of a giant Indian in "The Journey," he immediately thought of Richard. He was no Indian, but he stood seven-foot-two. As Rudd said, it was easier to make an Indian out of a giant than a giant out of an Indian. Richard got the job.

He was HUGE, like a whole building, but a gentle giant in both body and spirit. He was also the only one happy about working on Thanksgiving. Working holidays meant double pay. When we went into overtime that day, it meant quadruple pay. The Wrathers asked him to settle for regular pay, promising to use him again on the show, but Richard stood his ground. The show was a runaway success. The Wrathers's cup runneth over. They did not have to be that cheap. What was that song Lloyd taught me, "The rich get rich and the poor get poorer"?

Whitey Hughes: I came in on *Lassie* for stunts only. I also stunted for Bobby Diamond on *Fury* and Johnny Crawford on *The Rifleman*. Things like that have made my life so interesting . . . doubling kids. It gives me a great thrill, much more than what I started out to be. I wanted to be a tap dancer and I wound up a stunt man, and I enjoyed it. Got hurt a few times, but it was real rewarding. I came in for Jon on "The Journey." I was about forty-two and at that age, I was all man. Some of the girls wrote that I was spring steel . . . spring waiting to unwind. I was very handy at gymnast stuff. Swimming was one of my favorite things and diving. I loved it, and I was in great shape in that time.

Whitey and his brother Bill Hughes Sr. were two of the top stunt guys in the business. Bill was the father of Billy Hughes from our Christmas episode. Hollywood was still a small town and show business still a family business. Whitey was a great guy; he loved kids and was always upbeat, I really enjoyed having him around.

Whitey: I had worked with Bill Beaudine before. I can understand that a director might get a little lost thinking about the shot he wants. And I can understand that he wanted a closeup of Jon in the rapids and the danger that he and the dog were in, the dangers of the raft breaking up and getting separated. I can imagine how he felt about getting this shot of this desperate boy, but there are times when you're thinking of the shot that it outweighs the safety of it. The rapids in this river, the kids did that for sport up there; they shot these rapids. One local boy walked over and asked me, "Whitey, you ever shoot these rapids?" I said, "Son, I've never shot *any* rapids." The kids talked to me plenty about the water, the ins and outs of it, the danger. But I was a great swimmer, a strong swimmer. Mr. Beaudine was . . . I take my hat off to him . . . a great director, but, man . . .

The time came for the raft scene, the one Whitey was so worried about. Not me; I was really excited. This looked like a great story to bring back to Ron and Mike. I got to wear a full wetsuit under my clothes—as much for warmth as for buoyancy. My wardrobe included leather hiking boots and a heavy wool coat. Without the wetsuit, I'd sink like a stone.

We'd gone over and over the shot. Whitey was pushing to do it, but Mr. Beaudine said he only had one raft and could only shoot the stunt once. He needed my face in that water. Every precaution had been taken, at least that's what everyone told Mom and me. I assume my teacher was there, but evidently she didn't object either. If Catherine Deeney had been there, I'd never have gotten wet, but Whitey was the only one to express concern out loud—not to me and Mom, only to Mr. Beaudine. And so it was done, I was doing my own stunt.

Baby and I walked into the shallow water toward the raft. As we boarded and prepared to move downriver, the crew shot from several well-placed cameras. They all knew they had only one chance to get it. I pushed the raft along in the shallow water with a long pole. Lassie and I headed a little further downstream. In a second, everything changed. Water swirled around the raft in all directions. Rocks and tree limbs obstructed the path. We got the cue to jump off and leaped into the water. Even with the wet suit, it was freezing. Poor Lassie! The water felt like pins and needles stabbing any exposed skin: my neck, hands, and feet. I struggled to get my bearings as the water carried me through what I could clearly see now were treacherous waters. I had absolutely no control. My wet jacket and jeans were heavy and made moving difficult. My leather boots filled with water, pulling me down. I struggled to keep my head up as I hurtled downstream. The safety line! I had to keep my eye out for the safety line strung across the river, just out of view of the last camera. All I had to do was reach up and grab it, but the water spun me in all directions. I couldn't see the cameras anymore. The shoreline rushed by. I tried to focus on the safety line.

Whitey: I could see that he was really in trouble. I wasn't really interested in the dog because I was watching Jon. That was my shot. I was doubling Jon and protecting him. It was wicked water, wicked, wicked water.

BAM! I slammed chest-first into the edge of a sharp rock hidden beneath the water and all the air was knocked out of me. I couldn't breathe. I gasped, completely panicked, and swallowed water. I flailed my arms wildly. I went under. Out of the corner of my eye, I saw two of the crew get in the water. My arms felt like jelly. I couldn't feel my legs at all. I gasped for air, weak from the fight, relieved to see them. They reached out their arms and scooped Lassie out of the rapids as I sailed by. I went under again. Whitey heard someone say, "The kid is great. What a performance. Hope the cameras are getting this." Exhausted, choking, I went under for the third time.

Whitey: You can't describe the feeling I got when I saw this kid come by the camera. I made the dive of my life and I came up right under him. I just made a real big push and aimed. I pushed off that bank and went out just the right distance. When I came up under him, I just picked him up and that water carried me and him on down that river there to the rope. I reached up and grabbed that rope with one hand and had a handful of Jon in the other and I just held his head up out of the water until I walked along the edge of that bank. It makes me feel great that I was there.

There's no question Whitey saved my life. I'd never have had the strength to grab that rope and hold on. I would simply have been swept away. The incident was glossed over. Mom wasn't the type to make waves, so nothing was ever said . . . except to Whitey.

Whitey: I got a $100 bump on my paycheck ($1000 today) and I asked Mr. Beaudine about it. He told me, "That was for quick thinking, Whitey. Thank you for quick thinking." They were very, very humble about the whole thing.

Trouble Brewing

Tommy, not quite twenty-one and just five years out from Jeff Miller and Lassie, was twice a dad, struggling to keep regular employment. "The Child Star Syndrome" did not yet have a name, but he was living it. He had been the center of his universe for fifteen years. As an adult, he'd outgrown his "cuteness," and the business that had once embraced him now callously cast him aside.

November 1962
26: Deane Allen Rettig born to Tommy and Darlene Rettig

Darlene: He took odd jobs. He worked in a men's store; it killed him. I thought if he'd just get used to it, it would be OK to become normal . . . a 9 to 5. He was always looking for that fast buck. He got about $90,000 when he turned twenty-one. He let Ricki invest it in the stock market. We formed our own production company and we had a ball. That was a good time in our lives and we were successful at it, but Tom had a destructive mechanism. As soon as we got a little ahead, he would do something to make us lose. He tried to punish himself because he felt he wasn't worthy of success anymore.

Timmy as Santa

November 1962
28: Beverly Hills Christmas Lights Festival with Jay North

December 1962
"Personal Letter from Santa" shoot for Post Office
9: Pomona Elks's Lodge Christmas party, visited two boys' homes
17–18: San Diego with Flip and Charlie Herbert to attend a flurry of dinners and appearances while visiting thousands of children in the San Diego area

Dad: The final big event in 1962 was when, in December, Cecile and I talked Jon into buying William his first car, which was a 1963 Plymouth Fury. Bill was then eighteen years old and a senior in high school. In 1964, Jon bought Francile a 1964 Austin Healey Mark III when she graduated. Jon's gift of a car to Bill and Fran was his way of saying "thanks" for tolerating his affect on their lives.

Fran: I was eighteen when I got my car. My mother said she, Daddy, and Jon discussed it and, that since Jon had taken her away from me and my brother, he would be responsible to buy us cars. It never made any sense at all to me. I never understood why this should be my brother's responsibility, but there's an old saying: You don't look a gift horse in the mouth.

It showed up my father in a way, because I think that's his responsibility. I don't think there was any question in my father's mind about buying any of his children a graduation gift. In those days, that's what every kid from an upper income family got—a car when you graduated. I don't think my brother should have ever been responsible. Under the circumstances, I think my mother should have bought us cars—she was paid by the studio every day—not that it would have made any difference in how I felt because, I mean, a car over a life with your mother? A childhood? No, no. . . .

My parents explained that I had taken my mother away from the family and I should give back to them, something that would really be important to them. A kid's first car is huge, so we settled on that. I never questioned it. I shouldered that responsibility: I took Mom away from William and Fran. I told the story just that way, just the way it was told to me for more than thirty-five years before I ever really thought about it.

Life Imitates TV

Dad wasn't a strong presence for me at home and Paul Martin was also MIA from the show. In one episode, Ruth mentions that he's visiting Uncle Petrie, but the truth was Hugh Reilly was going through a tough time in his private life. His marriage was coming apart, but he'd had little warning.

Bob Weatherwax: Hugh was a very quiet man, very soft spoken. He was pretty devastated when his wife left him. . . . I went through that part with him at Tahoe. She left him for a woman. I guess that was even more devastating than just to be left for a guy. He went through a lot. It was during our last couple of seasons. He bought a Corvette, tried to get his second wind in life, to date some young girls and stuff. That divorce didn't leave him in good shape mentally.

Fireworks for Fran

Fran: I met Bruce on a weekday at a place called the Chez Paris on Fairfax Avenue in Los Angeles. I was with five girl-friends from Beverly High and Fairfax High. They got me a fake I.D. and said we were going dancing in a place where girls had to be eighteen and boys had to be twenty-one to get in. I was sixteen. Bruce knew all my girlfriends and came over to dance with them all. He was older and was home on leave from Army boot camp. I wanted to know who he was. I was just taken over by this guy. I said to these girls, "I'm going to marry him." "What are you talking about? You're going to marry him? Number one: you haven't met him and, number two: he hasn't even asked you to dance tonight. And you think you're going to marry him?" I was serious. He did finally ask me to dance in what little time was left, and somehow, I gave him my phone number. I had a cur-few—11:30 or so—and my parents were very strict. Bruce came from Beverly Hills and thought that every girl that lived in Beverly Hills had a Princess telephone in her room. He didn't know my parents. We had two telephones in the whole house—one in a little telephone parlor area downstairs and upstairs in the hallway next to my parents' bed-

January 1963

room. About 2 or 2:30 in the morning that phone rang. I go running out my door, but my father got to it before I did. And I just remember him saying, "Don't you ever call at this time, ever again. Don't you ever call this house." And that was Bruce; that was Bruce.

Soon after, he asked me out. He talked to some of his buddies, who said, "You're taking out Fran Provost? Do you know who she is? Jon Provost's sister." Bruce says, "What? Oh, my God." Before he came to pick me up, he was sweating bullets; he must have changed three or four times. He was practicing saying hello in front of the mirror, just in case my brother answered the door. He was twenty and he didn't know what to say to this little twelve-year-old.

Bruce: Are you kidding? Jon was a huge star. I was so nervous, every time I pulled up to their house, my mouth went completely dry and I'd speed up and drive around the block. Finally, I went to the front door and, of course, Jon opens the door wearing his "Timmy" red-and-white checked shirt and all this thick pancake makeup on and I just manage to choke out this, "Hi, hi . . . is . . . is your sister home?" And he says, "Yeah, just a moment. I'll get her." Then he turns around and yells, "Frannnnyyy!!!" and I cracked up.

Fran: I took my time coming downstairs, and so Jon checked out Bruce and Bruce checked out Jon and they liked each other immediately— absolutely immediately.

The First Miniseries

February 17, 1963

LASSIE®

Headlines read, "Princess and Dog to Star in Color." ABC and NBC regularly showed color programs. CBS was way behind and the year before they were widely criticized for doing "A Tour of the White House" with first lady Jackie Kennedy in black and white. The number of color TV sets doubled in 1962 and doubled again in 1963, but it was still a small percentage of the country's 50 million TV sets. So it was a big deal when, on Sunday, February 17, CBS had not one, but *two* color shows: "A Look at Monaco," hosted by my second movie mom, Princess Grace Kelly

Ranier; and the first of the five-part *Lassie* episode "The Journey." Americans tuned in by the millions.

Bonita provided the narration for the previews to next week's episode: "A frightened boy and his courageous dog, adrift in endless space, with all chances of a quick rescue stacked against them . . . I know you'll want to be with us next week to see how Timmy and Lassie make their escape from their airborne prison, only to encounter more dangerous predicaments. Remember, next week, the exciting part two of 'The Journey.'"

The press congratulated her on the success of the multi-part show. One production assistant told the *LA Herald Examiner*, "Bonita has brought a new concept to the show since she's taken an active hand. Lassie used to be the story of a boy and his dog. Now it's got more of a family feeling about it. We have almost as many adult viewers as children since she's taken over as executive producer." Bonita added, as she always did, that the contribution she was most proud of was me.

It was really Bonita who ran the show. This was her baby all the way, and yet her title remained associate producer all seven years. The glass ceiling was pretty low in 1963.

Greeting the Public

I shared the morning with fellow birthday boy retired Sheriff Biscailuz, as he turned eighty and I became a teenager. My official party was at Sabu, a Japanese restaurant across from The May Company at Wilshire and Fairfax. Mom planned everything. Again, it was a coat and tie affair, again a professional cameraman and again, Lassie on the cake.

March 12, 1963

> Susan Gordon, actor: The party was lovely, but I couldn't eat the food. I thought it was awful . . . and then I ended up living in Japan for thirteen years! It was really high class. Kids didn't normally have parties in a fancy restaurant, so it was different, definitely a celebrity party.

The season ended and I returned to Beverly Hills Catholic School to finish seventh grade. At recess or

April 1963

San Diego *USS Ticonderoga* with Flip and Jimmy Fields

14: *TV Guide* Magazine Awards, NBC Studios, Burbank. Lassie was nominated for an award. We all went to support Baby, seated between Bonita and me, but he lost to Disney.

break time, I was in the play yard with a few friends when I heard someone shout, "Hey, Provost!" I turned directly into the path of a paper bag flying toward me. BOOM! Right in the face, hard; then I felt something warm. I reached up; my hands were covered in blood. The bag held a Coke bottle, and it split my lip open. The nuns came running and sent me to the emergency room in Beverly Hills to be sewn up. They couldn't reach my parents so they called the Wrathers. Bonita had gone to great lengths to make sure I wouldn't get injured. I wasn't allowed to participate in most sports. My parents had to get permission to take me more than fifty miles away. They could not believe something like this could happen in school. Bonita panicked. How bad was it? How fast would it heal? Would it leave a scar? She sent me to Elizabeth Taylor's plastic surgeon, who said the stitches looked great and didn't touch me. At home, my brother and sister tried making me laugh to split it open. I do have a scar, but it worked out OK in the end.

The bottle had been thrown on purpose, and not only that, it was an actor's child who'd thrown it—Steve Carey, MacDonald Carey's son. I know the nuns called Steve's parents, but Mom was surprised we never heard from them at all.

May 1963

May 1963

18: Jr Grand Marshal with Lassie at the Santa Rosa, CA, Rose Parade

William graduated from Beverly Hills High School. May 12 that year was Mother's day. All of us forgot it this year, and Mom was terribly hurt. She broke down, crying that none of us thought about her or were grateful. I ran upstairs and pulled out my stash of pure silver dollars—ten of them—and gave them to her, but, of course, she didn't want them. It was a very bad day in our house.

June 6, 1963

John F. Kennedy's motorcade was driving down El Cajon Boulevard near 54th Street in San Diego. Thousands of people lined the streets, cheering and waving signs and American flags. I was in a reviewing stand near the intersection along with Miss America, Miss San Diego, and many others. I presented someone with a plush Lassie for Caroline Kennedy, who was a big *Lassie* fan. And someone presented me with a ceramic collie, along with placards welcoming JFK. In a moment, it was all over. He drove by, waving from a black convertible . . . and then he was gone.

Sum-sum-summertime

Now that I was out of school, Mom amped up the personal appearances. We must have started working later because the month was packed full.

> *Stan Stamper:* Is it possible that you remember a couple of trips to Oklahoma? My dad, Jack, invited you to throw out the first ball at the annual Little League summer baseball program. We enjoyed having you in our home for a couple of weeks and taking you "to the mountains" where we shot a dozen guns and introduced you to some of the "folks" in the Oklahoma Hills.
>
> Almost a half-century has passed and now I'm publishing the *Hugo Daily News* as my dad did before me. Our paths haven't crossed for many years, but I wanted to let you know you touched our small community during those two years.

June 1963
Santa Rosa Society for Crippled Children and Adults
Port Hueneme, San Diego, with Flip Mark and Diane Mountford
Opening night guest of Hugo, OK, Little League
Tweetsie Railroad, Frontier Land, and Ghost Town appearances in North Carolina

I discovered I had lots of cousins in Hugo and the surrounding area. I stayed for a week getting to know them, during which my cousins took me snipe hunting. They talked about it for days and I have to admit, I was pretty excited. It was a nighttime hunt, and I'd never done anything like that. Finally the night arrived, and we all ventured cautiously into the woods. My cousins told me to stay put and they would drive the snipe out to me. I stayed out there a long time, but I didn't see any snipe. Then I started hearing things . . . noises, sort of scary noises. After a while, I realized they'd gotten me pretty good. When my cousins finally came back to rescue me, they were laughing pretty hard. I love a good joke, even one on me.

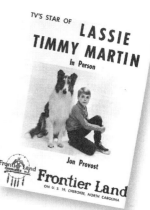

Tweetsie Railroad, Frontier Land, and Ghost Town in North Carolina and Six-Gun Territory in Florida were good, clean, family attractions. The theme parks featured Western streets and wooden boardwalks, cowboys and Indians, saloon

girls, stagecoaches and bank robbers with six shooters spitting lead, and a real steam locomotive. Robert Coburn owned the last three. He and his family were real nice Southern people and were so generous to all the celebrities who appeared there—people like Lorne Greene, Jerry Mathers, Clint Walker, and so many more. Everyone stayed in an apartment on the property; that's where Mom and I stayed. I worked anywhere from a week to a month. Mr. Coburn had a private plane, and he even let William and me fly it . . . wonderful guy.

At their peak, these G-rated parks attracted ten to twelve thousand visitors a day. The cowpokes, Indians, and saloon girls were mostly high school and college kids from the area. And for the only time in my career, I got to play a bad guy—every hour in a gunfight in the streets. People would come running out of stores to watch us. A couple of stunt guys got shot and fell off a roof. Afterward, I posed for pictures and signed autographs. It was a great job; I loved it.

William: I went down and spent a couple of weeks and had a blast at Frontier Land; they had a trail there too. We lived in a little apartment behind one of the facades for the main street for Western Town. It was really fun.

Janice Coville, fan: My friend Marie and I were on summer vacation with my parents. It was pretty much the norm for us to go to the mountains as we lived in Charleston and it was always so hot. We had been to Ghost Town before, but this summer was the best because Jon Provost was there!!! He played the bad guy in a little story and the "sheriff" shot him down dead in the street. Then of course the "undertaker" had to do his measurements (comedic) in preparation for his funeral. Afterward, Jon took pictures with members of the audience and one of those was me. Jon probably had his picture taken with a gazillion others! Anyway, on the trip back home, Marie and I were in the backseat just ecstatic from the whole incident. She wouldn't get her picture taken because she thought she was "fat," but she said the way Jon looked at her made her feel great.

Bonnie Ray Webb Campbell, fan: We had seen on TV that Timmy was to be at Tweetsie Railroad, so I begged to go! We only got to go one place in the summer, and that was where we went. Gosh, there were so many people there that day and all the girls were all over him. The only reason we even talked was because he was sitting there letting people come up and have their picture taken with him and he got tired of sitting so long. He got up to leave, and I asked if I could take just one picture of him alone. He said yes, but he wanted to walk away from the crowd. So, of course, I said yes and we walked off. I already had a crush on him; meeting him just enhanced it. We got on the train, as did all the other kids, but he sat next to me and I WAS ON CLOUD 99—NOT 9—BUT 99!! It was all I could do to stay calm, but I did, and we just talked as if we were friends. We talked about school and how hard it was at times for him to do schoolwork and learn his parts, too. He said he was so glad that I talked to him like he was normal. If he only knew how hard it was to control myself!!! But I did just so he would remember me.

When I got home, I received a free fan club membership in the mail with a personal note saying he enjoyed spending the day with me. Of course, you couldn't touch me!!!!! Every month, I got something from his fan club, and once in a while, he would send me a personal note and all my friends were so jealous. I really thought I was special. In fact, to this day, when I run into them, some will ask if we are still friends. Memories are nice, and I still get that old giddy feeling when I think of that special day.

Frank Stafford: My sister worked there as a can-can dancer for a while. When Jon Provost appeared there, he came to our house to visit with her.

Oh yeah, like I said, I loved that job. All the attention from girls was great. My fans were changing and so was I.

Mom always liked to get the most out of a trip. As long as we were headed east to North Carolina, she suggested a little detour to visit friends. We stayed with Marvin Silverman's family in Brooklyn a few nights, then traveled to Long Island where we visited Roger Nakagawa and his family before heading south.

Marvin Silverman: Since it was summertime, my parents wanted to know if Cecile and Jon wanted to see the Catskill Mountains. She said she'd heard about it and all the comedians coming from the Catskills and she would love to see. So we went to the vacation hotel that my family stayed at, a kosher hotel called Epstein's Villa in Elleville New York. We ate the kosher meal in the dining room and showed her the mountains. They went from the Catskills to a Japanese household. That was the type of person she would have been. She did this all the time, whenever they would go to a city, contacting people she had been corresponding with.

John Mangoni: Marv actually took a Greyhound bus from New York to Los Angeles to go visit Jon. We're just little kids now, and we're writing back and forth and he writes, "As long as I'm going to Los Angeles, why don't I come and visit you for a few days?" So he comes to my house. My father picks him up at the Greyhound station, and he spends a couple of days at my house. And then he gets back on the bus and goes to L.A. It really was an incredible thing for him to do.

In 1963, cross country buses were safe and clean and an accepted mode of transportation. Still, it is amazing that Marvin braved the roads from coast to coast. On this second visit, I took him out to Rudd's ranch for a weekend.

Marvin: Outdoors people, Rudd and his wife. What amazed me was that he had so many dogs that looked the same that all could do different tricks. Jon had a rifle, and he was trying to teach me how to shoot. Obviously, being from New York, I hadn't had any exposure to that. When I went back to New York, I found that the Boy Scouts actually had a riflery program at one of the armories, which I joined and stuck with through high school. I ended up winning some awards.

Marvin is a doctor today. He's a proud father of three adopted children and a proud grandfather as well. He's written books, appeared all over radio and TV, and lectured to large audiences. I know Mom was a big influence on his life.

Marvin: Before I met them, I had never even left New York. I think the most important thing to learn was that these people, the showbiz, TV people, are just people and not to be intimidated, afraid, or concerned. Knowing that made it easier just dealing with people; everyone is approachable.

Home Sweet Home

I was back at Desilu for my seventh year, the last year of my contract—something I had begun to think about. At some point I'd have to make a decision, so I began asking questions. Back at home, William and Fran were doing the same thing.

July 1963

William: In the beginning, I felt like I was on the outside looking in, but after a while, I got used to it. I did get to go to Indianapolis and some other places. Some of them were great. But obviously there were times where the bad side was weighing more heavily.

I lived at home for quite a while because of a free place to live. I was basically leading my own life. My room was right off the kitchen. There weren't enough bedrooms. There were three bedrooms upstairs and a servant's quarters downstairs. I had the servant's quarters with my own bathroom. You opened the door and you were in the kitchen, which was the hangout place, so I ran into people a lot— a bunch of strangers most of the time—and I'd try and walk through, say "hi and goodbye" and out the back door. At that time in my life, I wasn't really interested in anything going on there—especially after I had a car and everything. I didn't want to be around the house; I'd rather be cruising Hollywood Boulevard instead.

For a while I did live in Northridge with my grandmother to go to college. Mom found a three-bedroom house about a block from school, and they helped Grandma buy it so I could live there and go to school. She rented the other bedroom to a student. After a while, I quit school. Then I transferred to another . . . and another. I went to Cal State Northridge, L.A. City College, Santa Monica City College, UCLA, then back to Northridge. I got tired of doing the same thing and going to the same place. I kept trying something different, searching for new experiences, meeting different friends and following them to different schools . . . not really finding myself.

It's no coincidence that William focused on that gypsy wagon the Wrathers gave us back in Pomona. He'd been trained to be one, what my family had done for generations. My grandmother and her three husbands, pulling up stakes over and over and moving on, Mom at her side. And a husband and kids didn't slow Mom's pace. Even before *So Big*, we'd moved every few years. We left Dad for Arkansas and, even there, we stayed at different places. Fran and William went with Lola, with church ladies, with Homer and Eula, boarding school. Mom and I were in the apartment, in Japan, at an appearance. There was a constant flow of people: renters, baby sitters, actors, friends, fans, club members. No wonder William wasn't able to stay in one place for very long or to sustain relationships. He didn't know how; none of us did. And with each move, each new experience, William hoped he would find himself there. Trouble was, he didn't know where to look.

August 1963

Adrianne Conflenti Neri: Jon and his family were a big part of us all growing up on good old Peck Drive. It's one of my fondest memories of growing up. Mostly, I remember Jon as being a normal kid and a good friend. In the summer, Dad paid him a dollar to mow our lawn. He and Frank did crazy things like jumping off the roof of our house into the pool. My sister Lucille and I used to autograph his pictures on the kitchen table. Mrs. Provost paid us 2 cents for each one we did. That summer, we all went to the drive-in movies in Culver City. Phyllis, our housekeeper, took us and we all piled into our Studebaker station wagon with the hood that rolled back. We went to the snack bar together and Jon was MOBBED!!! All these screaming girls!! He was quite embarrassed. All he wanted to do was get his popcorn and get back to the car. The same thing happened when we all went to Disneyland.

Dad: Cecile joined the Ebell of Los Angeles, a social and cultural woman's club founded in 1894. Cecile has been very, very active throughout the years, serving on many committees and helping in the various departments. I later became an associate member.

Fran: She paid more attention to strangers than she did me.

Mom: She didn't care for acting, but Bill liked the money. Jon's agent wanted to send Francile out on things, and she did some commercials . . . I think for Pepsi or something, I can't remember now . . . but she never did like it very much. And then she did a movie with George Gobel, a small part and she *still* wasn't too gung ho about it. Then she got a chance to go in for *Gidget* and she thought she might like that, but she didn't get it. She wasn't into it. If she'd tried hard, I think she could have gotten things, but a lot of times, she wouldn't even go. She would have been great.

Dad: A lot of girls went out for that part, but she was second choice. It was between Francile and Sally Field.

The *Gidget* audition, actually series of auditions, was a turning point for Fran. Physically, Frannie was everything they were looking for, the perfect California beach blonde to play the innocent teen who loved surfing and boys. Sally Field was a petite, adorable brunette version. After several meetings, the producers still could not make up their minds which girl they wanted. One of the producers invited Fran to stay with him and his wife for the weekend. I didn't think anything of it. I had to stay at Rudd's for three or four days to get *Lassie*. I guess Mom felt the same way because she packed her sixteen-year-old daughter up and dropped her off essentially with strangers and drove away. Mom and I did that all the time; but Fran was different. Fran was scared.

Fran: I felt so uncomfortable and so afraid. They acted so differently than my family acted. They were Hollywood people. Mom and Dad were very simple people. I was scared to be taken away to somebody's home for the weekend. I could never be sure Mom would be back when she said she would be. "Oh, you're only going away for the weekend," and then she doesn't come back for me. I didn't know from one day to the next. . . . My mother could tell a good story or a white lie. I never trusted her.

Add to the mix an added pressure none of us knew about: Bruce, Fran's boyfriend. They'd gotten real serious real fast. He barely got any time with her now. If she became the star of her own show, her life would become . . . mine. Bruce basically asked Fran to choose: showbiz or him. The choice was more complicated than that. Choosing showbiz and getting the series might bring her the love and approval she so desperately wanted from Mom. The choice was really between a life with her family or a life with him. Somehow, Fran made it through the weekend. At home, she announced that she never wanted to go on another audition. This was the last. She didn't get the part. That was a turning point for Mom. She let Fran return to Beverly Hills High for her senior year, return to her friends. She let go of the dream.

> *Fran*: I felt that, I don't know, maybe I failed her. You know, I couldn't be Jon. But I don't blame Jon for that; I blame my mother, because she tried to compare me. She wanted me to be as good as he was, and I couldn't. I was never her friend, never felt like a close daughter. As I got older, the more difficult it became, the further we separated from each other and the less we had in common, to the point where we had nothing in common . . . nothing.

Meanwhile, my contract with the Wrathers had run out. I don't remember having a face to face confrontation with Bonita. Maybe I did; maybe Mom handled it. I'd been wrestling with the decision for a while, but now I voiced it loud and clear. I wanted this to be my last year as Timmy. I'd had enough. I wanted to go to a school—with girls. I wanted people to call me Jon. I wanted some time to myself. I was sure. To the best of my memory, Mom did not try to talk me out of it. As I remember it, both Mom and Dad said that they would never force me to stay. I suppose, in her heart, Mom knew it had to end sometime. The Wrathers, on the other hand, did not want me to go, not for another three years. They made all sorts of offers—more money, a Chris Craft yacht (they owned the company), no more promotional tours—but in the end, I said no to it all. Bonita resigned herself to having to end the Martin years, but not before I was made to sign a contract agreeing not to breathe a word of my exit to the press.

Twenty years later, my mother told child actress Andrea Darvi, in an interview, "They wanted three more years from him, but my husband felt Jon should be in school with other children."

Is that really how she remembered it? Dad may have talked things over behind the scenes with Mom, but he never directed me in any way toward any decision in my life. This decision was 100 percent mine. Just like Tommy before me, I had suddenly become anxious to put the show behind me. I'd been Timmy for half my life. The majority of people that I saw daily called me Timmy. Only a small group of intimates called me Jon. That was OK for a long time. Timmy and I had so much in common. Now it was time for me to discover the differences . . . now or never.

Winding Down

Recently, I'd taken up SCUBA diving. I'd gotten all my equipment and was really excited about a planned trip to Hawaii with my parents for some great diving and my first ever real vacation. I couldn't wait. I'd tested my snorkeling gear in the Conflentis' pool and was set to go. At the last minute, I was needed for some re-shooting in Lake Tahoe and couldn't go. Mom and Dad went without me. While there, Mom was interviewed by the local press: "Parents of Timmy Martin of *Lassie* Show Enjoy Maui Visit." In it, Mom offers free 8 x 10 color photos of me to any-one who'd like one. Just write us at our home address.

> **September 1963**
> Salt Lake City promoting the movie *Lassie's Great Adventure*
> **October 1963**
> Buffum's Department Store appearance
> 16: Lake Tahoe on location for *Lassie* and a visit to Incline Elementary School

A month earlier, she'd told a reporter for *Hollywood's Citizen News* that she'd been stage-struck since she was a little girl and every member of our family helped with my career. "It had to be a family project or else it never would have worked. If we all hadn't worked together to help Jon, I would have been divorced long ago. My husband would have left me." Of course, Dad would never leave Mom. He went along with whatever she wanted. And as far as William and Fran "working together" for my career, they went along with what Mom wanted, too. These are some of Mom's little white lies; they don't hurt anyone, but they don't paint the real picture.

Bob Weatherwax: On November 22, I was late getting to the location. I had picked up my wife and newborn son at the hospital that morning and brought them home. I was on my way to work when the news came over the radio. President Kennedy had been shot in Dallas. By the time I made it to the location, he was dead.

Lloyd: We were shooting way out in the San Fernando Valley somewhere. I remember being on a railroad track with a baby duck; the story was about Timmy adopting a duckling. Bill Beaudine was directing. Bob arrived and told us the news and we stood momentarily stunned.

Bob: Then Beaudine says, "I don't give a shit. I didn't vote for him."

Lloyd: . . . then we went right back to work. The producers were so cheap; we were on location and we stayed and finished the work. The Wrathers did not have to be that cheap. After *Lassie,* I went to *Gunsmoke* and it was a world of difference, a world of difference. Once we were out on location and our sound man had a heart attack . . .

Bob: We were working on the poor guy, trying to get him to breathe, and they told us we were making too much noise. After he died, we covered him, but they needed to put the camera there. They had us move him out of the way and finish the day's shoot.

There were big discussions in Hollywood and Beverly Hills as to whether or not the Christmas parades should continue so soon after President Kennedy's assassination. In the end, all agreed we needed the lift. The show must go on.

December 15/22

My fourth and last Christmas episode, a two-parter called "Lassie's Gift of Love" aired. This is a sweet story with, once again, Lloyd Corrigan as "the old gentleman who just might be Santa Claus." In this one, he's Mr. Nicholson, a mender of toys, turning cast offs and throwaway toys into magical, mechanical wonders for Ruth's church giveaway. Timmy had been leaving food for the birds, and Mr.

Nicholson inspires Timmy to go one step further: start a program to gather food from the farmers to put out for all the wildlife so they can survive the snow (more soapsuds). The food attracts wolves, which are killed by an angry farmer, Mr. Krebbs, who forces Timmy to end his program. Mr. Nicholson explains to Timmy that Mr. Krebbs isn't just a mean old man; he's lonely, but "perhaps we've planted a seed." Meanwhile Lassie discovers the wolves' three pups in a cave, but is trapped inside by a snow slide accidentally started by Krebbs.

The Martins all must be in church that night. Timmy sings a beautiful solo of "Silent Night." I am notorious for not being able to carry a tune, but Lloyd Nelson says it is absolutely me singing. Jeanne Russell's mom must have had to work overtime with me on that one, because, even if I say so myself, Timmy does a beautiful job— puberty and all. Everyone is moved. Mr. Nicholson puts his finger to his nose and a big wind comes up outside, blowing away all the debris blocking the cave entrance. Lassie escapes and finds Krebbs, who helps her save the wolf pups—little collie pups sprayed black with colored hair spray—and gets them all home in time for the Martins' Christmas party. Mr. Krebbs tells Timmy he's learned a valuable lesson and he'd be pleased to help start up the wildlife program again. The Martins invite him to join the festivities inside. Mr. Nicholson takes the wolf pups . . . and disappears into the night, his work finished.

> **January 1964**
> 10: Six Gun Territory, Ocala, Florida
> Spotliters and San Fernando Valley Youth Foundation's Sports and Vacation Show
> **February 1964**
> Camp Fire Girls Pep Rally dinner with Bill Dana
> Cub Scout Blue and Gold Dinner, 54th Anniversary, Hollywood

Winding Up

Another five-part episode, "The Disappearance," aired February 2 through March 1, 1964. In the episode, Lassie is once again separated from the Martins. For part of her journey home, she spends two episodes with Robert Bray as forest ranger Corey Stuart. Once again, fans tuned in faithfully every week to follow the story.

And then finally, it was here . . . my last episode of *Lassie*. Bonita and Bob Golden worked with writer Jack Paritz to create "The Wayfarers," a three-parter. June, Hugh, and I appear only in episode one, the first show of the 1964–'65 season. The struggle to come up with a story that would make Timmy walk away from Lassie was no easy task. They threw out dozens of scenarios before locking onto the one they used. All of the Martins would have to go somewhere Lassie couldn't. After some research, they discovered that Australia had strict quarantine laws. It's funny that the producers looked so hard for a real reason while Timmy was a runaway orphan who lived with three different families in seven years and no one ever legally adopted him. I guess they knew children everywhere would protest that Timmy would never leave Lassie unless he was forced. So, Down Under it was. Paul Martin is offered an opportunity to help farmers in Australia. (June always thought that was so funny since Paul had never made a big go of it on the Martin farm.) Timmy's excited about the big move until he finds out Lassie can't go without being quarantined for six months in England first. Timmy knows Lassie would be miserable, might even grieve herself to death, but he doesn't want to give her up. He wrestles with his choice: making an enormous personal sacrifice so Paul can "do the right thing" helping farm Australia, or staying behind with Lassie and Mr. Cully. Timmy returns to the hollow log where, in "The Odyssey," he'd carved "Timmy and Lassie Martin" to make it their special place. He sits between it and Lassie and sobs his heart out. In the end, with a little help from wise old Mr. Cully, Timmy realizes he can't stand in the way of his parents' dream of helping people. Dressed in a suit and tie, no more familiar check shirt and jeans, Timmy leaves Lassie with Mr. Cully and his Yorkshire terrier, Silky, making Cully promise to write updates often. Then he turns and walks away. He stops, knowing if he looks back, he won't be able to leave. Lassie watches as Timmy pushes himself forward, walking, then running away.

At one point in the story, Cully says something very profound to Ruth. I sometimes wonder if the writer looked at my life for the line: "He's just a little boy in a grownup world, and that ain't an easy thing to be. Things sorta get decided for him and there ain't nothin' he can do about it."

The difference was I had made this decision. I think I know just how Tommy must have felt when he walked away from that soundstage for the last time seven years ago. The anticipation of all that freedom overrode any sadness or lengthy goodbyes. I couldn't perceive what it would be like to *not* see these people every day. Seeing them in this place was all I knew.

Lloyd: When it was time for him to leave, I remember walking on the set, looking at the farmhouse, the phony backdrops . . . it was sad, like giving up part of your family. He couldn't have known what it meant for him to leave.

Stan: For a kid, I think that's one of the things that you really, really miss—all the people that adored me—the crew, the techies, the guy getting the doughnuts—they are just the nicest people. You feel like you have a zillion fathers and mothers during the show. But when we stopped every year, we never knew if we were coming back. It was the last day, and we'd have a wrap party and it would be like, "Goodbye, I may never see you again." Then three months later, we finally find out we got picked up again. This went on for the whole twelve years. We were under contract but were never told until sometimes thirty days before the show. When it ended—fortunately for me, I was twenty-two or twenty-three, so I had more of an adult sense.

Grace Kuhn: I took a trip around the world afterward, and everywhere I went, I said I worked on *Lassie*. Everyone wanted to know everything about Jon and the dog . . . It was a wonderful six years for me.

Sondra Space Thiederman: I remember being in public with my father and people recognizing him from *Lassie* and coming up to him and how much I loved that. Once, in San Francisco, we took a boat to Alcatraz. Someone recognized him, and a whole boatload of children came around him which was pretty cool. He loved it, signed autographs, and was so proud to have his daughters there.

Lloyd: I was with *Lassie* for thirteen years, and it was the best of the best when Jon and June were on that series.

I was contractually bound to not discuss the plans for the show on talk shows or to the press, but June and Hugh made no secret over getting their notices. Still Bonita refused to admit it was the end of the Martin family, wanting to keep the fans guessing all summer. June was quoted as saying that the cast change was occurring because my mother asked for too much money. Bob Golden told the press that they'd done all the "boy-and-his-dog" shows they could think of. Only my parents and I knew they wanted me to stay for another three years. I didn't really care what any-one else thought. I was just glad it was over.

"In six sexless years of playing a country wife and mother, I was hardly ever allowed to kiss Hugh Reilly on the cheek," June said after leaving the show. Privately, she joked with Hugh that she'd been married to him longer than any of her real husbands. Still, she told columnist Bob Thomas she was sorry to leave. "It was an actor's dream—steady work, excellent pay, a wonderful cast and crew, and a chance to do a good scene now and then. Yes, I even liked Lassie. It's really a wonderful dog. . . . Now I'm ready to go back to playing all those tramps and neurotic and alcoholic women. They're good fun, but motherhood pays off better in the long run." That it did. June will always be my mom, and I share her with millions who feel the same way about her.

The last Martin family portrait.

TV Guide reported that Hugh Reilly was seen leaving the wrap party "many drinks later," driving off in his convertible with a Beatles wig on his head. He already had two new offers—a leading role on the daytime soap opera *Days of Our Lives* and the role of the professor on a new show called *Gilligan's Island*. He turned both down, opting to spend more time with his sons.

Nonetheless, the press continued to sniff out the story. They speculated on the departure of the Martin family for Robert Bray, the forest ranger from "The Disappearance" earlier in the year. The advantages of reducing four human salaries to one would have tremendous appeal to the Wrathers. Still Bonita said no firm decision had been reached.

Bonita: As far as what our plans are next year, they're up in the air. We have built up such an adult audience; we are looking for stories with a wider scope. That's what our whole purpose will be in making any change that people might think we're making . . . our ratings have jumped in the past two years and it's because we do new things."

LA Times, Hedda Hopper's column: Attention, Mrs. Jack Wrather. Lassie's most faithful fan, Cheryl Walter, age five, phoned me after her mother read her a story that Lassie and his owner Timmy would split up and the show would get a new format. She protested violently. "They will never be happy apart. Please do something, Miss Hopper!"

Diane Mills for TV Times: I discovered a delightful young-ster with the enthusiasm of a child and the poise and intelli-gence of an adult. He gets along well with his brother and his sister's boyfriend about whom he says, "I like him . . . he has a neat car!" It just wouldn't be natural, however, for a normal American boy to be completely harmonious with his "big sis-ter." Jon says, "She won't let me sleep with the dog and when-ever she's mad at me, she squirts me with her hairspray!"

I thoroughly enjoyed my visit with Jon Provost. He has a sparkling quality about him . . . yet he tends to be humble and almost reluctant to talk about himself. He would much rather discuss such things as the "Beatles," a new singing group, coin collecting, and tele-vision monsters.

February 1964
9: Speaking of new things, just around the time I quit, I tuned into *The Ed Sullivan Show* to catch an English band everybody was talking about. They called themselves the Beatles.

Can you remember a time when someone had to explain who the Beatles were? Like the rest of the world, I got caught up in Beatlemania. Timing is everything. The country's youth, so despondent in the wake of the death of the president, desperately needed a lift. The Beatles were an instant smash. We all wanted to imitate their style and, for the first time in seven years, I could decide to let my hair grow . . . my first decision as a free man!

And, by the way, Timmy was trapped in a pipe, a mine, in caves, on ledges, in white rapids, and runaway hot air balloons. He was rescued from lakes, from radiation and fires, from lions and wolves, and from armed bandits. He survived poison berries, appendicitis, quicksand, and a minefield. But never, not once, did he fall into a well.

Part Three: Life After Lassie

"It's like the Mafia; once you're in, you're in."

—DAVY JONES

The season ended and I went back to Beverly Hills Catholic. My weekends were still full of personal appearances, but at least after school I could spend time with friends. Ron and Mike and I had taken to riding our bikes north across Beverly Hills all the way to Sunset Boulevard and the Beverly Hills Hotel, the pink palace. We loved the penny candy in the sweet shop on the lower level. The three of us got into a lot of mischief in the neighborhood: fire crackers, cherry bombs—I even think we blew up someone's mailbox and the Beverly Hills Police took us in. Dad was really mad about that one. Mostly, it was kid stuff, just blowing off steam. It wouldn't last long. Mom had my summer entirely booked.

Dino Martin Jr. went to Beverly Hills Catholic. I liked him and his brother Ricci and went to their house after school a number of times. Dino put a band together with Billy Hinsche and Desi Arnaz Jr.—they called themselves Dino, Desi and Billy—and they were pretty good. I sat in on a few rehearsals, then Dino called with great news. They'd been hired for their first paid gig over at actor Rory Calhoun's house. He wanted me to come.

Billy Hinsche: It was a party for Cindy Calhoun's seventh birthday at their home on Sunset Boulevard, literally one block from Desi's house on Rexford Drive. He and Dino and I walked up Roxbury carrying our guitars and amps. We made $20 for the gig!!!

The Nakagawas had moved to the East Coast from Japan in the early '60s. Roger's father was a bigwig with Brother Sewing Machines, which eventually grew to become Brother International Corporation. Mom had stayed in touch with them, and when I was invited to the New York World's

Fair in July 1964, Mom invited Roger and his mother to join us as special guests.

We arrived at the Fair at 11:00 a.m. and went right to the General Motors Futurama Pavilion. We remained at the fair until 6:00 p.m., squeezing in lunch in Africa, a porpoise show in the Florida Pavilion, a ride on the monorail, a continental circus where Roger and I posed for pictures, and an interview at 5:30 just before leaving at 6:00 p.m.

> *Roger Nakagawa:* I remember vividly, Jon and I were given a VIP tour. I didn't have to wait in line for any of the rides. Getting that VIP treatment made me feel really special. Then Jon participated in this first video conference call—telephone video conferencing. It was a TV connected to Disneyland and I sat next to Jon in New York while he talked to one of his fans in California "face to face."

My last *Lassie* episode, "The Wayfarers, Part 1," aired on September 6, 1964. It's time for Timmy to go. Tearfully, he leaves Lassie with Cully. In part 3, Cully passes Lassie to her next owner, the forest ranger, Stuart Corey, from "The Disappearance," played by Robert Bray. And it is done.

The Age of Aquarius

As part of my new life, I started a new school, the Marion Colbert School for Individual Institute at 344 North La Brea, just north of Beverly Boulevard in a Jewish neighborhood. The school was a non-descript one-story building between a synagogue and a Hebrew school. Marion Colbert was a small, private, co-ed school with no religious affiliation. Jay North went there, and that must be how Mom heard of it, because it wasn't close to home. It was way too far to go on my bike, and Mom rarely drove me. Most of the time, she had me take the bus, not a school bus, but a regular city bus, two of them. I caught the first bus on Wilshire Boulevard in front of Saks Fifth Avenue and took it to La Brea, where I transferred to another bus, traveling north to Beverly Boulevard. I really hated

May 1964
2: Grand marshal, National City Police Reserve Association Parade
4: Panorama Pacific Show KNXT, L.A.
7: KTTV for *Jean Majors Show*
9: Lawndale Civic Center appearance
19: Church Welfare Bureau Volunteers Recognition Dinner

June 1964
5: Graduated Beverly Hills Catholic School
11: Closed-circuit TV appearance, Anaheim & Santa Ana City School District TV for Flag Day
15: Wolfe City Friendship Center of the First Methodist Church, Texas
17: Appearance at Greenville, Texas, library
19: Atlanta Humane Society—Honorary Chair of Be Kind to Animals Year
20–27: Tweetsie Railroad—Western theme park
28: Brooklyn—Marvin's/ASPCA NY
30: Taped March of Dimes Special in L.A. for Jan. '65 airdate

July 1964
11: Grand marshal, Steamboat Days Parade, Winona, MN
15: Fort Atkinson, Wisconsin, Camp Fire Girls fundraiser

August 1964
Coast Federal Savings Annual Picnic in Arcadia, California

it and couldn't believe she made me do it, but not because I was a snob. L.A. was not New York; public transportation was not an everyday way of life. I felt awkward and uncomfortable about going to school as it was. I didn't know anyone who took the bus, and I had never taken it before myself. I already stuck out. Ask any of the people on the bus who stared at me like I was from Mars, like "What are YOU doing HERE?" I'm sure Mom would say it was so I didn't get a big head, but it was too much in the other direction. But being ostracized on the bus every morning was nothing compared to what I was forced to endure at school.

I was a freshman, Jay a year younger. This was his second year there and he hated it. He was scared stiff in school anyway because his education had been so terrible. Jay was a smart boy who literally could not do any arithmetic and could barely read. The classes were small; I think there were ten or twelve students total in the ninth grade. To say it was not warm and welcoming would be an understatement.

Jay North: It was a very expensive private school. Unlike a public school, they allowed you to come and go if you got work. They would give us our assignments, so we could keep up and not be so behind when we returned.

The other kids were so mean to us, so hostile. The cruelty that I experienced—and I saw kids pick on Jon as much as they did on me—made us cling closely to each other at school. Kids would shove me and say, "Hey, you think you're something 'cause you're a TV star," and punches and verbal assaults. People would try to start fights with him, ridicule him, "Hey, you're not on *Lassie* anymore; what happened? You both are finished." We were child stars and other kids could not relate to us. We never felt connected to these kids. We always felt different. The ones who wanted to befriend us wanted to get something out of us, and the others tormented and taunted us because of what we did. I think Jon and I were totally unprepared for this. I don't know how our families could have prepared us. The teachers didn't understand how to deal with it or what we were going through. I wish they could have counseled us . . . or the other kids. They observed the behavior and didn't do anything. I think they were hard on us to show the other kids that they were not going to play favorites with the Hollywood celebrities. They almost went out of their way to not treat us as special. We sensed hostility from some of the teachers, too.

Jay clung to me; I didn't cling to Jay. I was able to weather the storm a bit better than he was, though I suffered all the same abuse. The difference was our home life. Jay was getting yelled at and punched at home by his aunt and uncle. I had a lot more self-confidence, but we needed each other during that tough time, no doubt. Our poor friend Jeanne Russell had her own problems at a different school.

Jeanne: I would get a reaction in public. People would go, "Oh, God! There's that monkey from *Dennis the Menace*—Margaret!" And then they'd groan like I was the villain. Playing the creep really took its toll. And that was how Hollywood identified me, that's what they wanted me for, so I guessed that was how I was. Confidence was an enormous problem for me because of this image.

Stan Livingston: I used to dread going back to a new school, which was happening all the time. I can't tell you how many fights I had in public school because I was the guy on *My Three Sons*. Almost everyone was cool. They all wanted to be your friend and talk to you. But there was always some asshole, "You're not so great, not so tough," and eventually you have to deal with it. Eventually, it would wear off. I never tried to be special. I tried to look just like them; I tried harder, really.

MY THREE SONS

I was at Marion Colbert for two years, and it never got any better. One muscle-brained bully with the initials JP wrestled me to the ground one day and took my initial ring off my finger. I reported him, but I was told I didn't have proof it wasn't his ring. Case closed. We hated the place. There was a park about a block or so away, and sometimes Jay and I would buy hot dogs at Pink's and take them to the park to eat lunch. There was a small playground there, and in '65 and '66, there were always a few hippies. These free-living folk often gathered up in Griffith Park for Love-ins and Be-ins: General Hershey Bar, General WasteMoreLand and Susie and her husband Vito, who were a prominent part of the emerging music and cultural scene on the Sunset Strip. They had a little boy named Godot, and he played in this park with his mom.

Trina Robbins, writer, former Strip denizen: I knew her as Sue Vito . . . Sue sewed, she was one of us—the sisterhood of the sewing machine—which included Genie the Tailor and this amazing, slightly older red-haired woman with a single name, Morgan, or something like that, whom I had heard was a witch and had driven at least one guy crazy when they went out to the desert for a month and lived on cottage cheese and peyote, and I was a little afraid of her and in awe of her too. I used to run into Sue Vito at this big fabric place where everyone who was anyone in the Sisterhood bought their fabric. And she would have Godot with her dressed in some bizarre thing she had made him, like brocade diapers and such.

At first, Jay and I didn't know who she was, but we couldn't help but notice her. She dressed colorfully and crazily: long, Indian-print skirts, beaded, braless, barefoot, wild makeup. I'm sure she had no trouble figuring out who we were. She climbed the jungle gym near where we were sitting, and our teenage hormones raced as we subtly tried to catch a glimpse of thigh. I guess we weren't subtle at all. She laughed, shouted something we couldn't make out, then raised her skirts and flashed us and laughed some more. I froze in shock while Jay turned three shades of red. Whoa, the times they were a-changin' all right. Jay and I had just received a crash course in counterculture. I couldn't speak for Jay, but I was interested . . . very interested.

November 1964
November Richmond Auto show—fundraiser for Salesian Boys Clubs

The Salesian Boys Club is run by brothers, one of whom, Brother Phil Mandile, has worked with runaway kids and boys clubs in California for decades and in 2001 was named a Knight of the Holy Sepulchre of Jerusalem, one of the highest honors the Pope can bestow.

Brother Phil: Jon and his mom came over to a spaghetti dinner at St. Joseph's retreat center. At the time, it was the seminary for brothers. I was really surprised how open and friendly she was, and he just seemed like a normal kid. Shortly thereafter, I wrote a thank you letter to them for coming by, and after that I started getting all kinds of letters from Jon. Every place he went I got letters and postcards and notes and stuff.

I don't remember how many times I knocked on Cecile's door for a cup of hot coffee. Sometimes I dropped in with a small group of the boys from the club and she and Jon—if he was home—were never too busy to greet them and give them photos. I don't ever recall meeting his brother and sister. But his mom and I would sit at the kitchen table talking. B.A. would be in the living room watching an Alabama game and he would come and sit and join us sometimes, but he was pretty quiet compared to Cecile.

Peace and Love

Mom: I get a telegram: "Bruce and I are married. I need your love." I am entertaining the Motion Picture Mothers, getting ready for a crafts sale when it arrives, and I am almost down on the floor, waving the telegram and asking the ladies to call my husband. He comes home. In a few minutes the telephone rings. It's Mrs. Rubin. "Did you know my son and your daughter just got married? What are you going to do about it?" "We don't know what to do about it! What are you going to do?" She says: "I don't know. I'll talk to my husband." After, she says, "We know where they are—the Desert Inn. My husband is going to call the hotel, send up a bottle of champagne, and give them anything they want." I told B.A. and he said, "Send a dozen red roses."

November 6, 1964

Dad: What a surprise! Francile said she and Bruce had been married by a Justice of the Peace. Naturally this was quite a shock to us, but we realized that parents can't control all actions of their children.

Fran: I had turned eighteen in March, but we had to save up to get our first apartment. We had it for weeks before we eloped. I kept sneaking toilet paper and supplies out of the house, saved up S&H green stamps for a toaster, and made sure I only bought gas at a station that gave away a set of glasses with a fill-up.

I really would have liked for my dad to be there. I know I must have hurt him, but he never . . . my father doesn't talk about anything. Never has, never will. It was pretty cold. My mother got a telegram from me saying, "Sorry, too late; we're already married." I understand that my mother broke down, that she cried. I think it made her feel ashamed. It must point the finger that something's wrong. Daughters just don't elope, run off and get married, unless they're hiding something. I wasn't pregnant, so I wasn't hiding anything there. The only thing I can think is that she knew how I felt. I didn't want my mother at my wedding.

Fran got her wish . . . sort of. When they came home, there was hell to pay on both sides. Mom and Dad wanted them to marry in the church, and Bruce's parents wanted them to be married in a temple. Fran studied for months to convert to Judaism.

Fran: Bruce's parents weren't members of any temple, and here's where Jon comes in. Jon had, for many years, done charity work for churches, schools, temples. He had done some charity work for Temple Emanuel in Beverly Hills. And Rabbi Zelman remembered all the work my brother had done. He raised a lot of money for the temple. So my mother went to Rabbi Zelman and pulled some strings and he agreed.

Mom had people coming to the wedding I didn't even know, people whose names I'd never heard. The temple couldn't seat as many people as my mother invited; they were standing in the back. I didn't know ninety percent of them.

Laurie Ackerman: Fran's wedding was a real media circus: Charlie Herbert, Flip Mark, Cubby O'Brien, Shari Alberoni . . .

Dad: Fran's been married three times . . . to the same man. Soon thereafter they bought a house near us in Beverly Hills and we enjoyed the closeness of them. This marriage has been a wonderful union of two very devoted, happy, and understanding people. And he's still crazy about her.

A Horse Is a Horse

1965 Guest-starring on *Mister Ed* was a lot of fun. I liked the show. It was popular, in its fifth season, but that's only part of the reason I was excited about it. The producer was Arthur Lubin, who I knew from *Escapade in Japan,* and this was our first opportunity to work together again. Big changes in me, not so much with him—as kind and as blubbery as ever. Twice as nice—he was directing too. Some things don't change. Series star Alan Young was warm and welcoming with a Scottish twinkle in his eye. And actress Connie Hines was one of the sexiest TV housewives around.

Alan Young: We had one little boy on that didn't get along with Ed—kind of frightened him. Jonny just fit right in; he was lovely.

Connie Hines: He had kind of a crush on me, which was so fun . . . he was the kind of little boy that you just wanted to take care of, so sweet and very precocious. He had a presence about him that was a little more mature than his age. I guess that was because he was in show business. He was just so adorable.

Little boy! Hey, I was fourteen. I knew Connie was out of my league, but a kid can dream. With Connie and Alan both—what you see is what you get. I love them, then and now. Alan still twinkles, and I still have a crush on Connie.

The episode had me—Jonny Provost—as the paper boy/star pitcher of the little league team Alan coached. Alan misses a pitch of mine, and the ball breaks a window at his grumpy, ex-military neighbor's, the wonderful Leon Ames. He wants me to work off what I owe for the window—even on the day of the big game. I have a real "heart-to-heart" talk about it with Ed in his stable. I mention that I usually talk to my dog because he really under-stands. Ed's ears shoot forward in disagreement. In the end, I have to admit, Ed made me feel a lot better . . . good, clean fun.

I told Joe Finnigan, UPI's Hollywood correspondent, that I felt the role was a little more mature than that of Timmy. "I'm a different boy in this show, and I live in a big town, not on a farm."

Connie Hines: He was right on time, knew all of his lines, upstaged us to death. I mean working with a horse is bad enough but with a cute lit-tle boy. . . .

Alan Young: He did have a sense of professionalism in that he never intruded. He did it with such love, such understanding. He dug what acting was all about. He seemed to like the horse, and the horse sure liked him.

Ed was such a sweet animal—and enormous. Alan rode him every morning. And if anyone understood how important it was to get along with the four-legged star of a TV show, it was me. It's the lesson I learned on *Lassie:* What's the name of the show?

Fran and Bruce were happily settled into married life. William was with Grandma in the Valley going to school. And I had easily cut through those apron strings Mom had tied to me. With more time now for her husband, Mom and Dad took their first tour of Europe. You can imagine how my mother loved it; so did Dad. Hooked, they took fifteen tours over the next seventeen years. This meant they left me alone a bit more. You can imagine how I loved that; I took advantage of every second. I had a lot of time to make up for. I was booked all of July and August as a gunslinger!

Timmy's mom goes atomic! June Lockhart made her debut in *Lost in Space* as Maureen Robinson, mother of three, two of whom were friends Angela Cartwright and Billy Mumy and all of whom were among the crew of a spaceship adrift in outer space. Instead of a dog, they had a robot.

Bill Mumy: Jon and I share the unique experience of being the two television sons of June Lockhart. I'm sure we could each write novels about that experience from our separate perspectives. I'm also sure we won't.

This Property Is Condemned

The film version of *This Property Is Condemned* was based on a one-act play by Tennessee Williams. A young, homeless girl comes across a boy playing hooky as she walks along the railroad tracks and stops to recount the story of her beautiful sister, Alva—once the town's "main attraction"—and her tragic fate in the Deep South.

The girl was played by Mary Badham, a thirteen-year-old who just received an Oscar nomination for her first film role as Scout in *To Kill a Mockingbird*. I was playing the boy, Tom.

Mary Badham.

Alva was played by the gorgeous Natalie Wood, certainly one of the main attractions at the box office in 1965 and one of the biggest movie stars around . . . a former child star herself discovered in Santa Rosa, California. I'd heard she was small, but I never knew how small until I saw her that first day. She was just five-foot-two and a hundrd pounds soaking wet . . . about the same size as I was at the time, but it looked a whole lot different on her. I was used to meeting famous people, but I was a bit in awe of her; she was so pretty. Costarring with Natalie was new Hollywood leading man Robert Redford, top Canadian actress Kate Reid, the sinister Charles Bronson, and former *Little Rascal* Robert Blake.

One of the writers was Francis Ford Coppola. One of the producers was the legendary John Houseman, who had founded the Mercury Theater with Orson Welles. The director was Sydney Pollack. Today that name swings a lot of weight, but in 1965 he was known more as a daring and original TV director, mostly on *Ben Casey,* and a frequent Emmy nominee. Just thirty-three, skinny, with black-framed glasses, Pollack had his hands full with *This Property,* only his second film. He was my first experience with a young director the same age as the stars. In fact, he and Robert Redford were friends from their acting days in New York and would make several more films together. Natalie and Redford were good friends too, until her tragic death by drowning in 1981.

Natalie Wood and Robert Redford on set.

Sydney Pollack: Natalie was great. She was a terrific lady and was a big, important part of my career. She had director control and costar control. I'd only done one film, and I don't think it was out yet. She looked at it, and she's the one who OK'd me; so I've always had a sentimental attachment to her. She also was like that with Redford. She chose Redford on *Inside Daisy Clover.* She saw him [on Broadway] in *Barefoot in the Park.* Both Bob and I really miss her, because she was so important to both of our careers and a terrific lady. She was really easy to work with. I thought she was wonderful in the film, and I loved working with her. It was a real tragedy to have her life end that way.

Mr. Pollack worked next door to me on the Desilu lot and I thought perhaps we got to know each other a little back then . . . maybe that's how he brought me into the picture, but no.

Sydney Pollack: I did not meet Jon at Desilu at all. His name came up in a casting session, and I had seen him on *Lassie* and I knew what a good actor he was. That's how I hired him.

So, hired I was. The picture was shooting in New Orleans and Bay St. Louis, Mississippi, in October and part of November. I'd had less than a month of my sophomore year at Marion Colbert before I was pulled out to travel to Biloxi with Mom.

Mississippi

All together, there were eighty of us and most were staying at the Broadwater Beach Hotel, a south Mississippi icon, considered the jewel of the Gulf Coast, with property that stretched back behind the swimming pool to private, quiet bungalows.

Jim Dalton: Jon and his mother had a cottage. So did Mary Badham and her mother. I know Robert Redford and Natalie Wood did. The bungalow she was staying in had been painted inside and out more times than it had been in existence. She constantly wanted the color changed. It got to be a joke amongst us . . . you know, elbow in the ribs "You won't believe this, but that bungalow's been painted again." It's decimated now, the entire area. What Camille didn't get Katrina completely wiped out.

Call sheet.

Shooting was to begin October 11. Natalie arrived about a week ahead. So did Mom and I. The World Series opened on October 6, with the Los Angeles Dodgers playing the Minnesota Twins. Sandy Koufax couldn't pitch game one because it fell on the Jewish High Holidays. We lost the first two in Minneapolis. Half the crew had transistor radios glued to their ears and passed the score to those of us without. The Dodgers took the series in game 7 with Koufax pitching possibly the greatest playoff game of his career. Everybody was in a good mood.

We got settled right away, and Mom hit the ground running—out meeting people, arranging for me to go to a local children's hospital or something similar. She was in the Deep South, and it agreed with her. On one of her excursions, she met Don Jaye, program director at WLOX in Biloxi, and Jim Dalton, a station employee.

Jim Dalton: Don was one of those people, you met him once and for about thirty seconds he was a stranger; and after that, you'd known him all his life. He had the gift of gab and a heart of gold. I don't think he had a mean bone in his body. He was a very giving person, a lot like Jon's mother.

Don met Cecile at some function and they struck up a conversation. She had some things she could be involved in and make a difference, and she didn't want Jon sitting in a hotel room the entire time. She wanted to make sure somebody was available to get him where he had to be at a certain times, and that's how it progressed into Don and me accompanying Jon. There were one or two other people who assisted in keeping Jon occupied when he wasn't in school. He had his tutor with him. She trusted him enough that he was going to be where he was supposed to be when he was supposed to be there. Jon was a little gentleman; he did what he was asked to do. There was no sense of being a caretaker and having to direct him or prevent him . . . it was just kind of a companion arrangement.

It wasn't unusual for Mom to take off; she'd always done that and always found someone to look out for me. I was certainly old enough to be me on my own, but the law required someone to be responsible and present. Don and Jim became those people. Mom and I were in Biloxi for close to a month, but I probably only worked just over a week total, so we had a lot of free time.

With Don Jaye.

The Gulf Coast

Jim Dalton: The entire Gulf Coast at that time was like Las Vegas and Reno today. There wasn't a gas station or convenience store that didn't have slot machines. All the night clubs and dinner areas had backroom casinos. Just a few miles west was Gus Stevens's club, where Jayne Mansfield was appearing when she was killed in the car accident. It was wide open. There was a New Orleans Mafia family-type group that controlled a lot of what went on along the Gulf Coast. The crew was right in the middle of all this. And another thing, I believe someone got mad at the state organization of Mississippi for allowing the production company through. People up in Jackson tell them Bay St. Louis is a perfect little town to represent a Tennessee Williams town out in the sticks . . . it was pretty close to bein' true, too. There are still places up here where you don't go unless you know somebody because of the moonshining and today, of course, it's methamphetamine.

I'd been going to the South practically since the day I was born. My great-grandfathers fought in the Confederate army. If anyone felt at home here, it was Mom and me. I was too young to know about the clubs and casinos, but at fifteen, I was aware of the civil rights movement and the struggle going on in the South. Mom bought the local paper to show me a story on the movie, but what caught my attention was a box outlined on the back page, the announcement of a plan for the desegregation of the Bay St. Louis Municipal School District. I'd heard about segregation on TV in Beverly Hills, but here it was, really happening.

Jim Dalton: There were a lot of hostilities with that. Bay St. Louis was mostly Cajun; there were some blacks. I would say if there were 2,000 people livin' there, I would be amazed. And, because of the number of Cajun people that lived there, there was very little support from the state. Racism was a problem.

Sharon Smith, fan: When I was a senior in high school in Mississippi, I didn't go to school with black kids. They had their own high school and elementary school. One family on my street had a black maid. I remember blacks sitting at the back of the city buses, black water fountains and white water fountains. My mom and I stopped for lunch at Woolworth's, and one time the waitress told a black guy he couldn't sit at the counter. We had no riots or anything like that. They had their place, they just stayed in it. Same with Jewish people. We had three successful Jewish families in my community, but the only thing I knew about Jewish people was what I saw in the movie *The Diary of Anne Frank*. I was totally in a vacuum. One thing I was very aware of, we definitely had a Ku Klux Klan.

Bay St. Louis

Preparations in Bay St. Louis had begun weeks earlier when a seven-vehicle convoy transporting cameras, dollies, electrical equipment, catering trailer, honey wagon, and wardrobe made it from L.A. in three days. I never did see Bay St. Louis as it really looked. I saw it only as a movie set dressed in the time of the Great Depression. The crew had masked TV aerials, air conditioners, traffic lights. They dumped dust and dirt on paved roads and brought in vintage cars and trucks. Within days, a whole neighborhood had been transformed. Store windows featured hot water bottles and Kodak Brownie cameras. Gas was 12 cents a gallon and eggs 10 cents a dozen. Unsuspecting "civilians" were getting off the train in Bay St. Louis and doing a double take. Mom sure did. It must have reminded her of the times she and her half-sister had run around with Al Capone. I felt like I'd traveled back in time. They even brought a 1942 steam locomotive to the Coast from Arkansas.

The mayor of Bay St. Louis, John Scafide, tried unsuccessfully to drive the Hollywood group out of town. He and the local newspaper publisher and a few others filed an injunction against the film being shot there. Among the complaints cited were the closing of a portion of a main street and the "kind" of picture it was. Locals who agreed with him stood in front of the cameras or made sure their reflections could be seen in store windows to ruin shots. They wanted no part of this dirty Tennessee Williams movie or our ethnically diverse group—read that as Jews and blacks. Over the eight weeks, about 1,000 locals were employed and close to a half million dollars were spent there. *This Property* was the biggest industry in Bay St. Louis's history. Personally, I never felt threatened or unwelcome . . . until the end.

Mary Badham: My father originally didn't want me to do *This Property* because he disliked Tennessee Williams. A lot of people from the South disliked Tennessee Williams because they said he put such a vulgar, bad twist on the South and made them all look like a bunch of fruitcakes. He was really very opposed to it. And I don't know what they told him, how they talked him into signing the papers; I have no idea. There were a lot of people in the South that felt that way.

Jim Dalton: Some of the people living in Bay St. Louis, the ones that were extras in the movie—they didn't want speaking parts, didn't want to be identified—they did their best to ruin the shots they were in or to disrupt the filming in some way. It was the old mentality there, more of a combination Cajun and other ethnicities that thought that they were being exploited. In fact, I know there was a time during the filming that it was "get in, do your scene, and get away, leave." Jon was away from the set more than he was on the set; all of them were because the people did not want them milling around in the area.

Sydney Pollack: I've done a lot of movies now and I find them all difficult. I don't know of any easy ones. But I didn't find this one so much more difficult than any other. It was a difficult location. It wasn't a friendly town, but nobody made death threats or anything. We drove every day to Bay St. Louis, we didn't stay in Bay St. Louis, we drove. . . . The locals were not in love with Tennessee Williams. It was only my second film, and I had my hands full. I had Natalie Wood, who was a big, big movie star at that time, and Robert Redford, who was a hot new movie star. But then I had Charles Bronson, Bobby—Robert Blake—and Kate Reid and a big cast. It was a difficult film, a period film, so I wasn't so aware that there was any danger or hostility. I just found the picture difficult.

Down South Magazine: Regarding Mr. Pollack, a human interest note is due about now. While in the midst of frantically interviewing potential extras in staggering numbers, all lined up on a dusty lot as Indian Summer temperatures hovered in the 90s, a local reporter–novice photographer struggled in vain with an unfamiliar camera . . . noting her utter frustration, the director patiently took reporter and camera in hand, unearthed the mysteries of F-settings, light meter, and distance reading, even took a couple of experimental shots, and all so tactfully, the ignorant one left without feeling even slightly embarrassed!

One of my scenes, the film's close, was the first shot scheduled. At 7:00 in the morning on Otober 11, cars and buses arrived at the Broadwater for the thirty-mile drive to Bay St. Louis. In the limo with Mom and me were Mary and Mrs. Badham and Mary's tutor, Mrs. Grotke. We caravanned on the winding coastal road for more than an hour.

Once there, Mary and I reported to the makeup trailer. Even that early, the humidity was staggering. Mary, sweet and a bit shy, was from Alabama and no stranger to humidity. Thank goodness I was used to it from going there most summers. And we always shot *Lassie*'s Christmas shows in summer, so the thick makeup and winter clothes were tolerable.

Our scene was shot on the railroad tracks of the L&N line—Louisville to Nashville. As Willie, Mary finishes her story, we say our goodbyes, and I run away down a steep hill, kite in tow. The camera rises with the kite and captures my charge in an aerial view. It was a difficult shot that started with a helicopter landing on a train.

Sydney Pollack: We had a Bell J-3 helicopter that was a reciprocal engine helicopter that vibrated like hell and it was state of the art. I did a couple of different helicopter shots there. The one with Jon and Mary that ended the picture was very complicated because we put the helicopter on a flatbed railroad car and pushed the car in order to get the last shot of the movie.

I was used to tricky shots, but I'd only been in a helicopter twice before, and never anything like this copter. Mary and I were both aching to ride in it. That request came back a firm no. Mr. Pollack, a stickler for perfection, did many takes before he was satisfied, each time waiting for the train car and helicopter to reset. It was a long first day.

The director of photography was James Wong Howe. This guy was living history. A two-time Oscar winner for *Hud* and *The Rose Tatoo*, Mr. Howe worked as a slate boy in 1917 for Cecil B. DeMille and within a few years he was behind the camera, where he became known as "the lighting cameraman." I wish I could tell you that I appreciated being in his presence, that I questioned him to learn as much as I could, but that's just not the case. It was normal for me to meet people like this. I mean, I knew he was famous. I knew Natalie Wood was famous, but no one in my family made a big deal about it. Decades later, my wife looked at photos of me with Buster Keaton, Marjorie Main, or Ernie Kovacs and was all over

With Sydney Pollack.

me with questions about them, but finally, she came to understand that faces in my life came and went in a day, in a moment, for as long as it took to click a shutter, and I never saw them again. Mr. Howe was older and a bit gruff, but nobody could beat Mr. Beaudine in that department, so he and I got on without incident.

Sydney Pollack: James Wong Howe was more than just set in his ways. He was a difficult man. He was a consummately gifted artist and operated on the cutting edge of the field of cinematography, and he had his own particular technique at that time, and that was really why I wanted him. And he did a beautiful job on the picture. But he was a difficult man. He was irascible and ill-humored. He was quite old at the time we did this, and he was not terribly diplomatic or respectful of other members on the crew, but he was incredibly good at what he did and therefore worth it in the long run. . . . We didn't fight all day long, but there was a certain amount of tension that existed between us. At times I had to sometimes step in, take him aside and say, "I don't want you talking to my actors in this manner. You're getting dangerously close to directing them, and I don't want you to do that." Or I would have to argue with him about certain shots. I certainly would do it all over again, absolutely. He was a real genius at what he did. I was a very young, new guy and he wanted to run the set, and I wanted to run the set. He let me run the set. He wasn't that deluded that he thought he was going to kick the director off. He was difficult, I guess that's the right word . . . difficult and demanding. It cost you something to work with him, but he was more than worth it.

Mary Badham: The tension was palpable on the set. It was hot as Hades out there on a lot of days, and there was a lot of sitting around waiting for them to get their act together. . . . If you put James Wong Howe, Sydney Pollack, and Houseman, John Houseman—oh my God, you got three mega people there, each with their own ideas and very strong feelings about what they want to do and what they envision for this picture. It was tough, I am talking major tough, and you could feel it. You could absolutely feel it.

I was not on set nearly as much as Mary was. She was in a tough position and didn't have much experience to get her through.

Mary Badham: I don't have a lot of specific memories of Jon. There's just sort of an overall feeling. He was very professional, very easy to work with. He was always prepared; he never missed a beat. No matter what happened, he rolled with the punches and went to work and did what he had to do—which makes life very easy for the person you're working with. He was very nice, and yeah, he was pretty cute. [Laughs] To me, he was so good-looking, he intimidated me. I felt inferior. Here's this guy who has done everything and I am just this lowly peon who is just getting started. That is where I was. I was a little afraid to say anything or do much. I was very shy around him. The only thing I can remember is his smiling face. That's it, that's the way I picture Jon with that big grin on his face.

Sydney Pollack: They were both really, really good professional kids. I mean, Mary was much more amateurish than Jon. Jon was a real pro and had such a beautiful quality. I loved working with them both. It was a pleasure. He was just lovely in the movie, he really was.

The Fans

Down South Magazine: Most popular pastime during filming was "watching the movie" and a sort of carnival atmosphere pervaded the roughly six-block section used as background. Many Bay residents were in evidence when work began promptly at 7:00 a.m. and remained until fading daylight forced shooting to end, usually around 5:30 p.m.

Sharon Smith: I lived in Gulfport when they were filming. I'd have been thirteen years old. . . . My brother was a lifeguard at the Broadwater Hotel. I remember Larry coming home from work saying, "Oh my gosh, the hotel is swarming with movie stars like Natalie Wood and Charles Bronson." We all knew Jon from *Lassie* and we all knew Mary Badham from *To Kill a Mockingbird.* We couldn't get there fast enough. Robert Redford was swimming laps in the pool and Larry said, "That guy's in the movie too." I asked who he was. Larry said, "I don't know,

Robert somebody." I thought he was cute, but I wanted to be with the stars; besides, he was old!

The whole time they were there filming that movie, my life and the lives of my girlfriends revolved around going to the hotel. The Gulf Coast was a very sleepy area, and this was about the biggest thing that had happened there. Every day after school we hung around the hotel getting autographs till 9:00 or 10:00 at night. Our parents dropped us off and my brother brought us home. No parent today would let thirteen-year-old girls hang around like that, but times were so different. . . . We would get dressed up in our nicest casual outfits and walk around the grounds. I had a pair of sharkskin Capri pants . . . oh, shoot, yeah! I got the most sightings. I screamed, "Oh my God, there's Charles Bronson!" and actually scared the day-

With Charles Bronson.

lights out of him. He ran as fast as his legs could carry him. Later, he spent two hours talking with me in the lobby one night. I spoke to Natalie Wood at length. She was sitting out in the backyard of her cottage and I was walking by. I told her, "You're the most beautiful lady I've ever seen in my whole life," and she loved that. She talked to my girlfriend and me for hours.

Down South Magazine: Luncheon served daily from Michaelson's Catering truck to those sitting beneath one large tent and a smaller canvas for the cast, appears to feed most of the town. In addition to all employees, actors, and a large number of policemen hired for traffic control on off-duty hours, many guests are fed daily. Menu for one day included filet mignon, boiled and fried shrimp, baked potatoes, broccoli, baked beans, vegetable or fruit salad, coffee, milk and always on hand are enormous coolers of grape juice to quench the thirst of the cast, workers and observers.

In fact, those lunches served up to 160 people. Fans and curious people milled around the location and the hotel from morning to night. There were always girls around. Most thought it was natural for me to be in the center of a group of giggling teenage girls. The truth was if they didn't come to me, I'd never have been brave enough to approach them. I'd had little experience with kids socially, and girls were still a big mystery. Besides, I was usually pretty tired from work, so . . . no stolen kisses, no hot make-out sessions . . . just innocent fun.

Sharon Smith: Jon and Mary spent thirty minutes with us almost every night. Maybe it was his mother letting him spend some time with his fans. There were probably five different groups of girls who went . . . not the boys . . . and we were all ga-ga. The reason we were going was Jon Provost. That was our reason for being. Everything was based on Jon Provost sightings, if he talked to you or you got autographs. If you got that autograph on a t-shirt, you wore it to school the next day. All we talked about were his dimples and his hair. Jon even autographed my arm. I remember not showering so I'd keep that forever. I went to my thirtieth class reunion and a bunch of us were talking about how we used to go to the hotel. *This Property Is Condemned* is one of my all-time favorites. The memory of the cast will stay with me all my life.

Belinda Meyer Marcum and Linda Lewis: We were both four-teen and our mission was to meet Jon and Mary. We ended up with them at the pool. Robert Blake was lying on a lounge nearby and there was music playing from somewhere. He wanted us to dance around for him and, at some point, we jumped into the pool, clothes and all. We all laughed and had a great time. That's our first memory of being with Jon. I guess we must have won his trust enough to be asked back to visit. Jon's mom was so sweet to us and she seemed to enjoy us being there.

Linda, Mary, and Belinda.

We actually got to spend the night with Mary in her room. We felt like we were in a wonderful dream by then. That night, Mary decided to drive the car they were using all around the parking area, with all of us in tow! She was very adventurous, and we followed her lead, of course. It was fantastic. The next morning, we rode in the limo with them to Bay St. Louis to the set. While there, waiting around for their scene, we could hear music coming from somewhere—the Rolling Stones' "Get Off My Cloud." Jon climbed up to the top of the train car and started dancing and singing the song to us. He had us all laughing so hard.

Later, in the scene, Jon and Mary had to roll down a steep hill

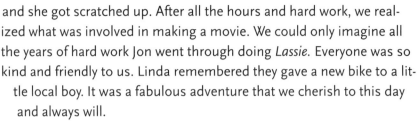

and she got scratched up. After all the hours and hard work, we realized what was involved in making a movie. We could only imagine all the years of hard work Jon went through doing *Lassie.* Everyone was so kind and friendly to us. Linda remembered they gave a new bike to a little local boy. It was a fabulous adventure that we cherish to this day and always will.

Down South Magazine: Probably most popular with the local youth, as far as actors go, is fifteen-year-old Jon Provost, for seven years Timmy on the *Lassie* television show. "Kids" from two to 92 flocked around his dressing room, and a more natural, typically all-boy, actor could be found nowhere. Much credit for his wholesomeness goes to his mother Cecile who made a hit with the town in its entirety. After hearing terrifying tales of Hollywood mammas, her attitude renews one's faith in human nature. She has not only strived to let her son lead as normal a life as is possible under the circumstances, but has succeeded in bringing up a happy, well-adjusted child.

Jim Dalton: When people look at and consider child stars, the impression that a lot of people have is that they're pushed into it by their mothers. I do not remember any impression that Cecile was that way. She made sure there were priorities in his life: his education. She didn't want the film to take away from his educational time. She was that way at home, too, when Jon was in school and not working. In fact both she and B.A. tried to bring all the kids up in a normal home environment. She was a semi-free spirit, and if you were going to compare her to somebody today from back in that time, someone who comes to mind is June Cleaver . . . she was serious about her children but open-minded. She would talk about things on her mind and she didn't hold things back.

Normal home environment? June Cleaver? Mom was more like Samantha Stevens on *Bewitched,* casting her spell over people, creating the image she wanted to project.

Soon after we arrived, we went to visit Dad's mom in Mobile, about an hour and a half east. Almost eighty-two, Grandma welcomed us and entertained some of the neighborhood kids for me. Mom called the local papers. Someone arranged a tour of the *USS Alabama*, which was really cool. I'm glad we made the trip, because it was the last time I saw my grandmother.

Dad called with the unexpected bad news. Grandma had suffered a stroke and died Friday afternoon, October 22. He flew out to Mobile and we met him there on Sunday for the funeral. We had to get back to Biloxi, but Mom continued to go back to Mobile to help tie up all the loose ends there. Don or Jim were usually around. I was on Don's radio show several times and made a deal to supply him with five-minute taped interviews with celebrities for his *Teen Time Record Show*. One free day when Mom wasn't around, I wasn't feeling well and stayed in bed. Don came into the bungalow and said some girls wanted to meet me. He let the girls into my bedroom, not in a group, but one by one to say hello. It felt really awkward, like he was trying to get something going for me. Mom would have had a fit. Besides the fact that I felt terrible, I just wasn't that type of kid. I never said anything to Don. I figured I'd never see him again anyway.

Mary

Working or not, Mary and I were both required to have at least three hours of lessons a day. Mary brought along her beloved tutor, Mrs. Grotke, who taught me as well.

Mary Badham: Wherever I went, Mrs. Grotke was my teacher, welfare worker. She was absolutely an angel from heaven. She took such good care of me, and I learned so much from her. She knew my school; she knew who to deal with; she knew how to deal with them; and she knew how to work with me to get the best out of me and keep me up to snuff. I had to keep my grades up because I was goin' to a private girls school and they didn't mess around. Mrs. Grotke made sure I had all my ducks in a row and my tests were in on time so, when I walked back in the door, I was right up where everyone else was—which was great. If I had anything to say about the film industry, it's whenever possible, make that happen for the kids—because having a teacher that you really love and admire and trust can be a real lifesaver. She was one of the best. I don't think there were many like her.

Mary really had a lot of pressure on her. She worked with everyone, and it was a rough, very adult movie. The set was not conducive to a young teenage girl. She kept close to her mother, but I'm not sure if that didn't alienate her more. And if you have never heard the language on a film set, it's like a locker room. The crew had been instructed to watch it around her, but when a hammer lands on a thumb instead of a nail, it doesn't matter who's around.

Sharon Smith: Robert Blake—all I remember is that he was in a verbal fight with someone in the parking lot one night. I grew up in a house where we didn't use four-letter words, and this was Mississippi in a different time. All I remember is everything coming out of his mouth was a four-letter word. It was the first time I'd heard the "F" word. I didn't know what it meant, but it had to be dirty because he was so mad.

Mary: You know how children know there's something that's not right? I didn't know what was going on, but I knew there was something very wrong. It never felt comfortable, it never felt safe . . . From a child's point of view, it was horribly confusing. I ended up in tears more than once in my trailer. At thirteen years old, the hormones are going; your chemistry is all screwed up, so you're happy one minute and then you're absolutely blue the next. That didn't help either.

This is going to sound really bizarre, but two people I have to thank for really holding me together a couple times were Bobby Blake, of all people, and Robert Redford. Both of them got me through some of the stuff that was going on. It's amazing how just a tap on the shoulder or a quick hug or something like that . . . a "good job, kid," little things I remember like that really pulled me up out of the well. Bob Redford was so incredibly caring and professional, just everything you could possibly want in an actor and a fellow co-worker. His wants and needs are very simple. He makes no outrageous demands; he's just a wonderful human being. Both of them, I remember at one time or another, giving me that confidence when they knew I was having a bad time.

Charles Bronson, oh my God, he was a scary individual. He stayed in character from the time he got on the set in the morning till the time he left. The last day of the shoot, I am leaving the sound stage and I'm excited 'cause I get to go home and see my friends, and he hails me from the side and wants to tell me "goodbye and nice working with you." He's all sweet and wonderful and I am just totally blown away. I was like, "What? No!" I didn't understand. I wasn't an actor. I didn't know method acting and all that kind of stuff. I had no clue. All I knew was that this guy had just been really uncomfortable to work around. We didn't get to know each other till those last two minutes while saying goodbye.

Natalie did not give me that kind of support. I never felt close to her, but there again, I was a little intimidated by her. She was so beautiful; all the guys were just so gaga over her. She turned everybody's head. She was very wrapped in her own world right at that point. I don't know my history on that, but it seems to me she was going with some prince or other.

Natalie

Jim Dalton: Natalie was dating a prince. The rumors were that she was wild.

Ladislow Blatnik wasn't a prince; he was a king—"The Shoe King of Venezuela." Hungarian-born, based in Caracas, this character was famous for toasting with a glass of champagne, downing the alcohol, then chewing the glass and swallowing it—bowl and stem.

Robert Redford shares a laugh with Natalie and Ladi.

Lana Wood, Natalie's sister: Natalie threw me a birthday party in a tiny back room in Le Bistro in Beverly Hills and Ladi did it—toasted me and ate the glass. I couldn't believe it. I'll never know how he managed it. I really don't know what the attraction was for Natalie, except that he was sweet and she was coming off a difficult time.

Natalie was afraid to be alone, which, for her, meant without a man. She was divorced from Robert Wagner, and her romance with Warren Beatty had ended. Only a few knew that she'd attempted suicide just before this film—not over Beatty as most speculated, but for the love of a happily married man, if there was such a thing in Hollywood, a director.

Sydney Pollack: She was certainly a very desirable, gorgeous woman. Everybody fell in love with her instantly. She was tiny, really small, and everything was perfect about her. She had an infectious good humor and vulnerability. It was part of that Russian thing. She was irresistible.

Natalie was excited about this film and told friends it was the hardest thing she'd ever done. Ladi, as everyone called him, was funny. He was no Warren Beatty, but he made her laugh and she needed to laugh. In May, they announced their engagement.

Sydney Pollack: He would come down to the location. . . . There was a set of swings in a park you take kids to out in a central area of this hotel we were all staying in, and I remember looking out the window and seeing this guy Ladi pushing her on the swing. They were running around like a couple of kids together. That's my only memory of them. The engagement didn't pay off. I mean, she never got married to him.

She liked to have a drink and she liked to have the cast come round at the end of the day. She got quite dark and emotional when she drank, like a typical Russian, very moody and emotional. Later, when we were shooting on the Paramount lot, it became a tradition at the end of the day's dailies; we would all go to her dressing room because she was the big star. She had an assistant—we used to call them maids, but we don't call them that anymore—but someone in her dressing room who got drinks for everybody. And Redford and Kate Reid and myself and Bobby Blake and everybody would go to her dressing room. I think quite often, we would go to her suite in the hotel when we were in Bay St. Louis and Biloxi.

She was totally professional. As a matter of fact, she was a huge help to me as a beginner. If I started getting too much pressure from the producers that I was a little slow or I wasn't making my day or something, she would back me up completely. She was terrific. She had special things in her contract where she could punish you. She was one of the few people who had in her contract that she was allowed to not come to work when she had her period; but that was up to her. In other words, if she felt that she looked bad or she was looking bloated or whatever, she was allowed to take one or two days off and we'd have to shut down if we didn't have anything else to shoot. She never did that while I can remember.

A Dark End

Sharon Smith: Jon and Mary—it was Halloween and we were all going trick or treating, and Mary wanted so desperately to go, but her mother wouldn't let her.

I think I was a little old to go trick or treating at fifteen, but that's not what stopped me from going. It was something a lot more sinister than that. Earlier in the day, the crew had reported that leaflets had been left on every production vehicle that said, essentially, "Don't come into town tonight if you know what's good for you." The next morning, we heard that a young black man had been lynched.

Jim Dalton: That's the recollection that I have, too. There was a faction, and I hate to use the term because it's stereotyping, but when you look at the way a people in a town were raised their entire life, I mean the people in Bay St. Louis knew very little or even wanted to about the outside world. And the Klan or klan-type organization was fairly strong. That part of Southern Louisiana and the western tip of Mississippi were all areas that the Klan had ties in. The Cajun people, a lot of them, were cut throat. I don't know how else to explain it, really.

Cecile was a dream . . . she was a real dream . . . I'm just thankful that I had the opportunity to spend a little time in her world and in Jon's world. . . . Just to give you an idea, before they left, she wrote down their telephone number. "I want you to promise me that you will keep that in your billfold and if you ever come to L.A., you had better call." I said, "Yes, m'am," and put it in my billfold. Three years later, I went through a real messy divorce. I knew Don was out in L.A. so I got on the bus and headed for Hollywood. When I got to the bus station, I was unable to locate Don. I was sitting there thinking I was really in a pickle, I didn't know anybody; and then I just happened to think. I reached into my billfold—I changed billfolds I don't know how many times in between, but there was the telephone number. I called and Cecile answered. I told her who it was and she said, "Where are you? This sounds awfully clear." I told her I was at the bus station. "You just stay right there. I'm coming to pick you up and you can stay with us." And it was like no time had gone by whatsoever. She, Jon, her husband, the whole family accepted me like I was part of the family.

Little Timmy Grows Up

I was glad to go back home. I tried to settle back in at Marion Colbert, just in time for the usual round of Christmas parades. At least I'd get to see some familiar faces.

Over the Christmas break, I got a present I'll always remember. Susan lived up the street. She was about two years older and not at all shy. She invited me over, making a point of telling me no one else would be home. She took me upstairs to her mother's bedroom and . . . gave me my gift: her lovely self. I had done some serious fooling around, but this was my first, official member-of-the-club, all-the-way time. Minutes later, we heard her mother coming in the front door. I scooped up my clothes and ran across the hall into Susan's room and into her closet where I dressed as quickly and as quietly as possible. Susan distracted her mom and, a few minutes later, gave me the sign to run. I flew down the stairs and out the door . . . a new man.

November 1965
Photo shoot with Lassie in a Datsun for publicity in Japan (Datsun was Lassie's sponsor there)
24: Santa Claus Lane Parade, Hollywood
December 1965
3: Pomona Christmas Parade
4: Another Christmas parade and also Optimist Club of West L.A. Benefit Christmas Party
25: Christmas Day— *Lassie's Great Adventure* opens in theaters. It is the five-parter "The Journey" released as a feature.
January 1966
14–16: Homestead, Florida, Annual Rodeo
February 1966
10–15: Hot Springs, Arkansas—Convent kids, hospitals, Ouchita Baptist College

March 12, 1966

Sixteen! This is the birthday I'd most looked forward to—old enough to drive! I'm sure I went to get my license that very day. For once, there seem to be no pictures . . . and just maybe, no Lassie on my cake. Just a note: my allowance was still $5 a week.

Anne Lockhart: Jon and I were in the same cotillion class as teenagers. Gawd! Once a week, we had to dress up—him in coat and tie, me in dress and WHITE GLOVES (they told us that boys had sweaty palms!!!!)—to learn ballroom dancing! It was called Beverly Hills Cotillion, and we took our lessons at the Daisy on Rodeo drive, which was at night the hippest '60s disco in town.

Jon and I were chosen to lead the grand entry dance at our cotillion ball in front of a couple hundred parents and grandparents at the Beverly Hilton Hotel—the big deal after our year of learning the cha cha and the mambo. I was so nervous I thought I'd die. I was so very grateful Jon and I had been paired, as at least this was someone I'd known since I was four. We both were aware that we'd been chosen because of who we were. The whole thing was really weird. Jon's mom was there to support us. My mom wasn't; I don't remember why. Never mind; gangly as we were, we were a smash and everyone complimented us. Both of us were tremendously relieved at the finish of the evening.

April 1966
"Share the Blessings" Easter brunch
May 1966
14: Benefit for Ventura County Association for Retarded Children with Tommy Rettig
June 1966
I finished the school year and left Marion Colbert for good.

Bill Mumy: The Daisy Club was a fairly wild place filled with the rich and famous and was always a magnet for the "young" crowd. People like Dino, Desi & Billy, Sajid Khan, Jay North, Jon, and tons of other actors and musicians would hang there, play pool, dance, and just schmooze. I went quite a bit, especially when I was in the last season of *Lost in Space*. I remember Jon there several times and we both wore Nehru jackets!

Fran announced she was pregnant. Because Grandma was a twin, there was some concern, because Fran is so small, but we soon discovered it was just one. Meanwhile, Grandma was nonplussed by the news. She told us she was tired and had made up her mind she didn't want to live anymore.

July 1966

In August, *This Property* was released in theaters. Natalie Wood felt it was some of her best work, and so did the Hollywood Foreign Press, which nominated her for a Golden Globe.

Press release: Jon Provost, after seven years of stardom on the *Lassie* TV series, returns to motion pictures as Mary Badham's friend, Tom. It is fifteen-year-old Provost's first screen role since 1956.

Anne Lockhart: I went to see him in *This Property* and I thought he was so good in it. It was so different than *Lassie,* and I thought he was great. I was so proud of him.

I enjoyed my experience on the film, but it had been very hard on Mary. Matter of fact, she quit acting shortly afterward because of it.

Mary Badham: It's a very up and down business, very egotistical. And if you don't have an education and something to fall back on, you're "here today—gone tomorrow and what are you going to do with your life?" We had family discussions, and they said, "All right, it's your choice. Do you want to stay in or get an education and have something else? You can always go back to it later if you want to." It just made sense to me to get an education. In just my short time in the business, I had seen people who were working one day and the next day, nobody cares. And it's very, very hard on them. If you don't have an education you end up waiting tables, and I knew I didn't want to do that.

I continued to enjoy my freedom away from a soundstage. I bought a motorcycle, a Honda 160 Scrambler, and I had a blast riding around all summer and getting to know the neighborhood kids.

Rosemary Hilb Shaw, neighbor: I don't remember the first time. I remember a million times with him. He was sixteen or seventeen. I was only about seven. When he was outside, the neighborhood kids would always gravitate to him. He'd do things for us to create a little fun on hot days. He'd splash water into the street and we'd watch it evaporate, and then he'd explain what was happening, why the steam would come up . . . stuff kids would like. Although he could have been doing anything that he wanted, he was most generous with his time, and he seemed to be having fun with us. It meant the world to me. Once, he went to the circus and brought home this monkey on a stick. He gave it to me and said he'd gotten it for me. I treasured that for many years. I went to school with a lot of celebrity children; still, he is the one who really sticks out as having this innate kindness in him. . . . He really was the All-American, clean-cut . . . I took a picture of him the week before we moved. He had on tight jeans and no shirt. I think he had the hose in his hand. It was the nicest picture. It showed how happy he looked . . . like the Golden Boy. He was my first real hero, and he lived up to his title.

Rand M. Bard, neighbor: I used to enjoy hanging with Jon. Strangely, I recall never talking to him about his show or movie star status, and we treated each other as just neighborhood chums. We weren't real close friends, but I liked him as a pal and never mentioned our friendship to anyone back then and never bragged that I knew him. I didn't see him that way, but I knew he was different just the same. And his confidence was unnerving to most who knew him.

Sandy McClusky, fan club president: He was just one of the good guys. I didn't think he was into any drugs or anything like that. He was just like the dream guy everyone wanted, like he would have been the perfect husband type or boyfriend! He had respect for people. He had very good manners.

The Beatles played Dodger Stadium to a sold-out crowd of 45,000. Tickets ranged from $4.50 to $6.00. Ron, Mike, and I popped for the $6.00 tickets. This turned out to be the Beatles' second-to-last public concert, and what a scene. The Fire Department put an eight-foot chain-link fence around the whole field from the bullpen around home plate all the way to the other bullpen so nobody could come onto the field. The stage, probably four feet off the ground, was at second base. From the moment the Beatles came out till the moment they went off, girls screamed continuously. It was great! Nine songs . . . thirty-five minutes of pure energy and joy, and they were gone. These days, just saying out loud in a room that I saw the Beatles live can cause a hush to spread through the crowd. Half think, "Wow, you saw the Beatles." The other half think, "Wow, are you old."

August 28, 1966

From Timmy to Teen Idol

Now that I had my license and my bike, I was able to "make the scene" a lot more: clubs like the Daisy, movie premieres, parties. As a result, I started appearing in teen magazines like *Tiger Beat, Sixteen, Fave, Outasite,* and a few others. "Win a Phone Call from Jon Provost!" "Jon's Secret Passions!" "A Dream Date with

September 1966

Jon"—which I went on with Angela Cartwright. From the first photo caption: "Veronica answered the door and rushed to tell me how lucky I was!" Ang and I laughed till we cried. And we laughed all over again with her kids thirty-five years later. It was all innocent and good-natured, filled with non-exploitative photos of everyone's faves, nothing at all like the tabloid stuff of today. These magazines put a smile on your face then as they do today. Mom saved a trunkload of them.

Ralph Benner, Editorial Director of Tiger Beat: We started *Tiger Beat* in 1965. Our offices were at 1800 N. Highland above Hollywood Boulevard near Franklin. A parade of people came up there, never people that weren't already established: Don Johnson—when he was trying to be a singer—would sit around all the time and want to be in the magazine; Linda Ronstadt—when she was with the Stone Ponies—came in barefoot in her hippie garb—big earrings, peasant blouse, long skirt—which she raised to flash me. We did stories on Jan Michael Vincent back when he was Mike Vincent.

Jon and his mother came up to the office a couple times. His mother I remember very well, small blonde. She was very sweet and I can see why Jon could survive, because she was one of the nicer people. There were good stage mothers and bad stage mothers. Boy, some of them were real tigresses, voraciously pursuing their child's career, knocking down people who got in the way. She wasn't one of them, like, say, Danny Bonaduce's mother, for one. Tony Dow's mom was lovely. Mrs. Provost was very much like her. . . . normal and sweet. She wasn't overbearing, but she knew what was going on.

Anne Moses: Oh, what a great guy! By the time we were doing stuff in *Tiger Beat*, Jon was past the little Timmy stage. I just remember him as one of the real nice kids of that time. A lot of them were not all that nice. He wasn't so wrapped up in the teenage idol thing.

The rock and roll scene was wide open. There were no rules, no past. Ralph and people like him blazed a trail. That's how a teenager like Anne Moses could find herself the Features Editor and later Editor of *Tiger Beat* magazine.

Anne Moses: I was eighteen when I went to work for them. I had been writing for a little local rock and roll paper these two gals down in Fullerton had started called *Rhythm and News.* They were real serious rock and roll people; they didn't want teenage fan kind of stuff. They used to send me to these black nightclubs down in Watts, and I would be the only white person in the building. I would go to these little dives and see these incredible black artists and interview them after the show. I was editing my junior college newspaper at Fullerton College and I did a few articles for *Tiger Beat* and met a few people in Hollywood along the way.

Tiger Beat said, "You can be the Features Editor." I got college credit for it, and I was still taking my college classes. In June they said, "We want you to go full time." I had been accepted at San Jose State, majoring in journalism. I had this whole thing mapped out . . . and they start sending me on tour with groups all over the United States. I'd never been out of California and that was that, the next seven years! I never got my degree. It was really wonderful. I had experiences that anyone would die for.

The Sunset Strip was emerging as the center of the scene. The glamorous clubs of the '40s and '50s gave way to coffee houses and Beat Generation hangouts. Now the hippies were taking over.

Ralph Benner: The strip was amazing. . . . streets at night filled with people. You couldn't drive, there were so many, especially around Clark where the Whisky a Go Go was; that was really the center, that intersection down to Holloway Drive. That was all people there—no cars—all hippies. It was like that every night. I lived around the corner from the Whisky, so I was there every night. I saw the Beatles when they came to check it out. They must have had the whole West Hollywood police force out there, but there were no riots, just happy people.

Anne Moses: On Friday and Saturday nights, it was jammed. I always got into Go Go because, at the same time I was the editor of *Tiger Beat,* I was the Hollywood correspondent to the *New Musical Express (NME)* in England. That was the number one British newspaper, so whenever any of the British groups came over, they would check in with me and I would be their host . . . Herman's Hermits or the Dave Clark 5 or whoever. It would be, "ANNE, show us the town! "Get us into Disneyland even though there is a haircut limit!" You couldn't get into Disneyland then with long hair, but I got the Dave Clark 5 in because I used to work there and went through the inside channel. That was the big deal for the DC5, more than the Whiskey a Go Go.

Stan Livingston: I ran into Jon at a party. We never really went to parties, Barry and me. I didn't do any publicity during the show. This was someone's birthday, but it was set up for publicity, and that's the stuff I freaked out about. The Righteous Brothers performed. They were taking pictures of people, and I was never really into that outside of work. I just didn't want to be there. I was shocked at how old Jon looked. He had long hair, and I was really envious. I had my hair short because we were still shooting. I just didn't feel cool, and I'd look at him and think, "I want to be like that." We talked more as adults at that point. At that age, you want to be an adult so bad, and I'm sure he was already in a car and driving. I was fifteen and I didn't want him to know my parents had to drop me off. I was totally embarrassed.

Bobby Buntrock, Sherry, Patty Petersen, and Lisa Loring.

I remember that party. It was a birthday party for a teenage girl named Sherry Smothers (no relation to the Smothers Brothers). She was just beginning to work as an actress under the name Diane Sherry, but everyone knew her personally as Sherry Smothers. Her dad, Bill, was throwing the party for her at his house in Beverly Hills. He was a financial manager in the music biz; I think that's how the Righteous Brothers were there. Sherry was a cute little redhead a couple of years younger than I was. I honestly didn't take much notice of her that night. I'd notice her plenty later on.

At sixteen, I didn't have any grand illusions about my work or my degree of success. I had nothing to compare to it, had no idea what other children's lives were like. What I did was all I knew. My earliest memories are not of my home and family, but of a movie set where I quickly learned what adults needed from me. But people my own age—that was something different. I wasn't sure what they wanted.

Besides the general awkwardness almost every teenager feels, I had so little experience with the social world of "regular" kids. At times, I felt like I had been tossed fully clothed into the deep end. Other times, I was so completely out of my element, it was all I could do to just hang back quietly and try to feel things out. I was shy. But "civilians" find it difficult to believe that someone who is a celebrity can be shy. After all, a celebrity appears before millions of people on TV and in films. For me, that only made the one-on-one stuff all the more difficult.

Some people interpreted my shyness as conceit. Several teen magazines of the day reported that I was "stuck up." And though I realize in these days of tabloid terrorism that I got off virtually scot-free, it always bothered me because it simply wasn't true; I was just insecure. I did not, however, suffer from low self-esteem. I was very fortunate to have come through the child actor years with a strong sense of myself when so many others did not. It was that very strong sense of self that resisted renewing my *Lassie* contract. I desperately needed to explore who I really was, without Timmy. Looking back, I think that need, that inner voice—whatever you want to call it—saved me from what would eventually come to be recognized as the child-actor-syndrome. I believe that if I had not made the break then, my own personality would not have survived. I may have continued adapting to each new situation, never putting down roots, never knowing who I am. I saw it with Natalie Wood when I worked in *This Property Is Condemned*—the steady stream of people to her dressing room, an insatiable search for love, acceptance, confirmation; her inability to be alone with herself. That image and the feelings surrounding it, stayed with me.

Rexford

With my new life came a whole new look: long hair, skin-tight pants. Friends compared me to Brian Jones of the Rolling Stones. In the fall, I

Dino Martin.

started at Rexford High School in Beverly Hills. This former house held a tiny, two-story school designed for working kids. I had about twenty-five people in my entire grade. Jay went there along with Dino and Ricci Martin, Burt Lancaster's daughters, some producers' kids . . . kids in or around the business. Nobody beat up Jay or me here. We were all part of the same club.

Jody Brisken, schoolmate: It was a duplex home, one living quarter on top of the other in a residential district. They turned it into a school 'cause they knew they could sucker a bunch of Beverly Hills parents into it. The headmaster or principal, Mrs. Axelrod, was my psychiatrist! It was a joke. I got tossed from Beverly and I went to Happy Valley where you couldn't get tossed from and I managed to get tossed from there. Then I was hanging out in town a lot 'cause I had nowhere to go. I couldn't go back home, so I would hang out at Rexford 'cause that was where my friends were. I would drive my mom's car and go out on their field trips. Their field trips were like to these self-realization parks. You sit and smoke weed and meditate. This is the cockamamie school Jon went to, and I am getting a real kick that he told his kids he was class president senior year! Ha!

Rexford was not as wild as Jody says, but it was . . . accommodating. Intimate, specialized, lenient, it was perfect for kids with a more "artistic" bent. And I wasn't class president; I was student body president!

Laurie Ackerman: Rexford . . . it was too Hollywood—you had David Cassidy, Dino Martin, Jay North . . . it was very small, very contained. It wasn't a real slice of what high school really is. For Jon, who had to be pulled in and out of school—that was the school.

Sherry Smothers: I was probably there because I wanted to be with the "wild" kids. I had been acting for a couple of years, and when I went to Beverly High I really got "lost" there. I started smoking pot and stuff. I was really lost in a big school and I wanted to go to Rexford . . . a wild school. It was partly celebrities' kids, kids that worked, professional tennis players, privileged kids; and there were a lot of scholarship kids. You were allowed to smoke cigarettes and wear jeans.

During those days, you had to wear dresses to Beverly and they had to be to your knees which was appalling. We all wanted to wear short skirts. There were drugs in school, but they were in every school at that time. I used to hide under the house across the alley and smoke pot with David Cassidy during recess.

Jody Brisken: I was seeing Billy [Hinsche] at fourteen and the two of us were completely removed from anything at all having to do with school . . . or with normal. Once I was with Billy, it was like swoop! I was modeling and he was in a group, touring. I was hitting airports at 1:00 a.m. and spending nights in recording studios and we were children. So I would hang out and see some fringe kids like Sherry.

David Cassidy: I started Rexford in the middle of the eleventh grade. I'd gone to two other public high schools; I'd never been to a private school before. I was a socially maladjusted, young rebel teenager and needed much more personal attention than I got at public school. I met Jon in one of our classes there and we became friends rather quickly.

David and I were drawn toward one another right away. We were both small physically, but more than that, immediately he was easy to be with, comfortable. His parents were actors—Evelyn Ward and Jack Cassidy—and David had been raised in that atmosphere. (His step-mother, Shirley Jones, would play his mother in *The Partridge Family*, but that was years away yet.) We talked about acting, but at that time, he wasn't sure he wanted to pursue it. Generally, we listened to music, thought about girls, and talked about political issues . . . mostly Vietnam.

Lookin' groovy.

David: I can remember Jon and me talking about his work. Having been around because of my stepmother and my father, I've known a lot of very successful actors in my life. I've been exposed to a lot of them, not kid actors or child actors, but I knew the climate and wasn't fascinated with it. I wasn't interested in hanging out with him because of his television experience or because he was an actor, other than the fact that we had some mutual interest there. It was mostly a mutuality with the time we were there and the times themselves. It was pretty much driven by the social climate, girls—we had a couple of mutual girlfriends, girls that we had dated . . .

Jon was not a stuck-up Hollywood kid at all, not at all. I don't think that was ever an issue for Jon. He was very personable. He seemed generally happy. We were always having fun, laughing, hanging out, groovin' and he was a very cool guy. There wasn't ever any arrogance, no attitude, like "I'm a big star" or anything like that. He was a guy that everyone knew from television when he was young, who was going through—I assume, and it's only an assumption on my part—probably a difficult transition as most child actors do.

Bruce and Fran clowning around; Fran's letter to fans.

I wouldn't call it a difficult transition. I was still being offered work, but I accepted less of it, to Mom's dismay. I didn't miss it either. I loved having free time, hanging out with Mike and Ron after school. I was too old now for Cub Scouts, little league, and other rites of passage, but new opportunities presented themselves now: fooling around with guitars, going to Dolores' Drive-In, the love-ins in Griffith Park. I still kept up with the personal appearances Mom booked. And the teen magazines gave her a whole new arena to play in. She worked with them, supplying photos and bits of news. Fran helped, too, with Francile's News and Photo Club. Fans sent in one dollar to be a member and Fran sent out packets throughout the year.

October 1966

6: Grandma dies at the age of ninety-six

22: San Gabriel PTA member Drive

31: Accepted invitation to be the Teenage Chairman for the Danny Thomas Teenagers March for St. Jude's Children's Research Hospital

Fran: That first year of marriage, those dollar bills came in very handy! I would have all the envelopes stacked up, waiting till Bruce got home from work. He'd walk in and see the stack and ask, "How much did we make today?" We'd open all the envelopes and put all the dollars in a pile on the table, $20 or $30 . . . that was a lot of money to us.

November 1966

Fran had made a clean getaway. She and Bruce were thriving, starting their own family. She was really happy. William was still struggling. Having me around more didn't make it any easier on him. About this time, we had a hell of a fight. It began as a typical disagreement between brothers, but quickly escalated. Suddenly, enraged, he grabbed me and shook me, shouting, "I could kill you! I hate you! I hate you!" He threw me down and stormed out of the house. A few minutes later, I heard his car peel out. I was shaken, stunned, and bewildered. I didn't know what happened. I rarely saw William emotional. I'd never seen him like that. I stayed out of his way for weeks.

> *William:* I buried a lot of my feelings. It was just my way of dealing with it. It was the natural way. Every now and then, little things come out.

December 1966

3: Huntington Park Christmas Lane Parade

21: Santa Claus Lane Parade in Hollywood on Santa's float!!

22: Brother Phil's Salesian Boys Club Christmas Party

The Summer of Love

It was the best time to be young and on a journey to find myself. The cultural scene opening up encouraged self-exploration and mind expansion. David and I got stoned and talked about things. We debated and chose sides. We listened to some amazing music. Make love, not war; that's how we wanted to live. Mom was aware of David's showbiz family, so anything the two of us wanted to do was fine by her, including staying out all night

1967

> *David Cassidy:* We started going out weekends. We'd go to After Hours at the Kaleidoscope, previously the Aquarius Theater and Moulin Rouge before that. They put on lots of different R&B acts, which were, at that time, cutting edge acts like Velvet Underground, Skye Saxon and the Seeds, the Turtles. We saw Wilson Pickett there; I saw Otis Redding. We saw some great acts, and it was really very cool. It didn't start until 1:00 in the morning, so it would end around 5:00. It was a good place for us to meet girls and be cool young bucks in Hollywood. That's sort of what we were. We really enjoyed listening to music. I was at his house a number of times and he was at mine. We used to listen to Country Joe and the Fish—all of those "Whoopee, we're all gonna die" kind of anti-, very much anti- the war in Vietnam; and, socially, we were into breaking down a lot of those barriers that were on all of our minds at the time. The draft was something we were highly concerned about. We experimented with smoking pot together

top: David Cassidy.

and doing the things that teenagers did in L.A. on the cutting edge of that scene; but, in discussing all of the social habits, my thrust was turning on, tuning in, being part of the political and social consciousness that was very much prevalent in all our minds and consciousness in high school. We weren't unusual in that respect.

I didn't support the war, but I always supported our troops. One opportunity to demonstrate that support was through the show Ace Lundon produced monthly at Camp Pendleton. Ace was in PR and personal management. One fateful plane flight, he fell into conversation with a young soldier seated next to him. He told the soldier what he did for a living and the young man told Ace he was leaving in two weeks for 'Nam. "Do you think you could bring some stars to Camp Pendleton before I go?" Ace promised to try.

With just ten days notice, Ace put his gorgeous actress-wife, Jean, along with a budding starlet in a pair of bikinis and got one of his most respected stars, Oscar-winner Jane Darwell, to see off twelve men. And every month for the next seven years and three months, he put on a show for returning and departing troops. The largest show had 80 celebrities performing for more than 80,000 troops.

Ace Lundon: More than 275,000 men saw these shows. Jon was one of the regulars. I'm sure he was there at least a dozen times, same with Jay North. That's how I met him. Jay's mother, Dorothy, introduced me to Cecile.

Jon would be brought on stage and introduced to the audience. Jean would interview him and open it up to questions. Then the pretty girls would take microphones into the audience and the soldiers were able to ask anything they wanted and they would get their answers straight from the lips of the star. We'd have a big finale and the boys would rush up afterward to get autographs and pose for photos.

Those wonderful days meant a lot to those men. I know because I get phone calls and e-mails thanking me " . . . for doing the shows and bringing the stars; it kept us sane . . ." Those were some rough years.

One soldier's wish on a plane came true for more than 275,000 because the right person heard it. I'm grateful to Ace to have had that opportunity. And thanks to the Internet, I have heard from many veterans who told me what it meant to them to catch an episode of *Lassie* overseas.

Jerry Stahl, vet: I wanted to tell you while in the hospital in Tan Son Nhut, Vietnam, they ran some of the *Lassie* episodes on TV by the base TV station. To be able to escape mentally, if only for a half hour, and forget my own pain and enjoy your show . . . believe me, you got quite a few of us through some hard times seeing those shows.

Anonymous vet: I was on R&R in Thailand for a week. I went to a brothel and paid for a girl for the whole week. The TV was always playing and *Lassie* and *My Three Sons* came on several times a day. I was just a kid, scared out of my wits and there, in the middle of this war on the other side of the world, I see Timmy. I'll never forget it.

> April 1967
> 5: Fran and Bruce welcome
> a beautiful daughter,
> Michelle
> 22: Photo op, Diabetes
> Association

And a vet from the Korean War told me that he once spent a night trapped with his unit in a valley below thousands of North Korean troops who called out to them all through the night: "We're gonna eat Lassie for dinner! . . . Down with Lassie!" The next morning, U.S. soldiers stormed and captured the hill.

June Lockhart took her "other" TV children, Bill Mumy and Angela Cartwright, to the Whisky a Go Go to see a band she loved called Hourglass with two brothers named Duane and Gregg Allman. The Allman Brothers were just beginning to attract attention. June had them play a party at her house too. Seems both she and I wanted to distance ourselves from the Martin farm.

Don Jaye came to Hollywood and opened offices in the same building as *Tiger Beat*. He added a few gigs to my schedule and lots of fan mail. I got it in droves. Mom had a little assembly line set up in the dining room and now, when fans showed up at the front door, she enlisted their help stuffing envelopes. For the most part, the girls loved it. The flow of people through the house was non-stop.

> Don Jaye
> Productions
> 1800 N. Highland Ave. • Suite 405
> Hollywood, California 90028
> (213) 466-5275
> Don Jaye

Sandy McClusky: The first time I met Jon was in a parade here in Palos Verde. He used to do the Christmas parade every year, two or three years in a row. I met him there with my girl-friend, Kathy. She and I were three years younger and lived in Torrance. I can't believe it, but our parents would let us take the bus all the way up there!! We had our own little fan club and we worked a lot with *Tiger Beat* and *Fave* magazines. We would come up on Saturdays and spend the day, just do little fan club thingies, maybe go shopping with Cecile or with Fran. Sometimes we'd spend the whole day, from early morning to nighttime over at the house doing something. Cecile was always so cordial and happy. And the dad too, they were just always happy to see you! It wasn't like you were a bother or anything.

Fran was married. Kathy and I babysat her daughter a couple times. And Bill, that's the brother, right? He was cute! He was in college at the time. He would come into the house and kind of just look at us like, "What are you doing here?!" I'd come through the door and he'd go to his room. Cecile would say, "Oh, that's Bill."

William was on his third college, directionless. We were two ships passing at home, friendly, but nothing personal. I never had to search for common ground with Fran; it was always there. We had a connection. She wore her heart on her sleeve. William was more internal, more difficult to read; more than that, he was emotionally covert. We were bound as brothers, but otherwise, he was a mystery to me. Our six-year age difference had created quite a gulf when I was younger. Now, we had a few areas of common interest—the same things that interested every other young guy: cars, girls, and music. I started bumping into him at clubs on the Strip: the Whisky, Pandora's Box, the Sea Witch.

William: At that time, his hair was longer and he had gotten away from the "Timmy" aspect of it. He was pretty well-known out there. He could go into any place he wanted. A lot of it had to do with Don Jaye. He was trying to promote Jon as a singer. He was going to start a group with Mike and Ron.

Mike played drums. Ron played guitar. I was fiddling around with the bass guitar. The Wrathers had given me a guitar one Christmas. I'd wanted an electric guitar, but they gave me an acoustic, a real beauty, which I still have. I never played it much, though, and instead took up the bass. We formed a group, trying to spin off of Dino, Desi and Billy. We never really did anything, went on a couple of auditions. One was for Disney and I think the song we played was "I'm a Long, Tall Texan," real corny. We didn't get the job, but I ended up at Disney for a movie about eighteen months later.

William: I enjoyed the Strip. I used to go up there quite a bit. The club I liked the best was next to the Whisky a couple of doors down called the London Fog . . . and Pandora's Box . . . that's where I liked to hang out before they tore it down. I used to go to Micky Dolenz's house up in Laurel Canyon, met him at a party or something; one party would lead to another. After awhile, people just knew who you were, so you could just go in. In those days on Friday and Saturday night, if you didn't know of a party going on, you'd go look for a party. When I lived in West Hollywood on La Cienega, I lived right across the courtyard from Steppenwolf; then he moved to Sweetzer. You got to meet these different people; then on weekends you'd just crash the party.

Those were fun days, the hippie days. Once, Jon was riding his motorcycle up and down Sunset near the Whisky and the Sheriffs pulled him over. I just happened to be there with my camera and started shouting, "You can't do that. I'm a photographer from the Free Press. I'm going to take pictures of this harassment!" I tried to come to his defense without saying he was my brother.

John Mangoni: Bill was very busy, dashing in and dashing out, a blur with a busy social life. Fran was delightful, really, really, really cute. Jon's dad was more laid back, and it seemed like he just stood back and watched this all happen. He seemed like a really nice guy who was an observer to all of it, literally an observer, very soft spoken and very nice.

Jon's mom always felt she had to buffer all the business. She felt she had to be the ambassador to everyone because Jon, at times, would not want to do all the things she wanted him to do, like go to an appearance. She would make up for the things he wouldn't do, so that everything worked out to the best advantage for Jon and his career. He was young and couldn't see the importance of doing some of these appearances, so she had to take command of it to further his career.

Davy Jones

Sandy McClusky: A few times Kathy and I just showed up and Cecile would say, "You want to see the Monkees?" And she'd take us over to Gower to see them. She just liked to have fun and seemed to enjoy everything that Jon was involved with and how the teeny-boppers reacted to everything.

I'd seen Davy Jones at events around town. You'd have to live in a cave not to know who the Monkees were. He was British and small, like me. Also like me, he'd started out as a kid, singing and dancing his way onto the Broadway stage as the Artful Dodger in *Oliver!* He'd heard of me, too, but we'd never met formally. It was Bob Custer who brought us together, one of the photographers for *Tiger Beat*. He thought of putting us together for a couple of photo shoots.

Ralph Benner: Bob Custer was a character: frantic, but a good guy . . . frantic and nervous. I don't think he ever had a lot of money. He was gay, and in those days we didn't discuss things like that much. We knew about it, but nobody ever talked about it. Bob was a gentleman . . . with really bad teeth. Davy Jones bought him a set of teeth.

Davy: I can't really remember that, what did I do? Fly him to see his mother or something? Oh yeah, photographer, bald-headed guy [laughs]. I did a lot of things. They always say that when you do an act of charity that you shouldn't flourish your trumpets as the heathens do in the streets. I did a lot of shit, flew people here, flew people there. As far as Bob Custer's teeth, Bob Custer took a lot of pictures of us and of me. *Tiger Beat* flew me to the Bahamas and did all kinds of stuff and he was instrumental in that. He was a nice enough guy.

Anne Moses: Davy was pretty remarkable in the way he would reach out to people. I went down to Texas with the Monkees when they played in Houston. Davy brought Jan Barry of Jan and Dean on tour with them for a few dates. At that point, Jan had had the bad, bad accident on Dead Man's Curve where he was brain damaged. There had been the movies for TV or whatever, that showed how everyone was using Jan and siphoning off his money and everything. I can remember sitting at a table at a restaurant next to Jan, telling me he'd learned his ABC's and he'd say his ABC's. But he was Davy's guest and Davy was working with him and it was really amazing. I thought it was really remarkable, in the midst of all the attention they were getting, that he would do that. I remember that so clearly as such a nice gesture.

Davy: I am not quite sure how meeting Jon all came about, to tell you the truth, but Bob came up with the idea and it was just pretty much a free-form thing in those days. Everybody that was around, whether it be the Buffalo Springfield or Sajid Khan, we were all these faces that were familiar and all knew each other. Jon was one of the faces that everyone was looking at at the time—same as me and a bunch of other guys; that was basically it. I might have said to Bob that I was a big fan. It was always a very, very strong memory for me—*Lassie*—that whole thing is like apple pie and ice cream and cookouts on the weekend, one of those childhood memories . . . that and *The Wizard of Oz*. He seemed like the young, fresh kid and he wanted to meet the Monkees and I wanted to meet the kid that was in *Lassie* and that is how we really got together.

Jon came up to the house a few times . . . this absolutely lovely Cape Cod style house, trees all around, sitting really pretty on its own acre of land there all the way up at the top of the Hollywood Hills. Phil Ochs was my next-door neighbor. Jon and I rode motorbikes. And we played pool, I remember that very clearly; he was a lousy pool player! [Laughs] No, just kidding!

There was camaraderie in our community. You go to the same parties and, some of the times, you dated some of the same girls. Jon was part of the same little clique because he was known and he had a TV series. It was just our time and that just happened to be the '60s. We were in a happy time; we were working; we had TV series. We were cute little guys and these girls were flashing on us and everything. What I'm saying is that it was a very fun time for us and it was a great time to be in Hollywood.

That it most assuredly was. Davy said it beautifully, it was "our time," and not just because we were well-known. It was our generation's time, a thrilling new wave of energy expressed in music, film, fashion, a new consciousness about ecology and the environment. In those days before the Internet, everything came into the United States from L.A. or NYC. We heard it, saw it, and experienced it first: Jimi Hendrix at the Whisky when his roadie was a young actor named Phil Hartman; Jim Morrison and the Doors at the Hollywood Bowl; some insanely weird guy named Alice Cooper singing with a snake wrapped around him. The Strip itself was always a scene, sidewalks packed with kids. Just walking a block or two could be overwhelming. My world for so long had been adults, all adults, but here, the world was all about "our time," kids with love beads, halter tops, and bare feet; long hair, bell bottoms, blue jeans; runaways from across town and across the nation. At night, it was a psychedelic carnival: long lines of orange-robed Hare Krishna chanting, dancing, and weaving their way through the crowds of kids, the Jesus bus stopping the ones who looked lost or homeless. We'd smoke a joint and go to the Strip, sometimes with no specific destination.

> *Davy*: Abbie Hoffman and Jerry Rubin, two of the Chicago Seven on the run—they stayed at my house around about the same time that Jon was there. Same thing when we were in England playing Wembley in '67 and Brian Jones was on the run and hid in our hotel. Who would have thought? We were the Monkees. Jerry Rubin? Abbie Hoffman? Staying at Davy Jones's house? They were there.

The Strip

The Sunset Strip was a unique piece of real estate positioned between Beverly Hills and Los Angeles, but it didn't have to answer to either one. Rather, this was West Hollywood, where they made their own laws. So, in the late '60s, a lot of nightclubs on the Sunset Strip were "eighteen and older," promising not to serve those under the legal age of twenty-one . . . but of course, they did, to kids as young as sixteen. Other clubs didn't serve liquor at all; those were sixteen and over. Alcohol wasn't the thing then, anyway.

Just last fall, the hippies had clashed with the cops in a showdown referred to as "the riots on the Sunset Strip." Buffalo Springfield wrote about it in *For What It's Worth*. It started with complaints from local businesses whose paying customers couldn't get to them through the sea of kids. The West Hollywood Sheriffs Department tried to enforce an ancient curfew requiring everyone under eighteen to be off the streets by 10:00 p.m. The kids rebelled, "singing songs and carrying signs," stopping traffic, dancing atop RTD buses for two consecutive weekend skirmishes. The flash point for the riots was a club called Pandora's Box. Word was that cops dressed as hippies had started throwing rocks and bottles to heat things up and make a few arrests. In the end, police won the battle but lost the war. Pandora's Box closed, but rock 'n' roll and hippies flourished on the Strip for years while relations between kids and cops remained strained. Seeing kids take a stand like that contributed tremendously to my sense of freedom and of belonging to a bigger picture.

Oh yeah, and the girls . . . lots of girls! It was my great luck to be seventeen and right smack in the middle of a sexual revolution. Hollywood was shaking off forty years of strict censorship in place after three enormous scandals rocked Hollywood in the 1920s, with rules like: timed kisses with closed, dry mouths only; if reclining, couples must have one foot on the floor at all times; no miscegenation, sexual perversion, prostitution, nudity, or swearing. These rules and more were still firmly in place in television. The Monkees did a show about the devil and couldn't say "hell." Lucy and Desi had a baby and couldn't say "pregnant." And not until the early '70s did Archie Bunker flush a toilet on the air. Not so with movies. *Bonnie and Clyde, Blow-Up, The Graduate*—the sexual revolution was in full swing on the big screen and in the very streets I called home.

And it wasn't just the Strip. You could follow Doheny Drive to Santa Monica Boulevard next to Abigail Folger's flower store to Doug Weston's Troubador for what was happening in comedy, rock, and folk with people like Lenny Bruce, Richard Pryor, Joni Mitchell, Tim Buckley, Lovin' Spoonful. Or walk a block south to Melrose and the Ash Grove, a Beat Generation coffee house that featured folk, bluegrass, and rock like the Byrds, Canned Heat, Kaleidoscope, the Chambers Brothers, Taj Mahal, Buddy Guy, Willie Dixon, Muddy Waters. It was a veritable feast, simply a magical time.

Davy: The Strip was full of performances all the time. Little Stevie Wonder and Bob Dylan were at the Playboy Club. I saw Sonny and Cher and the Byrds at what is now the Comedy Store, Ciro's. Sonny wore this waistcoat and like this monkey vest or whatever and puffy, bolero yellow shirt and cords and black boots. And that's what the Monkees had the first time. We just took that idea and thought, "Wow, that's a great visual! Could you imagine four guys dressed like that?"

Clothing for rock stars was a new business. Several women were part of the "Sisterhood of the Sewing Machine." Jeannie Franklin, also known as Genie the Tailor, was among the best of them. Small, vibrant, and really cute, she was close to twenty-four, worlds away from my sheltered seventeen. She got her start designing clothes for Paul Revere and the Raiders and was soon in demand by rockers like the Monkees, Mama Cass, David Crosby, Donovan, and Cream.

Genie, left, and Anne Moses, right.

Anne Moses: She was a really incredible person, she really was; she was very unique on many levels. I was eighteen or nineteen and not very worldly. Genie had been around. She hung out with the hippest of the hip. I looked at her like a mentor. It was always if you have a question you can go to Genie for the answer.

Once, she was doing the uniforms for Paul Revere and the Raiders and she had my mom come up to be part of this little production line in her little hippie house in Laurel Canyon. She didn't do grass or drugs at all and that was also the anomaly of what was going on at the time. She was a vegetarian.

She had a party at her house and had all these people and served baked potatoes and not much else. It was really different, but she was different in a real unique time. Everybody was trying to be different, but she was genuinely her own person.

Jody Brisken: She used to go with Jack Bruce of Cream; she was his girlfriend. She was making clothes for Cream and for lots of rock stars. And she wanted to open up a shop on Santa Monica next to the Troubadour.

Genie was adorable, but I was too shy to do much about it. Besides, there was a girl at school who'd caught my eye. Little Sherry Smothers had grown up. I'd heard she was pretty wild, pretty fast. All I knew was she was a little doll.

Sherry.

Sherry played Bing Crosby's daughter in TV's *The Bing Crosby Show* in '64. We thought it was funny we both played Bing Crosby's kid. She talked a tough game, but as I got to know her, I discovered the source of this tough outer shell. Sherry was living the life of a Beverly Hills kid that people in the Midwest read about: child of divorce, lost in the remarriage and new family. She was an only child until she was fifteen, then suddenly, she had a baby half-sister and was shuttled back and forth between homes and unseen in both of them.

> Sherry: I'd just been in *Hawaii,* with Julie Andrews, playing her sister. I was on my way to Broadway to be in a play with Lee Remick when my parents got divorced; and suddenly my career was just dropped. Then my sister was born. I would go home stoned and she'd be screaming and my mother would be yelling at the maid. It would be such a nightmare. I started smoking pot and kind of being "hip" and was of the mind that Hollywood was a negative thing. We were hippies. Money, property and prestige were evils.

> **June 1967**
> Mom and Dad travel to the Orient.

Sherry was fun, but I kept my options open. Some pretty interesting things were opening up.

Sal Mineo

I'd seen Sal Mineo on the Strip. By 1967, his career had slowed down, but you'd never have known it by the reception he received on Sunset Boulevard. James Dean had been killed a dozen years earlier, but Sal—the other Oscar-nominated star of *Rebel Without a Cause*—still turned heads. And my head was one of them.

Soon after we met, Sal offered me a part in a film he wanted to produce, *The Flower Children*. Nancy Sinatra was involved, and I went to several pre-production meetings at her house. Sal, Nancy, and most of their friends were a good ten years older. I thought sitting around Nancy's living room with Sal and his entourage—Sal always had an entourage—was very "groovy." And most important to me at that time, it was about as far from *Lassie* as I could possibly get.

David Cassidy: Sal had done a movie with my stepfather. He was very good friends with my parents and he and I became friends as well. I found him to be one of the finest people I've ever known. He was a very caring, wonderful person, someone who made an effort to try and support people who were creative and talented. When I became very successful, I would call him and talk to him because he had gone through it himself. When I was in London, he let me and a girlfriend have his apartment for three days during the madness; no hotels would take me because of all the fans. I thought he was just a blue chip person.

John Mangoni: He had this aura of someone wise and experienced. He always wanted to be in control of what we were thinking. He asked questions about what was in our minds. You were never allowed to sit there like a fly on the wall. He was in charge. He held court.

Anne Moses: Sal was non-existent at that time in the teenage eye. He was basically too old.

A lot of people thought of Sal as washed up. He clung stubbornly to his switchblade image: black leather jacket, black jeans, a choice firmly rooted in the past, which I believe hurt his chances for work at the time. But he was always working on something—a play, a movie project. To me, it seemed like he was working within the business. You could be out of work for six months and then BOOM! All of a sudden, you're doing a movie. That's the way things were. I didn't think of him as being a has-been, not at all. *The Flower Children* moved forward and one blurb in the *Hollywood Reporter* said that William had a part in it, too.

As we became friends, I learned Sal was bisexual, although I never saw Sal with a guy, only with his girlfriend, Susan. I knew some people thought I was one of Sal's boys—David, too—but that didn't bother David or me. Besides, he was so charismatic . . . Steve McQueen cool. Smart, talented, charming, and really funny, Sal was striking and could draw all eyes to him when he walked in. The way he carried himself, his whole image—he lived for that, for people to say, "Look, there's Sal Mineo."

One lesson I learned early on is that in Hollywood, everybody has their own agenda. If you could benefit someone, you were in; if you couldn't, you were out. It worked that way then and it works that way now.

The film project reached a dead end, but Sal and I remained friends, not because of any strong bond, but for our own aforementioned agendas. Despite my healthy self-esteem, I did wonder why Sal—clearly out of my league—hung out with me. I didn't have any benefits to offer him from where I stood. I didn't have a lot of industry friends; I couldn't help get him work. He knew I wasn't bisexual. So why me? I would discover the answer slowly, over time.

For me, the benefits were huge and instantaneous. He provided excitement, mystery, an older crowd. I loved going places with him. When Sal walked into a club, crowds parted like the Red Sea. I knew he wasn't rich, but when we went to clubs, he never had to pay; they just let him in. People rushed to attend to him, ushering us to a great table down front. When I was part of that—I was no longer Timmy.

Sal not only always wore black, everything Sal had was black. He drove a black-on-black Cadillac convertible, about five years old. Even the exterior of his house, a small, Spanish bungalow in West Hollywood was black. Inside, the furniture was dark and heavy or black leather. Thick drapes, always drawn, blocked out the sun. Smoke from cigarettes and pot hung in the air in thick clouds above the heads of his entourage, including his manager, Elliot Mintz, a radio personality who would later handle PR for John Lennon, Bob Dylan, and Paris Hilton; David Cassidy; a few other guys and lots of women. Women loved Sal, especially his girlfriend, Susan, but Sal was the center. All activity revolved around him. I realize now that he orchestrated the scene, a master manipulator so good at what he did that I believed I was the one in control.

William: Jon and I went over on our motorcycles and hung out, sitting around talking and drinking. Various people would be walking in and out of the house, always something happening. Sal was moody and very philosophical. He'd drink cinnamon coffee and it was like he was sitting on a throne and we were the subjects below talking to him. He was the leader.

Susan: Sal was a big pot smoker . . . that and "poppers."

Sal didn't do other popular drugs of the era: LSD, mescaline, magic mushrooms. All of these zapped his control. Sal made you think he took the drugs, but he didn't. Pot was all he wanted—and "poppers," capsules of amyl nitrate that make the heart race. Sal reserved these for sex. He told me he loved to break one open and inhale deeply when he had an orgasm, said it was like blowing the top of his head off.

Susan

I liked Susan. Pretty with long brown hair usually loose around her shoulders, she was soft and feminine, lace and velvet and devoted to Sal. She liked my parents; all my friends did. She and Mom strung love beads together.

> *Mom:* She was very pretty, very sweet, but I felt sorry for Susan. She told me how much she loved Sal, how she wanted to marry him. She was crazy about him and put up with his men. I told her he would never marry her. Whenever she and Sal came over, he was a complete gentleman; but I watched him like a hawk. I had two beautiful sons and I worried about them.

> *Susan:* Cecile expressed that she was worried about Sal and I told her I would protect Jon. She was also worried for me, but I didn't want to hear it. I didn't want to hear it.

If Mom had any concerns, I never heard them. Neither one of us realized how deep Susan's feelings for Sal went. She'd attempted suicide months before we met, but she went back to him anyway, stomach pumped, soul emptied, powerless to fight. She did what he asked, hoping she would win him.

> *Susan:* I met Sal in 1965. I was fresh out of high school, a baby, really. My best friend was going to his house and invited me to come along. He was living on Skyline Drive at the time, off Laurel Canyon. He didn't have a lot of furniture and you got the impression that he was not as well off as he had been at one time, even then. "Then" was the beginning of the end. He'd gotten hit with a lot of back taxes because his

business manager took him for a ride. He said something about the guy stealing $100,000, and in those days, that was a fortune, devastating. He'd had a maid and butler, a married couple, and he had to let them go. He lost his Bentley. All that had happened within the last year before I met him.

Anyway, we went over there and we went out dancing. He took us to a club on the Sunset Strip, I think it was the Trip, then walked us over to the Whisky. To be candid, I was seventeen and so naïve, that was my first time on the Strip. Everything was amazing. We were definitely treated like royalty. He was twenty-five, cute, a little weird, but very charming. We were dancing and hanging out, went back to his place, sat around; they were smoking marijuana. I had a couple of puffs with them, but I wasn't big on that. It was a charming evening. When we were leaving, he said, "Listen, I'd love to have your phone number."

Sal and I went out. He was a perfect gentleman. Before I knew it, we were seriously dating.

Now, I have to tell you that for the first two years of dating him, I did not have a clue—not a clue—that he was gay. People would tell me, "Hey, don't you know he's gay?" And I would say, "Hey, I'm his girlfriend and I ought to know and I'm telling you he isn't." And they'd say, "I'm telling you he is."

At that time, he and Bobby Sherman were quite close. One day, Sal told me he was going to New York to shoot something. He said, "I want you to stay here and watch the house and Bobby's going to stay here too." I said OK. Bobby and I flirted with each other and were attracted to one another, but nothing happened. When Sal came back—I don't know where the hell he went, but I heard he didn't go to New York. I heard he was staying at Elliot's—he badgered me, "Come on, I know you slept with him; you had to have." I thought, "This is so nice. He's jealous!" But he wasn't jealous. He was trying to figure out if we did and if we did, he wanted me to tell him about it. I finally thought, "I'm going to tell him I did and see what happens." He wanted more and more details and I started making it up. He got very excited behind that and I realized I was getting more attention from him than I ever would have if I'd said I hadn't slept with Bobby. Months

Sal on the
drums.

later, I told him I'd made it all up and he thought it was very creative of me. He had a motto: "Fantasy is better than reality" . . . a key phrase of his.

David Cassidy was hanging around the house then and he was teaching him how to play the drums; Sal was an excellent drummer. David was as straight as an arrow and Sal encouraged me to sleep with him too. The difference was that David and I really fell for each other and we got very involved . . . about a year before Jon came on the scene. He'd come pick me up at Sal's place, take me out and deliver me back to Sal's; and there Sal would be, waiting to hear all the details.

David Cassidy: Susan was an older girl who was dating Sal Mineo and very much a free spirit of the '60s. It was, you know, wild times at Rexford High. I think that the times being so different now makes the past sound reckless. They were wild and reckless, but they weren't dangerous. They were just fun and loose and wild and free. It was the summer of love and everybody was getting naked and having a really great time. Being the age that we could afford to do that—or so we thought—it was an interesting experience.

Susan: Sal was a very interesting person, very intelligent. I was having a tremendous growth period through him. He had a great sense of humor, very witty, very bright. We laughed all the time. I knew he cared about me and I knew he loved me in his own way, but I began to think that if he was, in fact, bisexual, maybe I was in the picture for the sake of the press, that if he had me around all the time, nobody could say he was gay. Without question, in those days, it was imperative that Sal put forth a heterosexual image. His career was not doing well and I don't think coming out of the closet at that point was going to do anything for him.

One day, I just confronted him: "I am really in love with you and I don't feel you 100 percent there and I don't know what it is. We're going on three years now. What's going on here?" He admitted to me, "You've been close to me long enough to know: I'm bisexual." Even though I sort of knew, I didn't want to hear it. I was devastated by it. I went home and took a bunch of pills. I was feeling very emotional and I basically took a few sleeping pills and called him. He came rushing over which is all I wanted. He made a fuss and called an ambulance. Then he called the press so they could meet him at the hospital. Nice guy, huh? He wanted it to get in the papers. "Sal Mineo's girlfriend attempts suicide when he tells her she's not the one." Sal was pretty much out for Sal. He had a selfish side—with no thought of how it would affect my life or my parents. Something changed for me. I didn't have the same feelings for him after that.

I didn't see him for about four months; then he started pursuing me again. And, when you're in love with somebody, you think maybe it will be different this time, so you go back. And it's not different; it's worse, worse than it ever was.

Now that it was out in the open, he wanted me to help him procure the young beautiful boys. At the time, I thought, "I'll play your game and I'll play it better than you. I'll get to the guys you want, only you won't get them; I'll get them." Then it became a competition. He enjoyed the challenge of the game for a while and I enjoyed it for a while; and then, Jon came into the picture.

My first impression of Jon was innocence, total, complete, 1,000 percent innocence. He was as awe-struck by Sal as everybody was, very impressionable and trying to keep up with the fast lane Sal was in.

Things started first between Jon and myself, but Sal was setting that up. I was fairly jaded by that time. What I mostly remember about my sexual experiences with Jon [laughing] was that I had to make most of the moves myself. Jon was such a breath of fresh air and, at the same time, that challenge again.

I was still very influenced by Sal. I was already hurt in this game. I was aware that other people could get hurt. I felt a little guilty about what was going on. Everybody else seemed to be able to take care of themselves. It was like, "OK, you want to play this game, you better be prepared." But Jon wasn't prepared. I tried to keep them apart. I enjoyed his company immensely. I thought he was absolutely adorable. I told Sal, "Leave this one alone; he's too innocent. He's not gay; he's not going to go there." And he said, "I'll show you that I can change anyone."

I was surprised when Susan initiated sex with me. "Sal and I have a very open relationship," she explained. "He won't mind at all." It was the '60s: peace, flower power, and free love. Susan didn't have to do too much convincing. The first time, we were in her kitchen one afternoon when she suddenly turned and began kissing me. She was warm and gentle and her hair brushed softly against my face. "Are you sure this is cool with Sal?" "Oh, yeah. He and I already talked about it. He thinks it's great." "He does?" I asked, incredulous, but Susan didn't answer. She had dropped to her knees and was unzipping my jeans.

Sal did his part, too. I can clearly remember him telling me it was cool if I wanted to get it on with Susan. Sal encouraged me to taste, to experiment. He and I talked a lot about sex, a subject I welcomed enthusiastically. Sal liked to talk about it . . . in detail from the beginning of our friendship. At the time I felt it was on the level of big brother/younger brother. I never saw how calculated these conversations were.

One beautiful L.A. day, I stopped by the house. Surprisingly, no one else was around. Sal and I smoked a joint, stripped and hopped in the hot tub. Once again, our conversation turned to sex. Sal only discussed his heterosexual experiences with me, and on this day, we were discussing the wonders of the orgasm. Sal revealed that he liked to hold back, get as close to orgasm as he could and stop. He'd do that for days, then have an explosive, incredible climax. My teenage hormones could only marvel at the idea of such control. It was then I noticed that while Sal told me his feelings on this subject, he had casually reached over to his Weimaraner, Dov—named for his Oscar-nominated role in *Exodus*, Dov Landau—and masturbated him.

> Susan: Sal told me he'd jerked off Dov, but I never saw him do it. I always thought he was lying about it.

I knew Sal was trying to shock me, so I pretended it was no big deal, but I was shocked, very shocked. This was one trick I had never seen Lassie do.

There's No Place Like ...

Dad: Would you believe we have been married twenty-five years on July 18, 1967? Just to make sure that everyone did know, we had a wonderful celebration in our Beverly Hills home. It was a great party and Bill and Jon snuck off with a couple bottles of champagne, YEAH!

July 1967
Visit to Rudd's with
  Tommy, Darlene, and kids
18: Parents' 25th wedding
  anniversary

Since William's bedroom was right off the kitchen, Mom and Dad were chilling the champagne in his bathtub. We liberated a couple of bottles and we drank and laughed. I don't think I'd ever laughed so much with William before. It felt good . . . till I got sick . . . for many hours. Mom and Dad figured I felt bad enough without having to punish me further.

Tommy Rettig
and his family.

My fan club stuff still kept a steady stream of people filing in and out of the house. Mom's attitude was always to share the wealth. She realized most of the kids that hung around wanted only a glimpse of me and she provided that for them and so much more. She wrote letters to many—guiding them through rough times at home or school; she sent gifts, birthday cards, photos. She welcomed the world into our home. She made people feel special . . . everyone except William and Fran.

Cheryl Gonroski, fan: When I was about twelve or thirteen years old, I wrote Jon to request a photo. I was so happy to receive a personal letter from Jon. I called his house every Thanksgiving and Christmas to wish him Happy Thanksgiving and Merry Christmas, but I only caught him home one time; that didn't matter. I was happy talking to his parents, especially his wonderful mother. She was Supermom.

Sandy McClusky: Cecile took us to Lucille Ball's house one day, to meet her. She might have been planning a party or dropping something off for Christmas. Lucille Ball came to the door. Cecile introduced us as friends or presidents of Jon's fan club. She loved us girls and wouldn't mind taking us places with her. Jon wasn't around; she would just be doing this with us kids. We stayed in touch for years. Cecile and B.A. came out to Torrance to my wedding, and I remember stopping at the house several times after I got married.

Ruthel Hawkins, fan: I was going through a difficult time, not knowing what path was right for me and not sure what choices were best. Jon's reply to my letter was very heart-touching. He told me that his mother offered to let me stay in their home while looking for a job and an apartment. That was very thoughtful of her, considering she had met me only once for a short visit. To this day I appreciate how very kind and compassionate her gesture was.

Marvin took a Greyhound down from New York to see me in North Carolina at Frontier Land. We stayed in touch for a short time after, then went our own ways. That was the last time we met.

August 1967
Appearance at Frontier Land
22: Greensboro, North Carolina, with the Ford Philpot Crusade Rally

Marvin: Jon was a senior in high school. Girls were about the only thing on his mind. He didn't change; he was never different or difficult to talk to. What was incredible was seeing Jon have access to the rides and the park after closing, access to do as he pleases with an entire amusement park.

Margaret Cartwright, mother of Veronica and Angela: Jon's mother asked if we were interested in going to North Carolina, so Veronica, who was working on *Daniel Boone* at the time, could sign autographs at Ghost Town. Mr. Coburn had a private plane and flew Veronica and me to North Carolina. They put us up in an A-frame house on the top of a hill. The way down the hill was very narrow, filled with curves and water flowing down from the top. We had to drive down every day to go to the restaurants to eat. One day our car got stuck halfway down the hill and I was terrified. I had my six-year-old son, Chris, and my sister with me and, I must confess, I was too scared to move in case I went over the edge. Luckily for me, Jon happened to be driving up the hill and stopped to ask if there was something wrong. He was like a Guardian Angel and drove my car back to a safe section of the road. Thank you again, Jon! I will never forget the day you saved our lives.

Our neighbor, Mr. Martin Conflenti, worked with Dr. Ford Philpot, an evangelical preacher from Kentucky who traveled the country holding crusade rallies. Like Bob Hope and the USO, Dr. Philpot used some of the former Miss Americas who were Christians to present in these public meetings.

Martin Conflenti Sr: Jon and I flew to Lexington, Kentucky, where he appeared on the Philpot TV show known as *The Story,* in which Jon gave his testimony about his life as a Christian.

The Reverend spoke in a Southern drawl, always opened with a funny story, then drove home his message. Mom was a Baptist, so these crusades really appealed to her, and she jumped at the opportunity to get me involved. I would be asked to speak, to testify. Later, when Dr. Philpot spoke, I witnessed people wailing, speaking in tongues, and falling on the ground in seizures. None of that bothered me. What bothered me was that good, hard-working people brought their families here to pray and, though some couldn't afford to put shoes on their children's feet, they were still asked for money at the crusade.

The summer had been a blur of music, sex, pot, and travel. School gave me a little more structure, but not a lot. One thing it did do was put Sherry Smothers in front of me.

Sherry: I think I'd had a crush on him when I was five years old, from the TV show. We really cared about each other already. We really connected.

> **September 1967**
> Senior year at Rexford, student body president, photographer for the yearbook

Sherry and I heated up again, but I was still seeing Susan. And I'd just run into Genie the Tailor at the Whisky. She wanted to make a shirt for me, but I had no time to see her or any of these ladies. I was preparing to fly to Manila in the Philippines to make a film called *Has Anybody Seen Chris?*

The Secret of the Sacred Forest

Every actor has one movie on their résumé like this. Today, it would skip the theaters and go straight to DVD. In the '60s, it went to a double bill at a drive-in theater. It was an independent, not affiliated with a studio, written and produced by William Copeland.

William: It wasn't really that bad. It was a B movie, no doubt about it. It certainly wasn't a great movie, but it wasn't a bad movie and I don't understand why they could never get it distributed. I know my parents invested money in the movie.

I have no idea how this all came about, how William Copeland and my parents got together. To my knowledge, this was their only dabbling in producing, but it makes sense. Mom had wanted to start her own school. She was great in real estate. Now she had an opportunity to invest in her son's next movie; it's no surprise she went for it.

October 1967
14: Ford Philpot First Methodist Church, Park Ridge, Illinois

In the story, I sneak into the Philippines to search for my brother, Chris, an investigative reporter whose plane crashed in the jungle while he was trying to expose a drug-smuggling ring. He is assumed dead, but I won't accept it. An American embassy official learns I've entered the country illegally and heads off into the bush after me. I manage to stay one step ahead with the help of Bayarti, a local guide. The two of us are pursued by black marketers, government agents, and headhunters, as well as the embassy man. Eventually, I find Chris and I am stunned that he has joined the drug-smugglers. In the end, Chris explains that he staged his disappearance to join the smugglers so that he could expose them. He and I go home together.

Chris is played by Michael Parsons, an American artist and sometime actor who lived in Manila. Bayarti was played by Leo Martinez, a popular Filipino actor close to my age. The embassy official was played by Gary Merrill, a stage, screen, and television actor who had been famously married to Bette Davis. Mr. Merrill had marched with Dr. Martin Luther King Jr. two years earlier in the Selma to Montgomery marches and was outspoken against the Vietnam war. I was anxious to spend time with him. The director was Michael du Pont, one of the du Ponts.

The shoot was three months long, and there was no time for me to attend school. We made an arrangement with Rexford that I would graduate with my class in June, but I would make up the three months the following September. I was working all summer, so summer school was out.

top: With Mike Parsons (center) and du Pont; *above:* Merrill, Copeland, the Filipino cast, and du Pont pose on the set

November 1967

Mom and I landed in Manila and joined Gary Merrill, Michael du Pont, Michael Parsons, and a few of the other Americans already there. The streets were congested and noisy and filled with a funny, colorful kind of vehicle called Jeepneys. Fil-ipinos modified U.S. military jeeps left over from World War II, stretching them, adding roofs, and decorating them in crazy, bright designs. Mom and I loved them.

Arrival at the Manila airport.

The Filipinos were great people, warm and very friendly. Ferdi-nand and Imelda Marcos, in the palace, had welcomed us warmly and extended a dinner invitation. From the kids running in the street to the adults to the folks on our crew, everyone spoke English, even the natives; but the poverty was extreme. It was black and white—either they were incredibly rich or incredibly poor.

The country's film industry was thriving, rivaling that of India's, with more films made per capita than in the United States that year. The Filipino crew was very professional and had all the latest equipment—unlike *Escapade in Japan* where we had to bring in both. Though they also had fully-equipped studios, we shot only on location or at private residences like Michael Parsons's place. His house—all of the houses or mansions, I'd call them—had walls separating them from the street and big gates to keep people out. Parsons's place was beautiful with servants, girls, the whole bit. I spent a lot of time there with some lovely ladies while Mom was off at dinners and formal affairs.

We stayed in a new hotel on Manila Bay, forty-five miles outside of the city in an area called Angeles. Nearby, a hotel and restaurant called the Swiss Chalet on Santos Street with its dark, smoky, European bar was where Mr. Merrill spent most of his free time. Weathered and rumpled, smelling of cigarettes, he and I had only a few scenes together. I regret there were so many distractions for this teenage boy; I didn't spend much time with him.

There was an enormous American military presence there and cer-tain businesses catered to the soldiers and all of those businesses were about girls. I was offered "an introduction" to a girl every time I went out.

Michael du Pont and Parsons were both a good ten years older and, as I was doing back home, I pushed to keep pace with them. The night Mom went to the dinner with the Marcoses, I hit the clubs with the guys—the striptease-type joints and the bars—eating peanuts and drink-

With du Pont.

ing San Miguel beer all day and all night, arriving back at the hotel late, totally smashed and violently ill. I told Mom it was bad peanuts. I didn't even know if there was such a thing, but I was in no condition to think. I was so sick, the house physician had to attend to me. I'll never know if Mom believed me; I suspect not, but she didn't have to say anything. I'd sure learned my lesson. I was so sick, I couldn't work for a couple of days—the one and only time in my entire career. Luckily, since the director had encouraged my behavior, there were no repercussions.

November 15, 1967 *Manila Times:* Sporting a Beatle haircut, the youthful Provost said that he has seen some Manila discothèques and described them as "really swinging. . . . Your teenagers are good dancers. And those combos can really play. I like the Manila atmosphere. I've tasted your bangua (milkfish) and I found it very tasty. I also like puto seco (butter cookies). But I think I could never eat your balut."

I love food and cooking, and this was my first trip to a foreign land as a young man. I wanted to try the local dishes. Food vendors set up little shacks all along Manila Bay and wonderful aromas filled the air. Men who looked like ice cream vendors with small carts walked the streets yelling, "Balut! Balut!" Someone said, "Let's try one," and off we went. Then I saw it—fertilized duck eggs about two weeks old with the duckling cooked inside the egg. The vendor would cut off the top of the shell and you were supposed to eat the little duckling and drink all the juice and everything that was in there; it was absolutely gross. It became the thing—everybody had to eat a balut to be macho, but there was no peer pressure in all the world that could get me to swallow that. Just the thought of it now makes my stomach do flip-flops.

One night, I went with Michael du Pont and a few others to get some barbecue from the vendors along the bay. We were handed bite-size barbecued meat on bamboo skewers. It resembled a pork chop and was pretty tasty. When we finished, we were told the meat was not pork; it was dog. I felt my stomach doing flip-flops again. Horrified, I swore everyone to secrecy. I couldn't exactly have people knowing that Timmy ate Fido. That was my last meal on the streets.

The food on location was simple local fare—rice and a piece of dried fish, some fruit and the ever-present San Miguel beer and orange drinks. Orange drinks like orange soda were as popular as Coca Cola was here, maybe because it, too, was manufactured by San Miguel. There wasn't a lot of real beef, at least what we were used to. The closest was the caribou, the water buffalo, like beef but a little tougher. We drove back to Manila every night.

With Leo Martinez.

On location in Luzon or up in Baguio, outside of Manila, the natives constantly chewed this stuff called beetle nuts, a fruit they wrapped in leaves with a little lime and chewed all day. I'm told it produced a mild stimulant along with a red juice that stained their mouths and teeth. I wanted to try it, but I didn't dare.

One morning, on location way up in the mountains of Baguio, one of the crew nudged me and gestured toward an immaculately dressed woman. "It's Mrs. Marcos." Imelda Marcos had driven alone to check things out. "Jon, do you want to see something?" The crew member motioned me toward Mrs. Marcos's black Mercedes Benz. "Walk over and look under the driver's seat." Mom wasn't usually on location. Matter of fact, most days I didn't see her at all. On this day, she was here and had engaged Mrs. Marcos in conversation, so I quickly walked over to the car and glanced in. To my surprise, under her front seat was her personal submachine gun.

The New Year

Michael took us all to Hong Kong for a respite, a week's vacation; that was absolutely fantastic. Our first-class hotel rose high above the shacks across the street. In the harbor below were tens of thousands of people living on little junks—boats—while closeby, ocean liners docked with hundreds of passengers from around the world. In between, people flocked to huge, floating restaurants; we did, too.

January 26, 1968

Mom and I explored the streets and alleyways, through the little markets in Hong Kong where we saw caged dogs, cats, and snakes and different things they considered delicacies. The Hong Kong tailors could make anything you wanted in two days. I ordered shirts and two suits (it was really tough finding a hip-looking suit when I was still five-foot-three and a hundred pounds). Everyone ordered things—Mom, too. I also bought myself a nice camera outfit, which I still use. And, for my friends back home, I bought copies of the *Little Red Book*, Mao Tse Tung's bible, along with pins and buttons and stamps from Red China. Back home seemed very far away.

We returned to Manila refreshed and finished the shoot in about ten days. Mom and I went home carrying Christmas gifts for the family; we'd missed the holidays. I went back to Rexford, filed for unemployment, and tried to pick up where I'd left off.

Lloyd: I met Jon in line in the Hollywood unemployment office. He'd just gotten back from the Philippines, and we had a big hug there in front of everybody; we didn't care. Then all of a sudden he was gone.

February 17, 1968 Lassie and I walked the runway at the Beverly Hilton for Celebrity Moms and Moppets on Parade, a benefit for handicapped children, along with Steve Allen, Carl Reiner, fashion designers like Rudi Gernreich—who invented the topless bathing suit—Bill Blass, and a host of others.

Making the Scene

Jay North: Jon was getting involved very heavily socially. He was trying to divorce himself from Timmy; that was his way of rebelling against the squeaky clean image. He wanted to enjoy being Jon Provost. He probably felt a sense of freedom after years of doing what was expected of him. I wished I could be like him, but I was too terrified of my mom and the punishment. I think B.A. and Cecile realized that it was time to let Jon have some normal experiences. I sensed a lot more freedom in his life as a teenager than I had in mine. They were a stable influence in his life.

I continued to see Michael du Pont back in L.A. He had a great house in the Hollywood Hills, lots of girls, lots of good times. I was still driving my mom's car, a '66 Chevy Malibu and was looking for a car of my own. Michael drove a Ferrari and his ex-wife had this little Lotus

Élan. The Ferrari was over my budget, but the Lotus Élan was pretty hot. Emma Peel drove one in *The Avengers*. I borrowed the car and it fit like a glove, just this teeny little go-cart, a little two-seater. I loved it and immediately got a speeding ticket on the test drive. I ordered my first car.

Tiger Beat magazine: Genie the Tailor Opens Shop: *Tiger Beat* always featured articles about the tailor to the beautiful people, Genie. Her shop opened in early 1968 and some hip scenesters came to support her. They included Anne Moses, Micky Dolenz, Samantha Juste (who seem to go to EVERY PARTY), Sajid Khan, and Mark Lindsay.

Jody Brisken: She was amazing . . . here was this girl right in it, right in the middle of the rock scene and she found a way to do business. The Plaster Casters were right in it and found a way to do business, but not make money. Genie was signing leases on stores, she was cutting fabric, taking orders, hiring contractors, ordering materials. I think it was phenomenal. I was constantly marveling.

Davy Jones: I was a little leery, wary, I wasn't a part of a lot of that stuff going on. Genie the Tailor to me—that was like going swimming naked in the pool; I didn't do it. I said Hare Krishna, slept in waterbeds and all that stuff, but I never went to the Monterey Pop Festival because I thought it was just a bunch of weirdos smoking dope, taking acid, and taking their clothes off. And Genie the Taylor to me was kinda freaky. I thought she was all part of that hippie thing. It's stereotyping, I know, but I can't help it; I have to remember what I remember at the time. I wouldn't do it now.

Ralph Benner: She was wonderful. She was like a free spirit, always had beads on, always. She was a vegetarian, but mostly all she ate was potatoes. I took her out to lunch and she was trying to get me to be a vegetarian; she wouldn't drink of course. Once, she came in the office really excited because one of her best friends had just gotten his first big break in Hollywood. He was going to star in a new movie called *The Graduate*. She knew everyone.

She gave a party and I took my cousin there—a midwestern guy from Chicago—and I mean, the marijuana smoke was so thick you could get high from just walking through the door. He still talks about it! People were sitting on the floor. Genie was running around. Sajid Khan was there, Rodney Bingenheimer. . . .

Genie was great to me, sweet and exotic and unique. The opposite of laid back, I'd rarely seen someone so passionate about her craft; Genie was always working on something. I ran into her on the Strip and she told me I'd missed the opening of her tailor shop. She invited me to stop by and I promised I would. Sherry Smothers seemed to have missed me and Susan and Sal wanted to see me, too. It was good to be home.

The Plot Thickens

Susan: Jon and I had sex on our own, at my apartment. Then I initiated sex with him at Sal's and Sal asked if he could watch—typical.

I thought it was weird, but who cared? Whatever, yes, let's try it. My hormones were racing at top speed. Susan and I undressed and made love in his massive bed as Sal, smoking a joint, situated himself in a chair at the end of the room and watched. After a while, just like the camera, I forgot Sal was even there. Just before I came, he raced over to the bed and shoved a popper under my nose. He was right about those; they were incapacitating. My heart raced, the room spun around and the top of my head blew off.

Susan: That's right, that whole amyl nitrate thing. This happened a few times and Jon felt very secure there. I thought I was the winner. "OK, Sal—you wanna watch? Watch this!" But in my heart, I knew he wasn't watching me. It was Sal's vicarious way of getting to the man he wanted to get to. I really cared about Jon and I felt guilty I was partici-pating.

Soon after, Sal and Susan invited me to join them in the bedroom for a ménage à trois—something that up until then, I'd only read about in *Playboy*'s Forum. Mike and Ron would flip. Susan lay between us, fac-ing me, and Sal respected my boundaries. Everything was very cool. I really thought this was wild. I'd left Lassie and the farm behind in the dust.

Susan: I told Sal he wasn't going to change him. I was protective of him—Jon was such a beautiful person, so sweet—and Sal would say, "You're wrong. You're wrong. You're wrong." And I said, "I'm not wrong. Don't do it. Don't do it." Sal had to be in control of every situation and it would drive him crazy when he didn't have control. And he'd find another way so that he would have control.

Sew and Sew

A week or so later, I stopped by Genie's new shop, next door to the Troubadour on Santa Monica. There was no sign; you either knew it was Genie's shop or you didn't. She had a few pieces already made in the front, but most of Genie's clothes were custom made. She sat at a counter in the back where she could watch the store. In front were large mirrors, dozens of bolts of fabric, two or three sewing machines, and all sorts of related accessories. She asked me if I wanted to see the fitting room and led me to the back, behind a curtain where she . . . took my measurements in a very creative way. Older women were amazing. She invited me to her place. We made a date.

People thought I was a real player, but if a few older women hadn't taken me under their wing, I don't know how long it would have taken me to work up my nerve. Maybe that was the problem with Sherry. I was too shy to push and she wasn't offering.

About a week later, I went up to Genie's place, north of Sunset up in the hills behind the Whisky. There, she did something beautiful for me and I will always be grateful to her. I've already said I wasn't terribly experienced and certain ways of pleasing women were still a mystery to me. Genie let me unravel that mystery that beautiful afternoon. It remains one of my sweetest memories.

Anne Moses: Well, that's so much Genie, I can't even believe it. Of course I didn't know, but knowing Genie . . . yeah, it has to be in like a beautiful, graceful way. She was a really incredible person, she really was.

Baby, You Can Drive My Car

Perfect timing—my Lotus arrived just before spring vacation. Ron and I drove the couple of hours to Palm Springs every year. This year, we went in the Lotus. The desert town became a haven for bikini-clad girls. The sidewalks were full of them. We were cruising the main street and I'm behind the wheel of this brand new, shiny white little Lotus Élan convertible—belly-button high if any girls walk over. I'm looking at all the chicks, being real cool when Ron yells, "Look out!"—never a good thing. I turned my head just in time to see the rear end of a Cadillac. BAM! My beautiful new car was so small that the bumpers never met. I slipped right underneath his rear end, lifting both of his rear tires off the ground. His bumper crashed my windshield, took the hood of my car right off and ripped the top of the engine off. We're sitting there looking at the tailpipe and rear end of this Caddy sitting right above our noses. I called my dad and he made arrangements to put the Lotus on a flatbed and have it brought back to L.A. I had an interview or a personal appearance I had to do the next day. Then I hopped on a Greyhound bus home with my tail between my legs. That car had less than a thousand miles on. Nobody had to tell me what an idiot I was; I felt bad enough all by myself. I had it fixed up beautifully . . . and it's in my garage right now.

> **March 1968**
> 16: Lunch with fan club for my eighteenth birthday; I was now officially draft age

Sandy McClusky: Cecile invited us to a birthday party for Jon. I don't remember where it was held. It was a sit-down luncheon fan club birthday party . . . just Jon and about twenty fans! I still remember the dress I wore.

Dick Clark's *Happening '68*

Dom Priore, author: *It's Happening* was a Dick Clark Production from late 1967. It replaced the ambitious *Where the Action Is*, which the network dropped because the budget was larger than any teen show. Instead, Clark did this new show, *It's Happening*, in an L.A. studio and got Mark Lindsay and Paul Revere to host it. At the end, they featured three celebrity guests as judges and two completely unknown bands. The judges would pick the winner in this mini-battle, one episode every week for three weeks. The fourth week, judges picked the best of the three.

That's where I fit in. I was a celebrity judge along with Bobby Vee and my pal Sal. I don't know whether he suggested me or I put his name in the mix. It's our only recorded appearance together. Our four segments were all shot in one day at ABC Television Center. We changed clothes and pretended a week had passed . . . one of which would fall on my eighteenth birthday. They were shot on Saturday so they'd have plenty of kids for the live audience. We rehearsed first, then taped. It took most of the afternoon. Between tapings, the kids in the audience were allowed to wander around and hang out, very relaxed and groovy.

Columnist Sheilah Graham interviewed me for her *Citizen-News* column about my appearance on Woody Woodbury's talk show. I mentioned that the Wrathers had sold my episodes of *Lassie* into syndication for over $13 million and I had recently seen it in Japanese. "Even the dog was Japanese. They refer to Ruth Martin as Lassi Mama-San."

> **March 1968**
> 25: *The Woody Woodbury Show*

Daniel J. Webster, fan: Here's some trivia: When *Lassie* was being shown here in Japan, your voice was dubbed by a woman! Children's voices in this country are usually dubbed an octave or two higher than the originals, which makes them sound a little bit too "cutesy" to Western ears.

I've also learned I speak French, German, Swedish, Russian, Spanish, and more. Instead of dubbing the actors voices, most countries simply redid the soundtrack completely, so Lassie's bark was dubbed, too. In Mexico, I could swear they used a Chihuahua! I received residuals for the first three airings; that was done before the decade was out. That was it. I would never earn another dime for my work on the show.

The Trap Is Sprung

Back at Sal's one night, he and Susan and I passed a joint around. After a while, he suggested we move into the bedroom. The three of us undressed and lay down on the bed, Susan between us. Her pale skin against Sal's dark body made them a very erotic couple. Sal handed me another joint and I took a deep drag, rolling onto my back. I was stoned, feeling warm and good. Susan lay across my chest and smiled at me. "It's O.K. Jon, just relax. Don't fight me, just enjoy it." She opened a popper under my nose. The room spun around. Susan was clinging to me, holding me down. Sal scooted close and suddenly began groping me. I struggled to get up and he lay across my legs. How had this happened? I was scared, my heart was racing. "This isn't funny . . . let me up." I was angry, helpless. I screamed Susan's name and something in her snapped. She let go and I flew off the bed. Susan tried to calm me down, but I jumped in my clothes and headed for the door. I heard Sal say, "It's okay, let him go." He'd been down this road before.

> Susan: We had a terrible fight after Jon left. I was crying, screaming at him. I get emotional now even thinking about it. I was so upset. That event has never left my mind. And all the anger that I had at Sal was really anger I had toward myself for allowing myself to ever, ever, ever, ever be a part of that with Jon. The game had gone too far. Jon was so adorable, so vulnerable. Why I would have been part of trying to rob him of that is beyond me. Apart from that challenge and that game, I think a lot of it was because the man I loved was who he was. I shouted, "I don't think it's funny. You're hurting people. Jon is this beautiful, innocent person; what's wrong with you? How can you do this?" Sal responded by saying, "What's wrong with YOU? Can't you hang with the big boys?"
>
> It was a major turning point in our relationship. I stepped back and looked at the whole situation, how dark it really was. Jon was the straw that broke the camel's back.

Two days later, I finally summoned the courage to call Sal, still very upset. He was nonchalant: "I was waiting for you to call." I vented my anger, but he remained calm and in control. "It just seemed so natural. I thought it was cool with you," he explained, defending his actions. Victims of abuse can often be convinced that it wasn't that bad, that Sal and Susan, people I trusted, were not so terrible. If you kick a puppy, it will still come back to you. But it was terrible. I returned to Sal's house once or twice in an effort to convince myself I had regained control, then never went back.

> Susan: Sal was more gay than he was straight. I was his beard; that's probably why I was so long in his life. I'd almost bet I was the last woman in his life. I definitely have the real story: the double life he led, both sexual and social, walking into those clubs like he was still a major player and yet, when he went home, he couldn't feed his dog—what a dichotomy. At that time, it was more difficult to see stars, and Sal made himself very accessible to the public, to young people.

Younger, sure, like Susan had been and me, younger, naïve, impressionable kids who could be molded, influenced, and ultimately controlled.

> Susan: In my opinion, Sal tried to rape Jon; that's how I perceive it. I think he and I saw each other twice when Sal was not around.
>
> I sort of knew who Sal was sleeping with—no stars. He tried desperately to get Don Johnson in bed with him to no avail. Don was doing the play with him by that time and Don's girlfriend, Christine, and I turned out to be best friends: Elliot, Don, Chris, me, we were like a little family—the five of us. After Jon, I needed to get away from the whole scene and went to Europe for two years. Jon was not in L.A. when I came back.

I continued to see Sal around town. By the fall, he was in rehearsal, directing and costarring in a controversial play, *Fortune and Men's Eyes*, which tells the story of a young man who is jailed for six months for possession of pot. During his time behind bars, he is bullied, raped, and degraded by cell mates. Sal cast an unknown Don Johnson opposite him. Don and I were the same age, same soft, pretty features. In the opening scene, Sal's character rapes Don's. Sal told me he planned to do it for real on stage. He was still trying to shock me, but it only sickened me.

> Ralph Benner: *Fortune in Men's Eyes* was a critical success. I remember going to see it and it was terrific . . . big hit, ran at the Coronet for a long time.

Susan: In the late '6os, early '7os, by doing that sort of vehicle, Sal was saying, "Ah, hell, I can't fight it anymore; let's let the cat out of the bag publicly." They had the first gay parade and it was being accepted that actors and celebrities were gay and everybody was starting to come out of the closet. Sal was the first one to jump out.

Maybe James Dean really did get ahold of him when he was fifteen and Sal was doing the same thing. Looking back, I got caught up. I have great memories of it and memories that aren't so great. I came out of it sane and happy . . . probably much more sane than Sal would have. Christine and I were always saying that Sal would die a tragic death and we were 100 percent right.

He was a talented, charismatic, lost, messed up, selfish guy. An actor is never in control of his own life—particularly a child actor, which Sal had been. Maybe that's why he was driven to try to control everything around him. In the end, he controlled nothing and a random act would end his life.

I pulled way back after that. I was pissed off, but it was my secret. Who could I have told? It was the betrayal that was hardest to reconcile. I didn't feel foolish . . . for long, anyway. What had I done but trust these people, offer my friendship, bring them into my home and family? I had never been so purposefully deceived. I'd never been aware of the plot, the entire seduction. It's only recently Susan and I talked about it.

I never blamed her, even then. I understood she had been manipulated, trained from a young age. The betrayal came from Sal. It may never have been his original intent with Susan or with me. What had begun as "free love" over a few years became a dedicated hunt in which he carefully chose targets and slowly reeled them in. Six months later, Sal immersed himself in a play with that exact subject matter. And by casting himself in the role of the bully, he was able to live out this scenario—forcing himself on a straight, naïve, eighteen-year-old boy—night after night. Was it obsession? Had he been abused? Was this his ultimate control fantasy? I'll never know, but whatever it was, it consumed him.

Sherry Baby

Sherry: He was having an affair, I think, with Genie the Tailor. My girl-friend Jody said if I didn't hurry up and sleep with him—I was a virgin—he'd go off with Genie the Tailor. I had to sleep with him now. I was actually a little embarrassed about being a virgin because I was sixteen, I think, and that was over the age for Beverly Hills kids or the kids in the gang I ran with. You weren't supposed to be a virgin that long.

I knew I was jealous enough of these other women. I didn't want him to have anything to do with Sal. He was dark . . . like Genie the Tailor. There was darkness to these people; and to Sal, certainly, there was evil. I had had a sunny life, sunny and fun in a carefree '60s kind of way. My life was stable at that point; it hadn't gotten dark. Mine got dark later. Once we started sleeping together, we were never apart . . . for years. I don't remember much about the first time except that it was on my four poster bed in my mom's house late one afternoon.

Sherry.

I'd been all wrong about Sherry. She was always surrounded by guys whenever I saw her. I thought she was fooling around with half of them, but my imagination must have been in overdrive. She wasn't "fast" at all. I was her first lover; and I did not treat it lightly. When I realized my mistake, it made things even better . . . for both of us. She really had to make that leap to commit to me—which I think she'd been putting off. She opened her heart to me and I felt it all the way to my toes. She and I got serious quickly after that. Sherry was cute, fun, sexy, smart—a showbiz kid with my career in perspective. She was not at all impressed by my celebrity. It wasn't even a factor for her, which was a relief for me. She got it, and she got me. I liked everything about her, always did; and now we were really connected. No longer held at arm's length, I fell head over heels for her.

Jay North: I didn't really know Sherry that well. I just knew that Jon loved her to death and she loved Jon. She used to call him Long Jon because of his long hair, like Long John Silver. And they were always together and very affectionate together. I didn't have a steady, and I used to wish I had a girl who adored me like Sherry adored Jon. She was a very sweet kid, a typical high school girl.

Sherry's home life was nonexistent. A new marriage, a new baby, they weren't paying any attention to her. They'd quit "bothering" with her career. Just like Fran, when she couldn't get their attention by being good, Sherry rebelled. In an attempt to fill her time—or just keep Sherry out of their hair—her mom got her a job at a hot Beverly Hills clothing boutique run by Jack Hanson, who also owned the Daisy Club.

> *Sherry*: I worked at Jack's when I was fourteen, after school and on Saturdays. My mom sadistically thought I should have a "normal" person's job. She thought it was cute after being paid a lot to be in movies and on TV to have a normal job, so I worked at Jack's. His office was above all the dressing rooms and he had the mirrors set so he could see into the dressing rooms through holes in his office. He thought he was real cute. Jack would drive me home in his Rolls and make me lie down in his lap while he drove me . . . and he was always trying to kiss me. I'm not even sure I was aware that it was wrong yet. He was such a creep that I almost regret not confronting him before he died.

We both had our secrets. We both felt alone, odd and out of place, but together we found freedom. She didn't really like Ron and Mike much, but we enjoyed a few other kids from Rexford as well as a couple of her friends, Gary Alan Singerman—GAS—and Jody, when she wasn't in the "hospital."

> *Jody Brisken*: I was like every Beverly Hills girl who's in trouble; your parents put you in the psych institute and then, of course, you're still partying. GAS visited and brought me pot. I snuck out one night with Jon and Sherry in his little Lotus. We're getting hammered on so much weed that we can't think and I am just thinking, "Oh, my God, they're so small!" I don't even know where we went; we just went out and partied. I mean, it was the '60s! I know this all sounds like, "Did you grow up like this?" It's like my sister said, "I can't believe someone made money off *Girl, Interrupted*. Was that not all of our stories? Did we not all do that?" I mean, who wasn't committed at that age?

Mostly, Sherry and I enjoyed being alone. We'd throw a blanket and a bottle of wine in the back of the Lotus and take off for the hills above Malibu. The fire roads had chains across them, but if Sherry held the chain up the Lotus was small enough to drive underneath. We'd park on a bluff overlooking the coast and spend the day drinking wine and making love. Sometimes we'd rent a tiny cabin at one of the old beachside motels, which I'd pay for with my unemployment money. We babysat for her sister Cammie or for Fran and Bruce; and after my niece, Michelle, fell asleep, we'd make love. We created our own little dream world where we imagined ourselves as adults taking care of our own children; we even chose names for them.

> Sherry: Chester, Jessie, and Annabelle Lee. They were some kind of "living like the Band in the country" fantasy. . . . It was so wonderful. . . . really fun. That is why I say it was "sunshiney." I remember a life more like that, not dark. Our relationship was very symbiotic. We just clung together. Maybe it's "young and in love," but we wrote pages and pages daily and talked on the phone when we were away from each other. We were totally inseparable.

We needed each other. I no longer asked Mom's opinion about things; I asked Sherry. I started turning down appearances because I had plans with Sherry or because Sherry encouraged me to turn them down. She was teaching me how to say no, that it was OK to say no. It felt great to take a stand and claim some time for myself. None of this made Sherry popular with Mom.

> Sherry: I think I was kind of a jealous nag [laughs]. I don't like that I didn't have a more wholesome and supportive attitude toward his career, in retrospect. But I guess he was thinking that way, too. He became something else.

> Fran: My mother tried to break up their relationship because that was competition. Sherry would have nothing to do with my mother, and Mom didn't like her at all. She thought Sherry was going to turn him in a different direction and my mother still wanted to control his career.

> Jim Dalton: She was extremely protective of him dating in high school. Once, we were drinking coffee at the kitchen table when he pulled in the driveway. He'd been dating a girl Cecile was extremely leery of. She said, "I just know she's after his money and we've set up a trust for him and I'll be darned if anybody's gonna mess with him." She was

serious. The Provost household was run on Mr. Provost's income and she was very, very adamant that that was the way things were going to be.

Sherry: Cecile was a stage mother. It was competitive with her. I was trying to get him out of her clutches. He had all these appointments at these stupid things to go smile and shake hands! And I wanted to play! It may have been a good instinct of mine, to get him out of that. I think that was my job in life, at that point, to get him away from her.

Sherry was right; I was becoming something different, but what? It was as if these activities defined me. If I stopped going, who was I and how would I choose to fill that time? These were questions I'd never had the chance to ask. I didn't even know which direction to look in for the answers; but together, we were ready to strike out on our own in search of the great truth. We'd heard Haight-Ashbury was a good place to look.

San Francisco, and the Haight in particular, had become famous as the center for the counterculture, the hippie lifestyle. Janis Joplin lived there; so did Jefferson Airplane, the Dead, Country Joe. The Strip was the nightclub end of it, but the Bay area was about the lifestyle, the genuine center of the movement. We had to check it out. I have no idea what I told my parents, but Sherry and I packed some backpacks and flew to San Francisco.

Sherry: We had to leave at six in the morning because we wanted to get up there, so I told my mother that we were going to watch the sunrise at the beach. But the sun doesn't rise at the beach here!

We had no real plan except to go. From the airport, we made our way to Golden Gate Park to find the beautiful people with flowers in their hair. The scene blew our minds—thousands of people in the park making music, selling drugs, begging for money. At first, it didn't seem much different from Griffith Park in L.A. But further into the crowd, it got worse: bikers and speed freaks, runaways and burn-outs, some with weapons; it was a real bad scene. Sherry and I were wide-eyed and tie-dyed, eighteen and sixteen, looking even younger—lambs among the wolves. Some locals in their thirties, a hippie couple, spotted us and came to our rescue. They made friends with us, then asked our plans. Sherry and I shrugged. We didn't know; we figured we'd sleep in the park, wander around. "No, you're not, you silly children." Bless this couple whose names I have long forgotten. They took us to their tiny flat, fed us, and watched over us until it was time to go to the airport. They dropped us there, whacked us on the butts and sent us home.

John Mangoni

John Mangoni: So, it's April 1st, and I'm upstairs. Jon yells up, "Mom and Dad are out, so why don't I make some eggs or something?" Fine. I'm washing my face and I hear him say, "John, there's a fire." I knew it was April Fool's Day, so I just thought, "Yeah, sure," and keep washing. "John, fire!" I dry my face and go downstairs; and, as I hit the first floor, all I see is this thick layer of smoke. We called his parents, who were down the street at Fran's. They had to tell us to call the fire department. The fire was contained to the kitchen, but one of the teen mags said Jon was almost killed in a fire in his home while his friend visited from out of town.

April 1968

Dad: I put in a new kitchen . . . and Jon tried to burn it down. It wasn't bad . . . it was exciting.

John Mangoni: I stayed at the Provosts even if Jon was out of town. Cecile would ask me to answer the phone. She knew it would be fun for me—and good experience, too. His friends like Laurie Ackerman would call. One time, David Cassidy called. Another time, it was the Screen Actor's Guild. I felt like I was one of her sons, the way Cecile would treat me with such kindness and was just so entertaining. I thought she was the greatest thing.

It was a big, important part of my life. As busy as he was and as his life was, he found a place to allow me to come into it. He gave me experiences I reflect on and that help me get through experiences today. For example, right now, I could talk to anybody! I met President Carter's wife a few weeks ago. It was a positive influence for me.

John is a good man, a pediatrician and author of a book on child-care. He's still in touch with me and my family. He's been on television and radio, too, and yes, my mother had a hand in that. He represents one of dozens, maybe hundreds, over the years my mother influenced through her letters, her visits, her encouragement, and her support.

Along the Way

April 1968
New Castle, Indiana, and Tuscaloosa, Alabama, with Ford Philpot

When I was younger, I never questioned any of the events my mother lined up for me; I simply went. I "testified" at close to a dozen of these, but after this one, I said no more. I'm sure Sherry had everything to do with it.

The photo shoot with Keith and Kevin was fun and easy in a park in Beverly Hills. Just as Davy had posed with me, now it was my turn to pose with some younger heartthrobs. Don Jaye worked with them a bit, too. Mom was always into sharing the wealth, contact-wise.

April 1968
4: Martin Luther King Jr. is assassinated
Photo op, L.A. Fire Department
Photo shoot with the Schultz twins

Kevin Schultz: We were kind of new in the business at the time, and Jon had been in the business all of his life, and he was very nice and UN-starlike. We became good friends. He had a manager that was our manager, and we went out to dinner and to a couple of nightclubs. He was so good-looking, he always got all the girls. Keith and I were amazed at his looks.

Evelyn Schultz, twins' mom: They were very pleased with the way Jon accepted them and acted as if they were as big of stars as he was. *The Monroes* was their first series, and they appreciated the way he acted toward them.

Jon's mom was as sweet, if not sweeter than Jon—if that's possible.

It was an accident that I got the twins in the business. I never looked for it. The girl across the street told Central Casting about them. They immediately worked and went from that job to the next, just by word of mouth. Then somebody said, "Who's their agent?" and I told my husband, "I guess I'm supposed to have an agent." And he says, "I know somebody whose aunt is an agent," so I got that name and went to her and it wasn't until a year or two later that I found out she was a record agent! She was glad to have somebody she could send out for theatrical work. Her assistant left for a big agency and took my kids with her. She got them a series or two and lots of work, commercials and westerns, all the things that were going on on television.

Over the years, I had sent her people I thought were good for the business and they worked. She thought I had a good eye for it and said, "When the boys get to be eighteen, I'd like you to come and work for me." I went to work for her. She retired eventually and I took over, and I was an agent for thirty years! I was one of the top agents in children's agencies. Look what unfolded!

That was Ken Osmond's mom. That was almost my mom. I'm sure it's the story for dozens of mothers—schools like my mother had planned, agencies, guardians on the set. It was a natural progression.

May 1968
5: Palos Verdes charity event with Elvis, Angela Cartwright, Barbara Stanwyck, and more to raise money for a child's kidney operation

June 1968
6: Bobby Kennedy assassinated
Graduation from Rexford

FAVE Magazine: Jon is digging Hendrix, Cream, John Mayal, Canned Heat, *The Graduate,* and *Rosemary's Baby.*

One night, after the Ash Grove, I saw the light on in Genie the Tailor's shop and stopped in to say hello. She introduced me to her boyfriend, Richard Thompson. He was British and had a pretty groovy band called Fairport Convention. Business was booming for Genie. She showed me the shirt she was working on for Eric Clapton.

Jody Brisken: She had a brilliant idea to open a shop inside the Whisky. She approached Mario (the owner) and asked for one of the two dressing rooms upstairs. He gave her the little one. When I was living in the mental institution, I needed a job to get out. Genie, God bless her, went there and somehow got permission for me to stay out until three in the morning every day to run it. Every band that came through the Whisky started ordering clothes. We had this little dressing room with just a cloth hung over that you push to the side. All the bands sat there to get blow jobs from the groupies. This was my job to get out of the mental institution. While the rest of us were all fucked up, she was running a business. She was one of a kind, really a good egg. I do know she slept with my boyfriend, Darryl, but who didn't?

Genie, Richard, and I talked about a recent cover story in *Rolling Stone* on groupies and the whole Sunset Strip rock and roll scene. She was mentioned as part of the scene, but she was pretty pissed off about the "many lies and distortions" in the article. She wrote a letter to the editor and it had just been published. It began: "Sirs: Your article is really f___ed. You could have done something groovy, but instead gave up halfway through and settled for a cheap, sensationalistic approach—that's not journalism and certainly not worthy of *Rolling Stone*. Hopefully this article will pass away unread into oblivion and you can redeem yourself in the next issue. Just remember that the truth is the most important thing you can write. If you wanted to know the facts about many of the things you glossed over in the article, all you had to do was ask." It was so Genie. She wasn't afraid to say what was on her mind, while encouraging their next effort. I liked her positive vibe and I was glad I'd stopped in. Genie always got me thinking.

Meanwhile, back at the ranch . . .

July 1968

Another summer, another visit to Ghost Town. I'm sure Mom was happy to separate me from Sherry. And in those days before cell phones, communication by phone was expensive. We continued to write a lot of letters, and I missed her like crazy, but this kind of separation was my definition of normal—people being thrown together, then ripped apart because of work. The show must go on. On the up side, I really did love it there.

August 1968
Tweetsie Railroad, Boone, North Carolina

Tweetsie, another Western-themed park, sprung up around a 1917 steam locomotive, the only surviving narrow-gauge engine left from the East Tennessee and Western North Carolina Railroad. I did the same thing there that I did at the other parks, plus I got to ride the train.

Beverly . . . Hills, That Is . . .

That summer, of course, the Democratic National Convention in Chicago erupted into chaos and rioting. Police beat kids while "the whole world is watching." GAS and I talked about Vietnam and what we could do to avoid being drafted. My brother William, with a heart murmur and flat feet, was out. GAS joined the National Guard and I found myself a good lawyer.

I returned to Rexford to make up those three months I'd missed in the Philippines. It was great to be back home, back with Sherry. My schedule was relaxed and easy. Mom had backed way off. Maybe she was finding her own interests now that I wasn't her primary focus. As always, she and Dad had their clubs. The newest was the Hollywood Lapidary and Mineral Society. Big "rock hounds," while other people brought back sweaters or hats from their travels, they started bringing back shells, rocks, and sea glass.

September 1968

Fran was wrapped up in her family, trying to increase it by one more. William graduated from the Don Martin School of Radio and Television in Hollywood with a degree in TV production. He'd stayed on there and was just about to get his Radio Telephone Operator's License—First Class. He became a ham radio operator and really enjoyed reaching out to people across the airwaves. But he and I barely communicated. We'd only had a brief window of opportunity to share a few mutual interests: motorcycles, cars, the party scene. Now, it seemed the window had closed. We'd gone our separate ways. Our paths rarely crossed.

Sherry: I remember Fran as being really sweet. I don't remember William at all . . . oh, I kind of do; I think he was jealous.

Sherry and I attended the premiere of the Beatles' *Yellow Submarine* at the Fox Village Theater in Westwood.

November 13, 1968

Around the holidays, I caught up with Rudd and visited the ranch. Bob was there; he'd just seen June. *Lost in Space* was ending, and her new role in *Petticoat Junction* started in the spring. She was busy as always.

December 1968
1: Hollywood Christmas Parade
8: Southgate Christmas Parade

Bob Weatherwax: She is amazing. That's why I asked her one day, "June, how come when I was twenty-one, you looked thirty-eight, and now that I'm sixty, you look thirty-eight?" She put her hand up to her face and said, "I've had some great work and some young boyfriends." At that time, she was with the actor who played Jesus in [the touring company of] *Jesus Christ Superstar*. He was in his early twenties and she was over forty. . . . She was always a fun type of girl.

Tiger Beat reported that I attended Sajid Khan's seventeenth birthday party at the Century Plaza Hotel along with Jay North, Desi Arnaz Jr., Paul Cowsill, and more. Later that month, Sherry and I went to see Sal's play at the Coronet Theater.

> Sherry: Jon wanted us to go see him, so we went. We didn't stay long. He was pretty disgusted and we left. Later that night, he told me what had happened with Sal. I thought it was absolutely gross and so creepy.

Walt Disney was about as far away as I could get from the darkness of Sal Mineo. I was cast in *The Computer Wore Tennis Shoes*, a Disney TV movie starring Kurt Russell, who was under contract there. The shoot was scheduled for three weeks in March. I'd finished at Rexford. While I waited to begin filming, Mom arranged some TV appearances. I was one of three bachelors on *The Dating Game* (I wasn't picked). On *The Joey Bishop Show*, I promoted L.U.V.—Let Us Vote—a campaign to lower the voting age from twenty-one to eighteen. We could be drafted at eighteen, but couldn't have a voice in choosing our government. Tommy Boyce and Bobby Hart wrote a very hip theme song for the cause. Maybe they were on with me. I know they sang it later on *Happening '68*.

> Sandy McClusky: A couple years later, after Jon moved away, Cecile talked me into going on *The Dating Game*. When I got married, my husband and I went on *The Newlywed Game*. We were on *Gambit* and I was on *Hollywood Squares*. I didn't work when I first got married. It was wonderful! But Cecile is the one who talked me into going on in the first place.

The Computer Wore Tennis Shoes

> Mike McGreevey: I remember Jon's Lotus bombing into the Disney parking lot every morning. He was a madman with his cars.

It was great seeing McGreevey again. He was always fun. I hadn't met Kurt before. He was a year younger and quite an athlete. As a matter of fact, when the child star thing ended for him a year or so later, he

played pro ball until an injury in '73 forced him to retire and return to the screen. I missed baseball and most sports, so we didn't have much opportunity to meet, but I sure knew his work. He'd been under contract with Disney since he was ten.

The 1960s ushered in the computer age. Disney capitalized on that with *The Computer Wore Tennis Shoes*, about a group of students at Medfield college—Kurt and all us kids—trying to bring their small-town college into the 20th century. They manage to persuade the town's big businessman, A. J. Arno, played by Cesar Romero, to donate his computer—which, back in 1969, took up an entire room—to the school. When problem-student Dexter Riley, Kurt, tries to fix the computer, he gets an electric shock that transforms his brain into a computer: he remembers everything he reads as well as Arno's illegal business activity stored in the computer. When he begins spouting the information on a college bowl TV show, Arno's gang kidnaps him. But they didn't count on Dexter's gang. His friends, disguised as house painters, rescue him, with an all-out, crazy car chase.

As usual, Disney had put together a great supporting cast of adults. I'd known Cesar Romero most of my life and always loved working with him. The out-of-step college dean was Joe Flynn, the best at playing exasperated authority figures. Patty Duke's TV Dad, William Schallert, was our patient professor, and Dick Bakalyan was everybody's favorite hoodlum sidekick.

Dick Bakalyan: Disney had a nice feeling about it. Now, it wasn't the studio itself, it was the kind of people they hired. The kids looked like they belonged together; a lot of times you see films where they just cast people in parts and there's no common denominator. This was a great group and the attitude the kids had toward us was great. It made my going to work every day fun.

Mike McGreevey.

Mike McGreevey: Disney was always a warm lot for me. *The Computer Wore Tennis Shoes* was my return to the lot; I was twenty-one. It had changed because Mr. Disney was no longer there. I had memories of him coming on the set every day to say hi and watch you shoot. The

March 1969
12: My nineteenth birthday

family feeling was still there, because all the people involved with that production were from Walt's era. Bob Butler was such a nice man and such a good director. . . . it was a really fun experience.

I didn't make a big deal out of my birthday. Frank Webb sneaked a bottle of wine onto the lot, and we had a couple of drinks together after work. The Conflentis made their annual cake for me. I met up with Sherry later.

March 17, 1969

Kurt's birthday was a different story. He was finally eighteen, but still in school. We only saw him when he came into the scenes. He always had so much to do. We had a nice party by the houses on the back lot, the whole gang of us.

Mike McGreevey: Computer was originally a two-part TV show. They shot it in three and a half weeks and it was "so good" they decided to release it as a feature. Disney had done this one other time. *The Shaggy Dog* was originally going to be a TV two-parter; at least ours was in color.

We did *Computer* then *Now You See Him, Now You Don't* and then *Strongest Man in the World*. It was a trilogy. That first one was a lot of fun because that group of guys, Jonny, Frank Webb, Frank Welker, George Winters, Alex Clark. . . . we all got along really well. The set was fun because of the way Bob Butler directed. It was sort of our gang running around. We all felt it was a silly little show and I was stunned when it became a movie and a big hit. I still get fan mail about it. People have actually done college theses on "the Medfield trilogy"! It was a seminal movie for young people at that time.

Tyler Mark, child actor: I visited the set of *Computer Wore Tennis Shoes* while I was filming a project on another lot. Jon was sitting near the craft table, long dark hair and looking kind of alone, although he looked happy for the time by himself. I watched a few takes later on that day and thought Jon was a far superior actor, although he had few lines. He had a keen sense of himself by then and I was amazed he didn't receive better roles as he grew older.

Mike McGreevey: Jon was exactly how I remembered him, good with the work, quiet, and very professional. He enjoyed that group thing, but he was the quiet one among us. I think he liked being part of a group, but didn't exactly know *how* to be a part of a group. I remember Frank Welker being sort of starstruck around Joe Flynn and Jon. He just couldn't believe he was around Timmy from *Lassie*. I said, "Don't push that." Frank was struck with how unaffected Jon came across, at how he was handling not being the star of this because he was always the star. Jon was very comfortable just being one of the people . . . at least he seemed so on the surface. Yeah, a lot of guys would have been uppity about the whole thing. But I also sensed . . . he wasn't going to continue this. At some point, Kurt and I said, "I'm done working. I've been doing this since I was six." Jon was the same, even younger, and I just got the sense that it was coming to an end. I remember having a conversation with him about going to college. College seemed like a priority.

I guess my state of mind showed. The reason I wasn't getting the bigger parts was because I'd stopped pursuing them. Sherry was a tremendous influence on me in that regard. But she didn't drag me from it kicking and screaming. The seed had already been planted. She nurtured it, fed it, and helped it grow. *Computer* had sort of fallen into my lap. It was local, quick with a great group, and it conveniently fit my schedule. But Mike was right; I had one foot out the door. College was the only direction Dad ever gave me. "All my children go to college!" Of course, Fran didn't. And William had trouble sticking at one school. Still, it was a phrase I'd heard for years, and as with most things my parents told me, I didn't question it.

All Good Things . . .

April 1969

My parents sailed away to Greece, Egypt, Lebanon, and Israel while I began at West Los Angeles City College and continued to live at home. Late in the month, an arson fire destroyed the Ash Grove. A number of groups that played there over the years helped raise money for the rebuilding: the Byrds, Canned Heat, and Firesign Theater.

May 1969
12: Genie the Tailor killed outside London

I don't know how I heard: Jody, the Free Press, word of mouth. Genie had traveled to the UK with Richard Thompson and his band, Fairport Convention. Most of them, Richard, Genie, Simon Nicol, Ashley Hutchings, and Martin Lamble, were in a Volkswagen van on the way home from a gig in Birmingham when their roadie fell asleep at the wheel. Richard and Genie were up front. The van somersaulted forty feet over an embankment. The roadie went through the windshield and broke both of his legs. Richard suffered broken ribs and a concussion, Ashley Hutchings, a broken nose and cheekbone. Simon Nicol, who'd been asleep in the back, escaped with a concussion. Genie and drummer Martin Lamble were killed. Genie was twenty-seven, Lamble just nineteen. Word spread quickly.

> *Ralph Benner:* We heard she died, that she was strangled by her love beads when her car went off the road. I mean it was incredible, incredible . . . like Isadora Duncan.

> *Jody Brisken:* I got the word that she was in a car accident and was strangled by her scarf. I had to close up both stores. We packed everything up, shut down the stores . . . I was in shock.

> *Anne Moses:* Why didn't I spend more time with her? She was unique on many levels. And she just died way too young.

Genie touched a lot of people. Jack Nitzsche wrote her a song, "I'll Bet She Knew It." And Jack Bruce paid tribute in the title of his next album *Songs for a Tailor*. She was such a life force, and then . . . she just disappeared. It was a surreal passing, and it seemed to ring the death knell for the whole scene. The Strip had turned coarse and tough, the scene edgy and dangerous. Flower children grew into scores of runaways doing hard drugs and turning tricks to stay alive while unsavory types moved in to sell it to them or profit in some other way. Kids slept all over the street and washed in the fountain at Doheny. Susie and Vito's son Godot died in a tragic fall from a roof during a party. David Cassidy moved to the East Coast. The landscape was changing. Maybe it was time for me to go, too.

Only Sherry remained constant. She was the person I held close in the darkness. Together, we built our own refuge and locked out the rest of the world. And we were about to take off on the trip of our young lives—six weeks in Europe with a group of kids from Rexford and two Catholic schools. We were counting the days.

If It's Tuesday, This Must Be Belgium

We flew from L.A. to Amsterdam. Most of the Rexford kids headed straight for the coffee houses, where it was legal to smoke and purchase pot. The Rexford kids got stoned and quietly appreciated the city. The Catholic school kids got so drunk and rowdy that some of them were kicked out of the hotel. We were there a quick two days before we took a ferry to London. By the second or third day, it was apparent that our L.A. travel agent had been duped. Their European contacts promised decent accommodations and breakfast, but in London, our hotels were fleabags and the food slop. Some kids, like Monica Mancini, daughter of composer Henry Mancini, bailed right there and went home. To make matters worse, I was pick-pocketed in Soho—my passport, my money, everything. "Hello, Dad?"

July 17—August 29

In Paris, things got worse. The food provided for us was terrible, inedible. What a scam. We'd paid for decent hotels, but had been booked in dumps in dicey neighborhoods. Someone pocketed the difference. Sherry and I stuck it out and, in a few days, the tour guide was replaced. From then on, everything was great.

We left Paris by bus and crossed into Switzerland. At the border, the guards reached up to the bus windows for our passports. When he got to me, he looked at it, then back at me. He smiled and said, "Woof! Woof!"

Italy was amazing and the food was GREAT! Sherry and I left the group and got a hotel room on our own for a few days, a pension three flights up. It was cheap and clean and we loved it. It had cold running water in the room. If we wanted hot water, we had to drop coins in a box on the wall. We saw the sites, strolled the Via Veneto, and picnicked in the shadow of the Coliseum on bread, cheese, and a bottle of wine. It was absolutely an idyllic time for two people in love.

August 1969 We sailed to Athens and a beautiful Greek island, where I fell asleep on the beach and got badly burned. When we returned to Italy, we learned about a gruesome murder back home in Beverly Hills. Five people, including actress Sharon Tate, famed men's hair stylist Jay Sebring, and coffee heiress Abigail Folger, had been slaughtered at the hilltop home Sharon rented with her husband, Roman Polanski, who was in London at the time. The entire Hollywood community was paralyzed with shock and fear. The scene was getting darker still. A much smaller story was the three-day music festival in upstate New York in a place called Woodstock. Our tour headed for Venice.

> Sherry: I bought him this beautiful gold ring in Venice. It was $50 or something, a lot of money at the time. It was like two people making love on this gold ring. They took us to some resort on the Mediterranean. We went swimming and there was oil in the water and the ring fell off. I was broken-hearted; that was like his wedding ring.

I was heartbroken too. The ring was beautiful, and Italy had been so special for us. Everyone in our group pitched in, diving for it, but no one could turn it up.

Our remaining days were spent in Austria and Germany, where the Catholic school kids, up to their usual antics, were tossed from another hotel before we reached the end.

Limbo Lower Now

September 1969 And then it was over. Sherry and I were back in Beverly Hills, more in love than ever. I'd let my hair grow and grown a goatee. Mom walked right past me in the airport. When she realized it was me, she burst into tears. Poor Mom. I returned to West L.A. City College while Sherry went back to Rexford for her senior year. After a few weeks, Sherry told me she was worried. She'd missed her period; she thought she was pregnant. We had spent so many hours dreaming of what it would be like to share a life together, raise children. I loved her so much, but we were too young to get married and have children. I hadn't even lived on my own yet. The choice was gut-wrenching. And on top of that, I was famous. This is exactly what happened to Tommy and Darlene Rettig—nineteen and seventeen with a baby on the way. It would embarrass our families and wreck my image. And Mom, forget about it. A baby right now would ruin our lives.

Sherry: I thought I was. I think maybe I played it up for drama, I don't know. Maybe there was a part of me that wanted to get married right then and have kids.

I didn't know where to turn. Our family didn't talk. I couldn't turn to anyone there, not even Fran who was pregnant herself. Sherry's family was also out. Jody knew something about abortions in Mexico, but that sounded terrifying. The clock was ticking, and we had no solution. It was all I thought of. I couldn't concentrate in class. I cried. I had no appetite and tossed and turned all night. Depression dogged me and I had fleeting thoughts of suicide. And then, suddenly . . . Sherry got her period. Looking back, I think this was a turning point for her. In February, Sherry graduated from Rexford and, despite my pleading, left immediately for Sonoma State, north of San Francisco.

December 1969

15: Fran and Bruce have a son, Michael.

31: *Computer* released in theaters

Sherry: I just wanted to get away from my family more than anything and I needed to get out of town. My family situation was not very good at all.

I had to complete another semester in Los Angeles before I could transfer up north. The wait was killing me. I could feel Sherry slipping away from me little by little, but I didn't know why. I flew up every weekend I could. Back then, the midnight shuttle on PSA to San Francisco was just $10. I wrote her almost every day.

Fran and her family.

Letter dated March 2: You should have seen the rainbow today— real nice with you at one end and me at the other and all the cities and miles between us. Oh, how I wish all that wasn't between us because I want to hold you in my arms and sleep with you. God, I can't wait until Easter vacation, can you?

As for the business, I was completely disillusioned. I looked around at my peers. Some, struggling to remain in the business, grew bitter and resentful, Tommy Rettig, for one, Sal for another. Others seemed empty, soulless, and just helpless to function on their own. I knew that look in their eyes. I had seen it in my own from time to time, and it scared the hell out of me. From my earliest memory, I had been told where to stand, what to say, how to feel, what to wear, when to get up in the morning.

A voice in my head kept telling me that if I didn't get out of Hollywood and get out now, I might never have an original thought my whole life long. I'd heard this voice before; it had saved me a number of times. Call it my intuition, my instinct, my guardian angel—whatever it was, it was right. If I was ever going to find out who I was, I had to get out. Around this time, I had an incredibly symbolic dream I described in another letter to Sherry.

> I was in Saks [Fifth Avenue] up the block from home, and this salesgirl started telling me about their candles. She said they were getting in some candles with messages in them; as they burned down, you could read them.
>
> Then I saw Jesse White, you know, the actor, and he and I went for a walk. He gave me his cigar. I took a couple of puffs of it. Suddenly, I heard my name being called from a loud speaker; it was my mom in a police car.

I didn't have to burn out to get the message. Mom in a cop car said it all. And I didn't have to think about where I would go; I'd go to Sherry. But first, I had to work. Sherry had work too. She'd gone for an audition at MGM and, while there, was spotted by director Roger Vadim. She got a part in his new film, *Pretty Maids All in a Row*, and shot it over the summer.

June 7, 1970

The Ash Grove burned in a second fire. Caught and convicted of arson were a group of Cubans organized by the Nixon White House as part of a plan to control radicals. Sound familiar? In a few years, the whole world would know Nixon sent a group of Cubans to the Watergate Hotel. Davy Jones hiding Abbie Hoffman and Jerry

Rubin was more dangerous than I realized. It could easily have been fatal. A favorite slogan of the times: "Just because you're paranoid doesn't mean they're not out to get you."

In August, Don Jaye arranged for Gary Merrill and me to fly into the Gulf Coast for the premiere of *The Secret of the Sacred Forest.*

Mid-June to mid-July 1970
Frontier Land
Parents travel to Finland,
  Russia, Poland
**Mid-July to mid-August
1970**
Six Gun Territory
Premiere of *Secret of the
  Sacred Forest* in Biloxi,
  Mississippi

Ray Zollen, fan: It was less than a year after Hurricane Camille, one of the most powerful and devastating hurricanes to ever hit the Gulf Coast. So, you have this Hollywood premiere with Jon Provost and Gary Merrill coming less than a year after this big event blew away most of the Gulf Coast and it was a big deal. There never was another movie premiere there before or since.

They wanted to have entertainment before the movie. Don Jaye knew my band. We'd recorded a couple of our own records and had been really popular along the Gulf Coast for a couple of years, but this was an opportunity for us to play at "a big event." It was exciting.

There were also a few familiar faces from my days in Bay St. Louis on *This Property.*

Belinda Meyer Marcum and Linda Lewis: Linda and I went to see it at the Saenger Theater on the first day. We met up with Jon and he remembered us and invited us to come over to the Buena Vista Hotel. We sat and talked in his room for quite a while, and it was like being with a dear old friend again. He had grown a little beard, and we thought he looked so mature. He really made us feel important to him.

Part of the legacy of being Timmy Martin is that I have friends wherever I go. About this time, I met President Secarno of Indonesia and President Anwar Sadat of Egypt in Beverly Hills, a tremendous honor. Nearly fifteen years later, I met Sadat's daughter, Camille, at a TV station in Detroit. We chatted and she told me that the first Western show Egypt got was *Lassie.* I have also been told it was the only Western show allowed in the Soviet Union because *Lassie* showed no violence or capitalism.

Leaving Los Angeles

Finally, I moved to Sonoma County and Sherry.

Dad: One of Jon's friends influenced him to go north. He moved to Cotati and continued his studies in special education at Sonoma State.

One of my "friends"—Sherry was the love of my young life. My parents showed such a lack of involvement on any kind of emotional or personal level. Mom seemed only to care about the work and Dad didn't seem to care much at all. Feelings were never discussed. Advice was not given. I packed up my car and I drove away. When I left L.A., I left completely. I didn't speak to my parents for a year. I didn't call them and they didn't call me.

Cecile: Jon had been manipulated by all of us, but he was too young to know then. He was trained, almost like Lassie, to do as he was told. . . . He didn't let me go up to enroll with him. We never went to that college one time. He didn't invite us. I told him if at college he wanted to go on an interview to call me or Lola Moore. She called him, but he wouldn't come back.

Fran: I've always found it strange that he packed up and left . . . because he was the one to her, the one she gave twenty-four hours a day to his whole life. And he couldn't wait to cut those apron strings.

Lloyd Nelson: He was just a kid; he didn't have anything else. His career was his life. It's a trade-off. How many kids would have liked to have had his experience . . . and have been as good at it as he was? I hope he's happy now.

Jon Shepodd: You never retire from show business; there's no such thing. I fully understand Jon moving north, because you can get lost in all that soup.

Stan: Almost everybody at some point—because our show went so long—ended up doing a guest spot, but Jon was never on our show. I think I said something to our producer about getting Jon on. Somebody said that he wasn't doing this stuff anymore. I remember hearing

Jon say he was out of the business and was doing something real. He wasn't pink slipped; he chose the right moment to walk out.

It was really important to me to leave while I was still being offered work, but the work itself was no longer important. Things had changed. I had a personal life now . . . and it was in trouble.

Bye Bye, Love

Sherry: I think two years was the extent of my intimacy range . . . my ability to commit. I had an affair up at Sonoma before he got up there. He knew about it. This was a guy I knew from high school, from Beverly High. I didn't talk to anybody there. I didn't meet anybody. I was really withdrawn.

Sherry pushed me away almost from the moment I arrived. I moved in with her, but after I settled in at school, she pushed me to get a place of my own. I moved into another apartment in her small building, and we continued to see each other, but she saw other guys, too. I agonized whenever I saw a guy go inside her place. She'd made the break from home and everything that reminded her of it . . . which included me. I fought desperately to hold us together.

We still did things together off and on. Close to Thanksgiving, we planned to attend an antiwar demonstration in Sacramento. We decided it would be easier to catch a ride with another student than to drive. We got a ride part of the way and figured we'd hitchhike the rest of the way, a common mode of transportation amongst the peace and love generation as well as the Beats before them. Besides, it was the middle of the day; what could happen? Right away, a truck driver stopped for us. He said he was headed for Reno and offered to drop us in Sacramento. We climbed in the cab and hit the road. After a while, he told us he needed to check his load and pulled off at a deserted brake check stop. He removed a heavy metal bar from behind his seat and proceeded to walk slowly and deliberately around his vehicle, hitting the tires and the restraints holding the load with this heavy bar. We could hear his footsteps and then a loud thud as he hit the truck with the bar. Then he returned to us. He pointed to the back of the cab where there was a bed and spoke calmly as he twisted and pulled on the heavy metal bar, striking the palm of his left hand with it over and over in a threatening manner. "I'm taking her back there," he said. "I won't hurt her. I'll even pay you, but you're not going to do anything about it. Then I'll take you the rest of the way." I jumped to the ground and pulled Sherry out. The trucker flipped us the finger, pulled away, and left us . . . two little hippie kids on the side of a desolate stretch of freeway. By sheer luck, the CHP came by and we were able to flag them down. We told them our story, but they took one look at my long hair, tie-dyed t-shirt, and overalls and elbowed each other. The first major intersection we got to, they turned us out. We asked if they'd make a call for us. "There's a phone out here somewhere. You two are on your own." Everybody thought hippies were disposable. Our three-hour drive to a peace rally had turned into a nightmare. Seems like everything we touched these days turned bad. The darkness had come for us now. Our glory days, when all we needed was to be together, were gone; and try as I might, I could not get them back.

Breaking up with Sherry had much bigger implications than the end of my most significant relationship. Without her, what would I do? She was the reason I came up here, why I chose Sonoma State. All my plans included her. I had no plans without her. The thought was paralyzing. I was not ready to face those questions, to do the hard work and self-exploration. Instead, I held on, hoping she'd come back.

Midnight Dip

Turns out my brother was also trying to hold on, but none of us saw it coming. We were all caught up in our individual dramas—all of us kids anyway; Mom and Dad never had drama. Besides, William was so closed down. Just about the time he reached puberty, a time to explore your identity, he had one thrust upon him: Jon Provost's brother. Not only that, he'd been robbed of his own birthright; the firstborn son's ranking had been stripped. He'd dutifully ridden that gypsy cart from one home to another, one school to another, to Arkansas and back. Just when he'd made friends in one place, we'd moved to another. No wonder he'd quit so many colleges. He didn't know how to stay in a place for more than a few years. And more, he had trouble sustaining friendships for much longer than that. He never had to, just as he never had to plan a future more than two years out. Sure, when he got older there were perks to being Jon Provost's brother: good parties, free tickets, a few trips; but in the end, it's a lousy trade for a strong sense of self. So when I left L.A., William lost his identity completely.

Paul Petersen: When a sibling is famous, it upsets everything. One of the many side effects is that the other siblings become famous without their permission; another is that they have a much higher suicide rate than "normal" siblings . . . especially the older ones.

I was already aware that the relationship between Jon and his brother was strained because William was just straightforward: he didn't like his brother. He resented him, and it was manifestly apparent to a person like me who was living with that myself. I've had to struggle with that with my own siblings. William would never say that, oh, God, no! Everything was fine. Everything was lovely. No hard feelings. No anything; and it's all bullshit. I can remember saying to William, "How can you say that? Telling me Jon's success didn't affect you? Come on!"

William: Part of being a vagabond, being moved around a lot, must be similar to those with parents in the military never putting down roots, but basically everything revolved around Jon and his career. After a while, you think maybe you don't have a whole lot of control over what's going on. At that time, I was old enough to be living by myself, had a job, had school, but at the same time, it felt like I didn't have any control over this; it controls me. So, I just went with it. I think it's something that a lot of people go through. You try and find yourself, try to find where you fit into the big picture. At the time, I didn't have a steady relationship; I worked at a television repair shop. That was where I got the money to buy the car.

I was real upset one night. I'd probably been drinking. I drove my car, a 1967 Toronado, to Malibu, down the Pacific Coast Highway to Sunset Boulevard. I drove down Sunset to the beach and parked. I spent quite a while looking out into the water. Then I just floored it and drove the car straight into the ocean. I kept my foot down until it went into the water and stopped. The Sheriff came, took me in, and called my parents to come get me and get the car out of the ocean. That was a comedy of errors. The tow truck went down there and tried to pull the

car out and it got stuck. Then they had to get another tow truck to get the other one out.

Could William have died? Sure, he could have. Was it a suicide attempt? I'd say more of a loud cry for help. He didn't know how to get anyone's attention any other way.

William: It was a shock to all of us when we found out Fran was going to get married at such a young age. I probably knew a little more then most people because she confided in me. That was her way of taking control and getting out from under the family and what was going on; whereas I never made that move. Jon did the same thing when he moved away. Something inside him said, "It's now or never," and that was his way of getting out. I kept searching for something, I guess, just sort of wandered.

Fran: It was so dysfunctional and I don't think my father ever saw it. He just wore blinders. My mother wore the pants in the family. My father didn't have any more say-so than I did or William or Jon. He was just another child in the family. She controlled my father the way she controlled Jon, the way she controlled William, the way she controlled me, and the way she's controlled all of her friends and little groups. It's what you can do for Cecile, not what Cecile can do for you. That was my *brother's* career; but it was my *mother's* decision. I never, ever have a thought, even a fleeting flash through my mind, that Jon was responsible for any of it. My mother made the decisions in the family.

Mom held the reins, no doubt. And if Mom was controlled by fame, then it follows that fame controlled us. I had no knowledge of what happened to William. My parents hadn't called since I left home, and it wasn't something he wanted to talk about. Fran had her own worries. She and Bruce were having big problems. And I was losing Sherry.

1971

After the holidays, Sherry dropped out of school and moved back to L.A. I certainly knew it was coming. In some ways, it was a relief. The "other shoe" had finally dropped. And for the first time ever, I was alone. Also for the first time, most people knew me as Jon. Whenever someone said, "Hey, you look just like that kid from

Lassie," I'd keep walking and say, "You know, I hear that all the time." I believed I could fit into a normal life. When in Rome . . .

Sherry's apartment was upstairs and bigger than mine, so I took it after she left. I was enjoying school. I'd made a few friends. The area was glorious—the rocky coastline, the redwood forests and the hillsides studded with enormous oaks hundreds of years old. It reminded me of the San Fernando Valley when I was a kid. There was nothing for me in L.A., no reason to go back. I decided to stay.

A New Chapter

Adrianne Conflenti Neri: On Jon's 21st birthday, I brought our cake over—the last one we made for him—and his Mom had piles of U.S. Savings Bonds on the kitchen table. We helped her put the different denominations into stacks so Jon could go to the bank to cash them in. It was pretty unbelievable!

March 12, 1971

I returned home for the big day, which included a trip to court to collect that portion of all my salaries reserved for me under the Coogan Law. The bonds are what my parents additionally put away from appearances; at least that's how I think it went. How ironic that my father, who is a prodigious record keeper, kept no financial records of the money I earned. And among all the press clippings and magazines, publicity photos and letters saved, I have never found one contract. I'll never know what I earned before taxes, agent fees, and expenses were removed. All I knew of finance was the small allowance I'd received over the years. I was never told anything about my earnings or investments made on my behalf. I knew things that were midlife crisis stuff and was more advanced than the average guy my age, but I'd missed a lot of the basics my friends knew.

Many newspapers reported that I became a millionaire on my twenty-first birthday, but that wasn't even close. My portion of my earnings, the sum total for eighteen and half years of work—my childhood—was about $150,000. No question, in 1971 that was a lot of money, certainly more than I'd ever seen before; but I was not set for life. I received one check for the whole amount. My parents did not give me one word of advice. They never suggested that I buy a house and

rent it like they had done all those years and I never knew Mom bought and sold properties throughout her life until much later on. I think Dad suggested I take an economics class at school.

Paul Petersen: Can you think of a worse time to get your money? You work your whole life with this carrot dangled in front of you: At twenty-one, you get your money. And there are your parents saying "Be responsible." You just spent ten or fifteen years being responsible! Now you want to play!

That summed up how I felt in a nutshell. And I was ready to play. I'd noticed a pretty strawberry blonde who lived in a chicken coop on the property. Most of the old ranches had chicken coops, big structures for hundreds of hens. People in the area converted them to living quarters. Sarah shared her coop with a roommate. The owners also built little houses in unique shapes and sizes further back on the property. In a short time, Sarah and I were living together in one of them.

Sarah was a student, into modern dance, an artist type. She was quiet. We didn't go out much. We loved to camp and to explore the coast. She was into weaving, and I bought her an enormous loom, which we put in the second bedroom. We drank a lot of wine and smoked a lot of pot and just kicked back. I had no income to speak of, an occasional residual check, but it wasn't a real concern. Something would come up; it always did.

Meanwhile, things began to click for William in my absence. He got a job with Pacific Telephone—Pac Bell now—where he's been now for over thirty-five years. Within less than a year, he'd bought his first home and settled in with a beautiful lady named Sonia. They went to night school together and William got his bachelor's and eventually his master's degree. I was glad for him. There were rumblings with Fran and Bruce, but two toddlers can put a strain on the best of marriages. For the most part, the three of us were content. Mom and Dad took off for Yugoslavia.

A great guy moved into the apartment building on the property about that time, Arnie Cohen. He and I loved to cook and usually threw something on the barbeque once a week. We hitchhiked to school together, went canoeing, traveled, and best of all, he had no clue who I was.

Arnie: I didn't find out until quite a bit later, and I just laughed. "You're THAT guy? Timmy with a ponytail?" I thought it was great, but it didn't make any difference. Jon was very guarded. Trust was a big issue. People wanted to be friends with him for the wrong reasons. He had to be careful.

Close Call

Late one afternoon, while Sarah was at the market, I sat watching the news when I noticed a car across the street with the hood up. Two guys about my age, college students, were scratching their heads and looking around. One of them started toward the house. He asked if he could use my phone to call a tow truck and I said yes. The moment he came inside, I knew I'd made a mistake.

As he moved toward the phone, his friend walked to the door. He saw my three large aquariums of tropical fish and asked if he could go look at them. I said it would be all right, and he stepped toward them, behind me. In the next second, he grabbed my ponytail, yanked my head back, and put a knife to my throat. His friend dropped the phone and came over. "We want money, drugs, and jewelry." My beagle, Barney, brought his chewy over and dropped it at their feet, not exactly Lassie.

"There's fifty dollars in my wallet on the table. I don't have much jewelry, and I've got a little bit of pot in the bedroom." They pulled me in and pushed me toward the bed. "Lay down," he said, the knife still at my throat. His partner started to rip the room apart, then stopped and asked me where the stuff was. I told him. I prayed that now that they had what they wanted, they wouldn't kill me. One quick slice with that knife and I was a dead man. His partner took the goods and went outside to bring the car around. Then I heard a horn honking. The guy holding the knife told me not to move until they pulled away and he walked out. Instantly, I grabbed a pistol from my nightstand, only inches away the whole time. I got to my front door as he was sliding into the car. "Hold it!" I screamed. The pair turned white when they saw me, gun drawn, aiming for the driver. They ducked and the driver floored it. They disappeared in a cloud of dust. I went inside and threw up. We moved out quickly after.

June 1972 — Mom and Dad bought a beautiful French Normandy apartment house with four two-bedroom apartments on Sycamore Avenue.

November 1972
Parents visit five countries in South America

Former Star of *Lassie* Busted

December 1972 — *Darlene:* Tom never did any drugs on the set. He never even smoked cigarettes until he was eighteen, but during the time we ran our production company, Tom started smoking grass most of the time; for years he did that.

We had a beautiful farm; I loved that farm. We had the best time there because it was away from the city and the things that kept him in that realm. Out there, I really thought we were going to make it. If we could have made it on the farm, I believe we'd still be married and he'd be alive today.

It was in the last week of December. We had been down in L.A. with the boys, visiting family and exchanging Christmas gifts; we hadn't even unpacked. It was about 6:00 a.m. and we were all asleep. There was a loud knock at the door, then the door opened and police stormed in. They came right into our bedroom. I wasn't wearing anything, and they did let me put on a robe. They searched the house; we didn't have anything in the house. They went out to the small house, and that's where Tom had put about six pot plants before we left. They were spindly and pathetic-looking because of the freak frost that had taken place just before we left for L.A.

One newspaper said we had ninety acres of marijuana. We only *owned* fifty acres. All the plants loosely fit into two shopping bags.

The IRS came about three days later and took our tractors, our car, and every penny we had, including money the boys received as Christmas gifts. They charged us with $350,000.00 in taxes. In the end, it turned out they owed us $2,200.00. We never did recover financially and lost the farm, so I guess they won anyway. That totally hurt Tom and me. That was the beginning of the end of us.

June [Lockhart] was the first one to call us and ask if there was anything she could do. Jan was in New York at the time, but June found out and was THE first person to call. I was so impressed by that—what a wonderful woman. We only saw her at different functions, we weren't close, so it was very touching.

Roger Nakagawa: I remember hearing about the *Lassie* boy's drug bust and thought it was Jon. This is the first I heard that it was NOT Jon.

I was on my way home from Reno with Arnie when I heard the story over the radio: "Former star of *Lassie* arrested for cultivation of marijuana." A lot of people besides Roger thought it was me. Mom and Dad called to make sure it wasn't. I couldn't imagine the nightmare of it all for Tom and Darlene with two little kids. Most of the charges were dropped, and some minor fine was paid. Only some of their items were returned. And the story of the mistaken charges? Of Tommy's reprieve? Back page of the paper in an article just two inches high.

Strangers in a Strange Land

Weeks drifted into months and Sarah and I had been together more than a year. One day, I looked over at her and said, "We're going nowhere." She'd been feeling it, too. Our romance had run its course. We simply called it quits. No fights, no angry words, no real emotion, it was just over; she moved out.

1973

I was still at Sonoma State part-time, not taking a full load, majoring in psychology with a minor in special ed. I was living off my money, trying to generate some income. I made clocks with my friend Stephen Cohen, replicas of Regulator wall clocks. Steve's business started out slow, grew quickly . . . then slowed down again. I had a lot of time to do nothing. I loved having no set schedule, not having to be anywhere. Once I didn't shower for almost a week. It's almost as if I needed to do a complete 180 from my life in L.A., not just stop living like that, but vigorously push it away. I'd lost touch with Ron and Mike. I barely saw any of my old friends from L.A., just GAS and Sjimmy, his Dutch girl-friend he'd met aboard the *Orient Express*.

Bruce Dzieza, friend: Jon was lost. It wasn't uncommon for people our age to feel that way. It's a time in your life when you try to figure out what you will do. The difficult thing for Jon was that he already had done all this stuff . . . so, now what? He was coming from a completely different reality than ours. He didn't know what to do, but he knew he did not want to go back to Hollywood. He hated being recognized and was always self-effacing.

I have to say, it wasn't a great time to look for work. There was a recession going on. There weren't a lot of great jobs. I owned a denim clothing store and I was making great money—$200 a week. I encouraged Jon to work there. I encouraged anything he wanted to do.

I dated some nice women, including Cory, a college student who danced in a topless bar. She floated in and out of my life for years and gave me one of the best dogs I ever had, a black lab named Bess. And I dated Cathy, a cute girl who worked for Bruce. She was sweet, positive, easy to be with. We had fun together.

Cathy Jones Brazil: Jon and I dated for six or seven months. We just clicked. Bruce told me who Jon was, but it didn't really impress me; I mean, that's not what attracted me to him. I just thought he was cute. I liked his personality. He told me he used to write Jon Bion on his checks so no one would recognize him. He wasn't stuck up and never bragged about himself ever.

He lived in this really neat house he rented, like an old cabin but parts had been added on. It had a river in back in a wooded area, built-in Doughboy pool. We sat by the pool and played Pablo Cruise all day, hung out, smoked pot, played with Bess; that was a way of life back then. He lived a simple life, reclusive, a homebody.

Bruce Dzieza: He always picked quiet girls, always. Jon was a real homebody. I think a lot of the reason for that was because he hated being recognized. It was easier to stay home. And he was a little guy. He felt vulnerable, especially after the robbery. He felt his fame attracted those guys. Why else would they think someone in that funky little house had a lot of money? Quiet women, quiet life . . . no ripples. I think it was Jon trying to get real. He had cut his ties to the business and was trying to lead "a normal life." Once, on his birthday, I was there when he got a call. I remember jerking my head around because he started talking in a different voice—his actor voice. It was June Lockhart calling to wish him a happy day.

Cathy Jones Brazil: He'd go to L.A. for a week at Christmas or something, and he'd come back different; it used to bug me. I sort of felt like he got it all back in his blood again, just caught up in that whole L.A. fast life thing, maybe hopeful, not the down-to-earth person I knew in Santa Rosa. It would take him another week to become grounded again.

Jack Wrather Jr.—Jackie—was William's age and just five days from his twenty-ninth birthday when he died. A child of divorce with more money shoved at him than love, guidance, or discipline, he never found his place in the world. Mom had shoved Fran at him; fortunately, they didn't click. Jack eloped in 1962 with a different sixteen-year-old, Lana Wood, Natalie's sister.

> *May 4, 1973*

Lana: Jack was a very troubled boy. He attached himself to me and was quite handsome and dashing to a sixteen-year-old. He was volatile, abusive, and demanding . . . but seemingly lost. Unfortunately, he found another lost soul in me. We came back from Tijuana and moved in with Natalie in her house on Summit Ridge. He was very sweet and kind at times, proclaiming undying love; other times, he beat me. My parents had the marriage annulled after about six weeks.

> **December 1973**
> 8: William and Sonia marry.

Years after the annulment, he came to see me at my apartment and asked to borrow money. I finally gave in. Shortly afterward I was informed that he had committed suicide.

Looking back at seven years on *Lassie*, it was hard to distinguish year four from year six unless something special happened. Now one year up north seemed to be blending into the next without much change. I had never been the one to make things happen,

> *1974*

August 1974
President Nixon resigns.

a self-starter. I didn't know how to do that. I remained in school part-time, still no regular income. Cathy eventually moved on. I still saw Cory . . . and others came and went.

Bruce Dzieza: The women always left Jon; Jon would never be the one to leave . . . no ripples.

Gidget Wipes Out

1975

April 1975
Vietnam War ends.

Fran and Bruce hit a wall. Trouble had been brewing for a while, but this time, Bruce moved out. They had been together close to half Fran's life. She had two little kids. Initially, she was devastated and stayed in bed for days, a week, depressed, distraught. Mom thought Fran was silly, overly dramatic. She didn't understand a woman being so upset over a man.

More Trouble for Tommy

Tommy Rettig was in trouble again, serious trouble, accused of a felony for conspiracy to smuggle cocaine.

Darlene: Tom got this brilliant idea for a documentary: because cocaine was so big, he was going to go into this place in South America and watch them make cocaine and tell how they smuggle it in.

He took a trip to South America with this guy named Cliff, a smuggler, and when he got back, he was acting really paranoid. He said people were following him. This goes on for about a month, then one morning I'm washing my hair over the tub and the phone rings. I see Tom running past the door. A few minutes later, I hear all this banging. When I look up, there is a man with a shotgun pointed at me. I wrap a towel around me and my hair and ask what's going on? It was the DEA on a drug bust. They were at our home—without a search warrant—for sixteen hours. When they couldn't find any cocaine, they decided they needed an arrest warrant to take us to jail.

This really was the lowest, saddest time in my life. I also lost a great deal of respect for our law enforcement at that time. What were they trying to prove? After sixteen hours of tearing someone's home apart, wouldn't you think you would find something? They just didn't want to look like jerks or get sued.

Because they did not find any cocaine in our home, they arrested him on conspiracy to smuggle cocaine. This is the thought of smuggling, not the act of smuggling—a charge you cannot prove either way. It was a mess. Jan Clayton testified, but since the DEA has more pull, guess who won? The conviction was finally overturned. It still dragged Tom's name through the court. He got off, but it cost a lot of money. And what do they say? "Oh, gee, sorry." There's no retraction, nothing. I was just devastated because of the children, so upset. I didn't want to be in that element anymore. When I was thirty, I came out of the ether and left Tom.

The Thrilla in Manila

I was happy to see Fran bounce back. She'd been dating actor Hugh O'Brien, and the two of them flew to the Philippines for the Mohammad Ali/Joe Frazier fight—fourteen edge-of-your-seat rounds. Ferdinand and Imelda Marcos were there too, but by 1975, the country was under Martial Law, so no trips to the palace for Fran. The bout is ranked as one of the greatest fights of twentieth century boxing. Shortly after Ali was declared the winner, he fainted on the canvas. It was great to hear Fran so excited agin. She'd been through a rough time.

October 1, 1975

Late in the year, after trying to reach her for several weeks without success, I called Mom. "Oh, Fran's in the hospital. She has been for almost a month. She almost died." No one had thought to call me. My sister was diagnosed with something called mal-absorption syndrome. Her body was unable to absorb any nutrients from food or drink taken by mouth. She was literally withering away. They fed her intravenously which worked while they tried to get to the cause. All told, she spent fifty-eight days in the hospital. During that time, Michelle lived with Mom and Dad and Michael with his best friend's family. As soon as she was well enough to go home, I closed up my house and lived with her in L.A. for a few weeks, nursing her back to health.

November 1975

Dad: What do you do when the kids grow up and move away? What do you do with three empty bedrooms? After a period of thinking things over, and since the real estate market was up, Cecile and I concluded we should sell the Beverly Hills house and move into one of our apartments. And that is what happened.

February 1976
Sal Mineo murdered.

Sal, still trying for a comeback, hoped his appearance in a play would draw some attention. He made the headlines, but not the way he expected. On February 12, as he returned from rehearsal to his West Hollywood apartment, neighbors heard his terrified screams. They found him lying on the concrete, his chest covered in blood. He had been stabbed repeatedly during a fierce struggle. Despite efforts to save him, Sal died as paramedics were arriving. He was thirty-seven years old.

I guess I woke up to the news the next morning like everyone else. I hadn't spoken to Sal in at least five years; nonetheless, it was stunning news. But it was not surprising. The darkness enveloped him.

Susan: I think my husband and I were off in Mexico traveling and he told me Sal got killed. He died a very tragic and horrible death. That point in his life was absolutely bleak. I was devastated. He had been a big part of my life. But it was another part of my life. And I look back on it all and laugh. We did have a lot of laughs. Christine and I are still best friends today, thirty-odd years later. Elliot kind of went his way. Don and I ran into each other at a wedding a couple of years ago, but basically that whole crowd kind of dissipated. Jon moved away and I never really did know what happened to him.

Two years later, Lionel Ray Williams, serving time for forgery, bragged to his cellmate about murdering Sal as a random target, a "thrill kill," and was convicted.

Love's Labors ...

May 1976

Arnie graduated college and his first job was teaching special needs kids in Marin. Almost all Down Syndrome children were labeled "trainable mentally retarded" back then. Arnie needed a teacher's aide and offered me the position. I took a semester off, my last semester of college, to get this hands-on experience.

I loved the work with Arnie and I loved my kids, but I loved them too much. Each and every one climbed into my heart. After a full day, I was wrung out, absolutely drained. Some days I could barely make the hourlong drive home, I was so wiped out. Arnie warned me I was too emotionally invested in each child, that I'd never make it in this field being so emotional. I knew that already.

One spring day, I made the drive back from Marin to Santa Rosa and pulled into Montgomery Village for a quick errand. Shops lined both sides of the street with parking on either side. I pulled up and ran in a store. Five minutes later, I hopped back in my car and backed into the street. Bang! I'd just collided with destiny. Sandy Goosens, a petite brunette, handed me her license and we exchanged information . . . and had dinner together that night. A few months later, she moved in.

Sandy and I had few problems, but employment was always an issue. I had confidence, but not in that area and for a lot of reasons. I was very self-conscious about my reading and spelling. I couldn't do anything that involved typing. I'd studied special ed. only to discover I wasn't suited to it as a career. And though I only had a semester left at college before I graduated, it seemed pointless now. I never went back. So . . . now what? I had no idea. Add to that, no matter what I choose to do, I would probably never achieve the success I'd already had. That was a daunting mantle to carry out into the world.

1977

Then there's the actual looking. I had never looked for my own employment. I had an agent, a manager, and Mom to do that. I didn't know how to "sell myself." I'd never filled out a job application before. Actors are really helpless that way. And when I did get an interview, inevitably, they'd ask, "What are you doing here? Tell a story about *Lassie*," and then, "Thanks for coming in." I didn't know how to say, "I need a job." They thought I was a millionaire and didn't really need to work. The reality was I hadn't done anything right with my money. When I bought cars, I paid cash for the full amount; that's what Dad always did. I didn't build my credit. I didn't invest in anything. I was still renting. And even though I had not lived extravagantly, I had lived comfortably and my savings were rapidly dwindling.

Mike McGreevey: It was harder for me to become an adult than an ordinary kid. As a child actor, everything is provided for you and you come to just expect things to go smoothly. I was unprepared to be assertive or aggressive. Then as an adult, suddenly I had to pursue my career. That was a difficult concept for me—to go get it. I had to learn how to do that. Being a working child actor was the biggest contributing factor to that lag in my development.

Lag is an understatement. But while I stalled, my sister and Bruce were able to find their way back to one another. On November 26, 1977, Fran and Bruce married for the third and final time in All Saints Episcopal Church in Beverly Hills.

I'd been living with Sandy for close to two years and was typically content to keep on keeping on, but she was growing increasingly frustrated with my non-committal attitude. Her identical twin sister, Sue, was already married and Sandy was anxious to do the same. Finally, she issued an ultimatum: we get married or she moves on. All my life, my major moves had been decided for me; only one had been my decision alone—leaving *Lassie*. Sandy gave me the push I needed. I loved her. I wanted to spend the rest of my life with her, have a family together. We announced our engagement and picked a date. I bought the house we were living in with what was left of my savings, but because I hadn't established credit and didn't have regular employment, my father had to cosign the papers.

August 4, 1979 Sandy and I were married in a small wedding for family and friends. William, Fran, and family traveled north for the occasion. Mom and Dad toured Scandinavia, Holland, and Germany, returning just in time to attend. I didn't invite anyone else from L.A. Arnie, Bruce Dzieza, and another good friend, Ken Wiseman, stood up for me. It was a beautiful day to begin the rest of my life.

Jack Wrather created a flap when he obtained

a court order prohibiting Clayton Moore from making appearances as the Lone Ranger wearing his trademark mask. Wrather was planning a film version of the story and—get this—did not want the value of the character being undercut by Mr. Moore's frequent personal appearances. To millions of fans the world over, Clayton Moore will always be the Lone Ranger. He played him with honor and dignity and conducted his personal life in the same fashion. To unmask the Masked Man, to show such disrespect to a beloved childhood hero, was unconscionable. After having had his finger on the pulse of the entertainment world, how could Mr. Wrather now be so out of touch? He won his suit temporarily, but created a public relations disaster. The public responded loud and clear. In 1981, the movie flopped and, in '84, Mr. Moore countersued and got the court order lifted. Years earlier, Jack Wrather had said, "It's a case of a man with a mask and you can always find one of those." How wrong he was.

In 1981, Bruce Dzieza opened Willow Creek Properties, a real estate office, and thought I might enjoy the work. He encouraged me to get my license. I really needed something. We were expecting our first child. I threw myself into classes, studied, passed the test, and went to work for Bruce. Right out of the box, I sold my first listing. Things started off so well, but it was a bad time for the market, with double-digit interest rates. And for someone who had been told what to do from earliest memory, a job without structure was not the best job for me. I didn't know how to direct myself. It was a constant struggle and I lost more than I won.

September 1, 1978

February 1980
After months of problems, William and Sonia separate.
Mom and Dad join the Pacific Shell Club, then travel to the Balkans: Greece, Turkey, Bulgaria, Romania, East Berlin.
July 1980
My father discovers the broken remains of the last of the Northrup N9M Flying Wing test models in Chino. He begins a dream of restoring it and the long process to make it happen.
December 1980
8: John Lennon is murdered in New York. Hearts break around the world, mine included.

Lost

From the beginning of the pregnancy, Sandy felt something wasn't right. She complained for months, but after running tests, our doctors in Santa Rosa assured us everything was normal. Now, near the end of her second trimester, she was convinced something was wrong. Our doctor sent us into the city to the University of San Francisco's medical center for blood tests. The tests confirmed Sandy's feelings; there was something wrong. Doctors urged us to have an amniocentesis. It was very dangerous, but necessary, they felt. The results came back. When they said they wanted us to come in, we knew it was bad.

In the office, we held hands as we got the devastating news. Our baby had a multitude of problems, problems with such long names for such a little being. We cried as they told us they did not believe the baby would make it through to full term and if, by some miracle, it did, would never survive outside the womb. The only good news was that it was a once-in-a-lifetime thing. We should have no problems having children in the future. We made an appointment to have labor induced.

I was not allowed to be in the room with Sandy, but her mother, who had been a nurse, was with her. We had agreed not to see our baby; the doctors told us it would be better that way. It was a devastating loss.

Once More with Feeling

May 1982
Parents go to the Peoples Republic of China
September 1982
19: 34th annual Emmy Awards, Pasadena Civic Auditorium

Tom Rettig Jr.: They had the two Lassie families present at the Emmys, and my brother and I got to go with my dad. He had gone backstage and Deane and I were in the audience. Jon walked down the aisle, came up to me, and said, "Tommy? Jon Provost!" I said, "Oh, Jon, it's so good to see you!" And he thought I was my dad! I was shocked! I couldn't believe it. I don't know if I look older or my dad has always looked young, so . . . it was very funny.

I am still embarrassed about that. I can't believe I did it. Young Tom looked exactly the way I remembered Tommy. Of course, I knew it couldn't be him and yet, for a minute . . . time stood still.

Show hosts John Forsythe and Marlo Thomas welcomed the audience, then introduced us as the first presenters for the evening. The warm welcome was a memorable moment. June, Jan, Tommy, and me, Lassie with Rudd out in front—we all presented the first two awards of the evening and we had a blast.

What a reunion. I would remember it, too, because it was the last time I saw Jan.

More Dog Heroes

Something very significant happened to me this year. An organization in Santa Rosa called CCI, Canine Companions for Independence, contacted me to participate in an annual fundraiser for them called Celebrity Chef. I'd seen their assistance dogs around town, but I didn't know much about them. I learned that they supply highly trained service dogs at no cost to people with all kinds of disabilities (except the blind who have their own guide dog program). I thought what they did was great and I love to cook, so I accepted the invitation. The event was big, with dozens of local celebrities: radio personalities, the sheriff, the mayor, award-winning wine country chefs, as well as a dozen local wineries pouring. It was good people and a lot of fun; so when they invited me to attend one of their graduations a month or so later, I accepted.

1983

At the graduation, recipients receive their dogs, all golden retrievers or labs, and during the ceremony I learned the long and difficult journey from puppy to service dog. Volunteers care for breeder dogs and their pups. Then the pups are placed with volunteer raisers. These people take the dogs with them everywhere: in the car, on the bus or plane, to work, to the theater, grocery shopping—anywhere their future owners might need to go. And, of course, they love them. After a year and a half, the dogs go to one of the CCI centers for a program of advanced training by professional instructors; not all the dogs will make the final cut. Human candidates are matched with dogs and together, they undergo two weeks of intensive Team Training.

The dogs become incredible, devoted companions, performing up to fifty commands and giving someone a full life out there in the world. There were speeches and a slide show, and I was incredibly moved. Then came the moment when the puppy raiser symbolically turns over the leash to the new owner. After a few steps, they look back at that dog they loved, the dog looks back

Canine Companions for Independence is a non-profit organization that enhances the lives of people with disabilities by providing highly trained assistance dogs and ongoing support to ensure quality partnerships.

Learn about CCI dogs and graduates at www.cci.org

Reach us direct at: info@cci.org 1-800-572-BARK (2275)

August 1983
William and Sonia had gone back and forth for three years; in the end, they split for good.
28: Jan Clayton dies of cancer at sixty-six.

at them . . . and then, with a wag of his tail, he sits with his new owner. There wasn't a dry eye in the house. I was hooked.

As I got more and more involved with CCI, I was asked to join their local board of governors, on which I've proudly served for over two decades. Recently, I was made an Honorary National Board member.

The Circle of Life

The good news was that we were expecting again and everything was normal. Sandy felt confident that all was well. We relaxed, went to birthing classes, and enjoyed the exciting and happy time.

January 26, 1984
Sandy woke me around 3:00 a.m. and said she thought it was time. In a fog, I told her to go back to sleep. We did for a while, but two hours later, we headed to the hospital. We chose the Leboyer Method, with dim lights and soft voices. The labor was uncomplicated and brief. At 9:17 a.m., our son, Ryan Jonathan, was born. I squeezed Sandy's hand as the doctor held him up. "Hey!' he said. "He looks just like Don Knotts!" We looked . . . and he was right! Ryan looked exactly like Barney Fife. We laughed and cried and I cut the umbilical cord. He had ten fingers and ten toes and everything was in working order. He was a miracle and all was right in our world.

November 1984
12: Jack Wrather dies at sixty-six of cancer.
It was really important to me for Rudd to meet my son. He was as close to a grandfather as I ever had, and though our communication had been spotty over the years, our love for one another never waned. On one of the trips down to L.A. with Ryan, we went out to the ranch and I proudly placed my son in his arms, Lassie by our side. The circle was complete.

February 25, 1985
Sadly, Rudd died at age seventy-seven just months later. I rushed to L.A. as soon as I heard the news. I stayed with Mom and Dad but went to the funeral with my sister. The first person to approach me was a gray-haired gentleman with a beard who threw his arms around me. I hugged him back and took my seat with Fran.

"Who was that guy?" I asked her. "Jon, don't you recognize your own father?" It was Hugh! I hadn't seen him for almost twenty years, and the white hair and beard threw me. I looked around the room. We had all come together: June, Hugh, Sam Williamson, Frank Inn, Lloyd Nelson, Darlene and Tommy.

> *Darlene:* Tom and I went to Rudd's funeral together, even though we were divorced. Tom spoke at the funeral. He was *very* emotional. He had needed a father figure, and I'm glad it was Rudd. It's a good thing it happened to him. It kept him grounded during the short time they worked together and it provided an anchor for him for the rest of his life.

> **In Loving Memory of**
> **Rudd B. Weatherwax**
> BORN
> Sept. 23, 1907, New Mexico
> PASSED AWAY
> Feb. 25, 1985, Mission Hills, Calif.
> SERVICES
> Friday, March 1, 1985, 1:00 p.m.
> Pierce Brothers Little Country Chapel
> EULOGYS
> Tommy Rettig
> Frank Inn
> GRAVESIDE SERVICES
> Fr. Sebastian Meyer
> INTERMENT
> Valhalla Memorial Park
> DIRECTORS
> Pierce Brothers Valhalla Mortuary

We lost another beloved member of the *Lassie* family. George Chandler died three weeks shy of eighty-seven.

June 10, 1987

William had been romancing his recently divorced next-door neighbor, Hetty. They married in July. Her two young girls gave him an instant family, and William was a devoted stepdad. But just four months later, Hetty went back to her first husband, the girls' father. Deeply hurt, lonelier than ever, William sold his house and moved in with Fran and Bruce . . . a gypsy once again.

Mom and Dad bought their last home on North Detroit Street. Naturally, Mom got another amazing deal on the duplex and, after several months of renovations by Dad, they moved in.

Sandy and I also moved to a new house, one with three bedrooms to make room for our daughter due the first of the year.

Katherine (Katie) Amelia was born at 7:30 a.m. She, too, had all fingers and toes and, thankfully, did not look like Don Knotts. She was pink and gorgeous like a little doll. Our family was complete.

January 11, 1986

> **October 1988**
> 11: Bonita Granville Wrather dies at sixty-six of cancer.

Dad continued to work on restoring the prototype of Northrop's Flying Wing, the only one not destroyed. It was a labor of love, and he was interviewed on television about it a number of times. He got quite a kick out of seeing himself on the tube; so did I. In the summer, the BBC of Australia came out to do a piece on it. I am so proud of my father's contribution to aeronautics.

The Smithsonian

I was thrilled to receive a letter from the Smithsonian telling me of their plans for a History of Television exhibit. They very much wanted to include something from me and asked if I had anything to contribute. I called Mom. "I've got it all, your whole out-fit." And she did: the red-and-white check shirt, pair of blue jeans, and my high-top tennis shoes.

Jeanne Russell: The minute he pulled it out of the box and smelled it, he nearly swooned; it was like he was back there. He had this over-whelming sense memory. He told me what it was like to open the box, to touch and feel and smell it.

Jeanne's right, it was a complete rush of emotion to see it again. I'd been running from that check shirt for years. Now, it was an old friend. My son, Ryan, begged me for the high-top sneakers, but I had to say no. The outfit was packed up and shipped off.

Dad: Oh! What fun we had in Washington, DC. The Smithsonian Insti-tute invited Jon to come to the opening festivities of the first historic display of TV. Sandy went and Cecile, William, and I met them in Bethesda, where we stayed for three days. We were given very special treatment at the museum.

The opening of the exhibition itself was a seminal moment for me. The room was filled with people excitedly talking, pointing at items on display. Each piece evoked a special memory for people, and emotions poured forth. I moved through the room as the crowd did, ooohing and aaahing, and then I saw it—my outfit, displayed with photos of me in it, hanging between the Fonz's leather jacket and Archie Bunker's chair.

Wow. If I had not gotten the big picture before—the impact I had as Timmy—I got it now.

The New Lassie

Laurie Ackerman called me when she heard there was going to be a new *Lassie* show. "Maybe there's something there for you," Laurie said. "Call them." A soundstage sounded pretty good to me right then. Things were rough at home. Maybe this would help ease some tension.

May 1989

Arnie volunteered to act as my agent. He got in touch with the producer, Al Burton, and told him I'd like to be involved, even if it was in some sort of advisory capacity.

Al Burton: I am a wild dog lover and I loved the idea of working with that dog.

I thought of Dee [Wallace Stone] immediately because she'd be a star name, she's a perfect mother, and I thought she was contemporary, as opposed to say *The Waltons,* which was old-fashioned. I called Dee, and the only way she would agree to do it was if I found something for her husband, Chris. So I found something for him—and it worked out very well. We were very happy with that.

Dee Wallace: Lassie is a part of our culture. It is more than a word and it is more than a dog. It's literally part of our childhood. The show was an incredibly wonderful time in my life. I had just had my daughter after six years of trying, and Chris and I shared a humongous trailer. Al and everybody would give me time before and after lunch with her, and we were always finished by six at night; we never had overtime. I felt like I was doing good material with lovely people that were kind and generous, and I got to work with the person I loved every day. How much more could you ask for? As an actor, those things don't come along very often. Al was just a master creator.

Al: I was a fan of the old *Lassie* and very familiar with Jon's work from the time he was a little tyke. Somebody told me that Jon would like to do it if it came back on, and I called him. We immediately constructed a part that would be the uncle of the boy and girl. We designed the part for him and he was terrific from day one.

Al Burton was a small man with a huge résumé. Not only did he co-develop one of my favorite shows, *Mary Hartman, Mary Hartman,* but he also developed *Facts of Life, One Day at a Time, Diff'rent Strokes, The Jeffersons, Silver Spoons,* and *Square Pegs.* He had a great mind and a great talent for working with kids. I was anxious to see who he'd chosen for the next "Lassie boy." His search extended to almost seven hundred boys, which he'd painstakingly narrowed down to four.

Will Estes: There were six callbacks, so I knew I was getting close, because that was a record number of callbacks for me at that point. I felt like a veteran at the time. I'd done a bunch of commercials and I'd been acting for a year—a long time for a ten-year-old. I'd only gone on two or three callbacks before, so I knew that six was really something. Finally, they brought the dog in with Robert Weatherwax. I had grown up with dogs my whole life and really liked dogs a lot. Maybe some of the other kids were afraid of dogs and that's why I got the job, but I got it.

Will Nipper won the role. Today, he's known as Will Estes. And so there's no confusion, his character was named Will McCullough. Wendy Cox had been cast as his sister, Megan.

Paul Petersen: Al Burton was really concerned about how the children were treated. He thought that many mistakes had been made in the old show, and he didn't want to repeat those mistakes. I think he understands that the producers who employed us came out with the money and watched these kids kill themselves. These adult men, because of economic pressures, continued to exploit us, but when the game was over, they realized what they'd done. I know Al Burton was very sensitive to this whole thing with the new show.

Will Estes: I've heard horror stories where they wouldn't let kids run so they wouldn't get hurt and mess up production. Al Burton was so cool. He'd let me ride my bike around, in between takes. I'd jump in and out of these scenes, and in between I'd do my work and play so it really was a wonderful experience.

Wendy and I were in the same schoolroom together. We had two teachers at one point and later just one who was capable of doing all of it. We could bank hours . . . do four one day and two the next . . . but for it to count, it had to be at least twenty minutes. For most of the time there, my tutor was a great guy, really smart man. I probably learned more from him than I did from some of my regular teachers. I didn't feel shorted at all. I loved the way Al Burton ran that whole show.

Wendy Cox Hagen: Oh, I loved them all to death. They were like second family. I respect Dee so much as an actor. She's consistent, so talented. Just being able to work with her and having her helping me, that was just phenomenal; so is she.

Chris was really protective of me. It's so funny looking back now as an adult, because I didn't realize when I was a teenager, but some of the clothes they put me in were real tight, or just not . . . not conservative. And I didn't think twice about it. Chris would be like, "What is she wearing? What are those shorts?" you know, like a dad. And Dee would say, "Oh honey, relax!" But now, when I look back I think, "Oh, my gosh, he was right; I shouldn't have been wearing those shorts!"

Once, we were shooting a scene where Dee and Chris were going out to a fancy dinner or party or something, and they were all dressed up. We're sending them off, and Jon was there babysitting for Will and me. We say, "Have a good time!" And Dee pulls a condom out of her purse, looks right into the camera, and says, "And a safe one!" They just did that for the dailys. They were always doing little funny things like that.

Will: I watched quite a few episodes of Jon in his series, so when he came on the set, I recognized him. He was a cool presence; just to have him there made the show that we were doing somehow feel much more credible and genuine. I was just so pleased he was so nice to me and open to talking to me about his experiences.

Wendy: When Jon came on the set, I yelled, "Oh my God! It's Timmy with a mustache." Those blue eyes, so blue—and he didn't get a lot taller!—just such a nice guy, real upbeat, loving spirit, friendly, down-to-earth, fun.

We shot each episode in three days, no rehearsal. I appeared as Uncle Steve in every fifth episode and was away from home one week a month. I was still in real estate, so I could make my own schedule. Working on the show was better than I imagined . . . driving onto the Universal Studios lot, past the familiar guard gate, walking through the corridor of soundstages, grabbing lunch in the commissary. But nothing prepared me for stepping back onto a soundstage. You know how you catch a whiff of bread baking or maybe it's apple pie or pot roast—something that makes you say, "Smells just like Grandma's house." When I walked onto the stage and breathed deeply, I was home.

> *Al:* The thing that I most remember about Jon was how absolutely terrific he was with the boy who was playing the part he had played. Will Estes was, at the time, ten and eleven, and he thought Jon was the greatest. We'd made sure that he'd seen all Jon's *Lassie*s and he'd handled the part of the boy so well, and then he was so kind and so interested in helping Will that it made Will's job a lot easier and I've always thanked Jon for that.

> *Dee Wallace:* I just remember, truthfully, Jon as being a really available, loving, open-hearted person, earnestly wanting to make things work. He just kind of moved into the family heart of the group. His essence as a man and as a person, how he was with the kids—there just wasn't any room not to like Jon.

Al came up with a great idea to bring back other stars of *Lassie* from over the years, giving me the great opportunity to work with some old friends.

> *Dee:* That was all Al's idea, oh yes, "mister always looking for an opportunity for publicity." He's a master at it! You gotta hand it to him. We were incredibly thrilled with the choices.

> *Al:* I prided myself on the fact that I personally wanted to get all those people together and we really did succeed. We got June back; we got Roddy back. We had Gale Gordon, Patty McCormack. I had a lot of fun getting those people.

Tommy and I did one episode together. By this time, Tom had rebuilt his life and discovered he was a genius with computers. He wrote books, created a remarkable program, and lectured around the world. It was quite a comeback. We had always kept in touch, and I often made a point of getting together with him when I dropped down to L.A. Working with him again was a great treat. He cowrote the episode as well and, naturally, the storyline had to do with computers.

Tom, Will, and me: the "Lassie boys."

Deane Rettig: My dad was playing a professor who was Jeff Miller grown up, and he'd come up with this computer study for dogs. Jon and his nephew, Will, entered Lassie in the study. She didn't really perform well with the mouse, at least that was part of the plot; but when a fire actually occurred in the building, the other dog didn't click on the fire alarm. Lassie clicked on the fire alarm and saved everybody. Typical story—either dog saves boy, boy saves dog, or they both save everyone else. It was pretty cool, too, seeing Dad and Jon together.

Al Burton: When I first called Roddy, he absolutely did not want to do it and I asked if there was anything that would make him want to do it and he said, "Well, I always wanted to play a blind man." So he helped me construct the story of him being blind. We reached a lot for storylines to accommodate everybody.

With Roddy McDowall and Will.

Roddy McDowall: The extraordinary thing for me in relation to Lassie as a fellow performer was that I really related to the dog as if it was another human being. And of all the animals I've ever worked with, that is the most human one I have ever encountered.

I was really pleased to work with Roddy. To me, he was classic Hollywood, a real legend . . . the original "Lassie boy." Refined, charming, and so warm, Roddy was everyone's favorite. A talented photographer, when he wasn't working he was unobtrusively weaving his way through the set behind the lens of his own camera.

Naturally, June did an episode too, playing a woman who has discovered papers that make her Lassie's legal owner. She comes to the house to claim her dog and suddenly recognizes me. "Timmy?"

"Mom?" In a convoluted story, Ruth and Paul Martin couldn't take Timmy with them to Australia because they had never legally adopted him so they left him behind! Needless to say, Timmy was pretty upset, so upset that when he was adopted by the McCullough family, he changed his name from Timmy Martin to Steve McCullough. It was hard enough to believe Timmy would leave Lassie, but Ruth and Paul leave Timmy? Those fans who could follow the twisted tale didn't buy it. Sadly, it was just one of the problems with the writing. Bob Weatherwax and I went to Al and told him the stories moved too fast, were too complicated, took on too much. Simple stories were what worked for *Lassie*. Al asked us to come up with some story ideas, and I came back a few weeks later with five story lines. The one he liked centered around the inhuman treatment of research animals. I'm proud to say I received a Genesis

Bob and Lassie on the set.

Award for Outstanding Television in a Family Series for it. But story changes came too late for the show. Much to my disappointment, it was cancelled after the second season.

Will Estes: It's very cool to have worked with all of them. . . . I'm not sure if I knew what *legacy* really meant at that age, but I had a blast doing it, and yes, in some ways, in roundabout ways, I think I did feel the history of it.

Al Burton: I loved being on the set; there was nothing like it. I've always said it was my favorite show to do because of the animals. We had plot lines going with another dog, rabbits, and all kinds of good things like that. And Jon was always very helpful and added great good cheer to the set. He was a fun guy. I tried to include him in something we did after *Lassie* because we liked him so much as a person and I didn't sell anything that was apropos for Jon being in the cast or he would have ended up with another role.

The Well

"Success is the necessary misfortune of life, but it is only to the very unfortunate that it comes early."

ANTHONY TROLLOPE, ENGLISH NOVELIST, 1862

Rusty Hamer, child star, committed suicide. Rusty costarred on *Make Room for Daddy* for eleven years, but when he hit his awkward teens, the job offers evaporated. Aimless, bitter, with few job skills, he traveled the states working odd jobs. Deeply depressed and flat broke, a raging alcoholic, he spiraled into a violent and delusional state. At forty-two, he shot himself. I'd only met him once or twice, and I have to say, I didn't like him much. He was a bully; however, his inability to assimilate into society after his Hollywood career ended, his feelings of inadequacy and depression, his tendency to self-medicate with alcohol and drugs—these were all issues I could relate to, common threads in the lives of all kid actors.

January 18, 1990

Rusty's death came eight years to the day after the suicide-by-hanging death of child actor Trent Lehman, twenty, of *Nanny and the Professor* and just four months after the drug overdose of former child actor Tim Hovey, forty-four, best-remembered in *The Private War of Major Benson.*

> Paul Petersen: What people don't understand is there are long-term, life-threatening consequences to early fame, even more so in adolescence, when you most want your privacy to figure out who you are. This business lavishes great attention on children and turns its back on them when they're no longer useful. It's brutal. Any child actor will know that moment when someone says: "Didn't you used to be somebody?" Or, worse: "I used to love you."
>
> I knew each of these young men. I knew where they lived; I knew they were in trouble, but I failed to show up at their doors. And I promised my wife, Rana, the day after Rusty's suicide that that would never happen again.

Hamer, Lehman, and Hovey weren't the only former kid stars who were in serious emotional or financial trouble at the time. Todd Bridges from *Diff'rent Strokes* was in jail on attempted murder charges; Todd's costar, Dana Plato, was naked in *Playboy*; Drew Barrymore's autobiography detailing drug and alcohol addiction at age ten, eleven, and twelve was set to hit the stands; Danny Bonaduce from *The Partridge Family* had been fired from another radio job for drug use; Gary Coleman was about to sue his parents and management team; and, finally, Jay North, who played *Dennis the Menace*, was on a course to commit violence.

Jay North: I was so angry at the people in Hollywood who hadn't lifted a finger to help me when they knew I was in trouble. I just wanted to line them up, get an Uzi, and mow them all down.

Stan Livingston: A lot of the people really enjoyed being in the limelight. It's nice and it has its time and place, but when you're not on the show and you're slipping out of the limelight, the question becomes whether you can deal with that as a real person. I think a lot of people have a difficult time with that and they end up doing outlandish things to get themselves back into the limelight, things that have nothing to do with their career or regenerating their career. In our day and era, in Robert Mitchum's day and era, everybody goes through their own thing in their own time. If you're caught drunk driving or with marijuana, it's fodder for the tabloids. You always want to make sure that doesn't happen to your friends unless they want it to.

Paul wasn't exempt. He had a trunk full of personal problems, too, including alcohol, drugs, and a couple of marriages. He attributes his problems, in part, to "the result of diminishing fame and a loss of focus." At the time Rusty died, Paul was writing a book, his seventeenth—an examination of child stars and the consequences of early fame. He put the manuscript in a drawer and put the title on a new organization: A Minor Consideration.

In 1991, Paul got sober and A Minor Consideration got going, with the help of Rana Platz-Petersen, RN, then president of Studio First Aid. Jeanne Russell came on board pretty fast. I was really flattered when Paul called me to get involved, flattered . . . and relieved. I had some great friends in Santa Rosa, but there's something about the fraternity of kid actors. They can be from different generations, it doesn't matter;

we all had a similar experience which only we intimately know. We know what makes us "different" from "civilian" kids. I realized I was starved for the contact.

Davy Jones: It's like the Mafia; once you're in, you're in.

Jeanne Russell: When I look back on the hub of my childhood, the warmest fuzziest center of my childhood, it's that apartment on Fernwood; it's Cecile and Jon coming over, the smell of the makeup, the sounds of the soundstage that eclipses even my earliest memories of Christmas lights and tinsel. It defined my world and who I am, rather than the kids in first grade or the kids in kindergarten or the kids on the street. That vaudevillian troupe, tribelike feel—it's just sort of like a family. I feel like Jon and I are from the same planet.

Keith Thibodeaux: It's just automatic when you see other child stars when you're older, there's an immediate bond. And it doesn't matter who you are; it's almost like you're in the army together. You're there in the army and you understand the rules and you understand the life and you understand the problems and the heartaches and the things that come along with it.

Stan Livingston: I was fortunate in that my show ran until I was in my twenties. I realized that these actors on these shows that got lopped off when they were fourteen or fifteen had a hard time getting work or worked sporadically from that point on. You'd only work on a show where there was another kid, so there would already be a teacher there; or they would hire someone that was eighteen and you wouldn't get the job. Almost all the girls that played my girlfriends when I was fifteen and sixteen were eighteen already.

The day after your series stops—even if you're number one—the guard at the gate you waved to everyday can't let you back on the lot. You start feeling yourself edged out. That's why we feel like kindred spirits, because we know everybody that's done what we've done has gone through that metamorphoses—the realization that maybe "I'm not needed anymore" or that you're living on your past laurels as a performer. "What am I going to do to keep my career going? Get a new career? How do I reinvent myself?"

Jeanne: It wasn't until I realized that it was up to me to survive after show business, that I realized this could go either way. I could be embittered and turn this wonderful experience inside out on itself and hate it or I could embrace the memory, be grateful that I was one of the chosen, and get the hell on with my life.

These revelations were long in coming for all of us and all hard won. When Paul Petersen's career crashed and burned, it was former child star Mickey Rooney who went to him and told him to get out of town. "The industry is not going to help you." That's all there was for a kid star in trouble in terms of advice—another kid star reaching out. Most, like me, felt isolated, alone out there in the "real world." We had no one to talk to about how we felt, no one who could grasp what it had been like. I barely had anything in common with most people. I hadn't done sports, or Scouts, or camp. I hadn't worked in a store or office. My schooling was entirely different, and I have no high school reunions. I was always the oddity in the room, almost like having two heads.

Paul Petersen: Adults were mystified by what us kids went through, this phenomenon of being a child star.

Plus, there was a major difference between child stars of the silver screen and TV kids. People saw us differently. They didn't have to drive to a theater and pay to see us like they did to see Shirley Temple. We came to them, into their homes, right into their living rooms week after week; and later, in reruns, every day. They knew us intimately. When fans saw a movie star, most stood back, mouths open; but a TV star was like an old friend. People had grown up with us, and they weren't afraid to approach. They talked to us or shouted out their opinions when they saw us in person, in a restaurant or on the street. I was even asked for my autograph once while standing at a urinal. There were no boundaries. You're always "on."

Tragically, some of us never find our way out. I had three things going for me that other kids stars didn't: Everyone loved *Lassie,* and I am always greeted warmly and with affection; I wrote my own pink slip. I wasn't edged out or pushed out or tossed aside. I left while work was still being offered with my self-esteem intact; and there's my family.

As dysfunctional as it was, as much as Mom pushed me and booked me and separated me from everyone else, she never let me live a privileged life.

Ron Howard's parents, McGreevey's parents were in the business . . . they understood the business, knew what pitfalls to avoid, knew there *were* pitfalls. People like my mother didn't even know what an agent was, much less a pitfall, and didn't have anyone to ask about it. Lola Moore sure wasn't going to tell her, not as long as I was earning money for her. As Jeanne said, Mom was a pioneer.

Sea of Love

Dad: As the summer of '91 approached, I said to Cecile, "We have talked about having a big celebration for our fiftieth anniversary next year, but it will be the same old thing: champagne, music, eating, etc. What do you think about a nice cruise for our family?" And that's what we did! We celebrated our forty-ninth wedding anniversary on a Caribbean cruise in July of 1991. There were eleven of us, including: William, Fran, Bruce, Michelle, Michael, Jon, Sandy, Katie, and Ryan.

1991

Vivien: Both B.A. and Cecile spotted me and told William I was the most vivacious girl on the cruise and he should try to meet me. It wasn't until the cruise was over that I met him along with B.A. and Cecile. I just happened to get on the same bus going back to the airport and William turned around and introduced himself and his mom and dad. As they say the rest is history!

Dad: At our fiftieth anniversary party, Fran gave a great talk, had everybody crying. And Bill is the business type. He called us Bion and Cecile, never did call us Momma and Daddy. Jon had everybody laughing. You know what this character said? "Everybody's talking about how great this couple is to be married fifty years . . . what do you think of a couple who would turn their kid out to work at two and a half?!" Everyone laughed so hard.

July 19, 1992

Within months, Dad would celebrate again when the Northrop Flying Wing prototype he'd worked on was ready for a test flight. He and a small crew had worked on it almost every Saturday for eleven years. Dad had spent years tracking down the original team of men who built it, including the original test pilot. When famed test pilot Chuck Yeager heard about their plan to test the Flying Wing, he wanted in, but the team turned him down and let the original pilot take the wheel. You can see it today at air shows around the country and at its home at the Planes of Fame Museum in Chino, California.

Coming to an End

1993

My family meant everything to me. I fought for it, fought to save it as best as I knew how, but Sandy and I were in trouble, real trouble. There were problems on both sides, and neither one of us knew how to fix them. We did the best we could, but in the end, our marriage failed. She took the kids and moved out.

Ryan: I came over one day and Dad was sitting on the floor in the back hallway, leaning up against the wall and just sobbing. I'd never seen him crying like that and I was scared and so sad. The divorce was really, really hard on me.

Arnie: I was very worried about Jon. He was really hurting. It was a huge loss.

September 1993

I was scrambling for work. I could only see my kids on weekends, so selling real estate was out. I worked for a time in a hardware store. Somehow, by osmosis, I'd absorbed a lot of information from Dad. I knew my way around tools and household repairs. Things started looking up in the fall. I was offered a job at a title escrow company. I was to start when I returned from Germany! A talk show in Cologne invited me on the show and offered a first class ticket and accommodations for four days. I really wanted to share that with my son and, using a little trick I learned from Mom, I asked if I could exchange the first class ticket for two business class tickets. Ryan and I spent three full days touring Cologne and sailing the Rhine. It was a ball and a great lift to my spirit. It didn't last long.

My divorce was final. I came home from a weekend personal appearance and Sandy had cleared out the rest of her things, most of our furniture, even our bed. I knew it was coming, but seeing that empty house and what my life had come to . . . I never felt so wrecked in my entire life.

I spiraled down hard and fast. I drank too much. I binged on ice cream. No matter what I did, the depression never seemed to let up. It was especially bad when I was driving. Going home from work, I'd get this incredible feeling like there was a heavy, heavy weight . . . like a lion or tiger was on my back digging into me, gripping the back of my neck. I envisioned suicide. I could see myself pressing the gas pedal to the floor and aiming straight for an abutment at 100 mph. Only thoughts of my children stopped me.

I was in the deepest darkest well I'd even been in and there was no dog in sight.

Fran: Yeah, it was devastating. He just fell apart. He cried on the phone, and I knew how much he hurt. I had been there before. I remember saying, "Bruce, I just don't think he's going to make it. I think he's going to drink himself into a stupor, get into his car, and drive into a wall." Jon's very emotional. I'm very emotional. My family means everything in the world to me, and I think Jon's family meant everything in the world to him. The divorce was real bad, real bad.

Jeanne: He couldn't understand how this was happening to him, how the mother of his children could do this; and what could possibly be so bad to make someone walk away from their life.

Paul Petersen: The breakup was devastating to Jon. I will never forget the look on his face. It looked like somebody just hit him with a club.

Stan: I saw him at an autograph show and he looked kind of blown away. He seemed really depressed. I sensed something weird was going on and asked what was wrong. He said, "I'm getting divorced . . . and I've got kids . . . and oh, man." What can you say except to offer a shoulder to cry on? Having been through it myself, sometimes you just need to know that somebody's there if they need to talk about it.

These autograph shows were something new, and boy, did they come along at a great time for me. A room full of nostalgic celebrities, together with vendors selling all kinds of Hollywood memorabilia gather for a weekend to meet and talk with fans and sign autographs. If ever there was a time to be with old friends, it was then. And the fans felt just the same way.

> Stan: I got to know Jon again as an adult through these shows; and, with the advent of Nickelodeon, all our careers got rekindled. We got a whole new audience, and we were kind of back in the limelight again, and people wanted to interview us. For TV and radio, they usually had more than one guest, and I would get to see Jon at some of these.

It was a return to the fold. Funny, I spent so many years trying to bury this part of my life; now it felt like coming home. *This* was my high school reunion. I'd never gotten much chance to know them when I was young, but these weekends away with friends in cities around the country gave me the opportunity to know them now as adults. Slowly, but surely, I began to climb out of that well.

Hollywood Ending

February 1, 1994   I received my star on the Hollywood Walk of Fame (Location: 7080 Hollywood Boulevard). My old friend Laurie Ackerman and Mom worked hard gathering signatures to make this happen for me, and it remains one of my proudest days in Hollywood. It was a really special event. Thirty-six years earlier, the Walk of Fame was dedicated and 2200 stars were unveiled on the Boulevard, 1500 with names on them. On this day, a silver gazebo saluting women in film, held aloft by silver likenesses of Mae West, Dorothy Dandridge, Dolores Del Rio, and Anna Mae Wong was unveiled and an additional 150 stars were added between Highland Avenue and La Brea, thirty with names, among them Sophia Loren, Katy Jurado, the Dead End Kids, Efrem Zimbalist Jr., and mine. During the ceremony, we were each presented with a plaque by Hollywood's Honorary Mayor, Johnny Grant, and given a moment to speak to the large crowd. Here is what I said:

This is a pleasure and an honor. I never expected anything like this. I've had a lot of famous mothers in my career—June Lockhart, Grace Kelly, and others, but the most famous of all is my own mother. Without her, I wouldn't be standing here today. I want to thank my fans, my friends and my family.

Jay North: I'm proud that Jon was able to survive what he did, come through it, move on in other areas, and not become a victim of the business. He's never been in the scandal magazines, never the center of controversy. He had inner strength and individuality.

Jay North and Jeanne Russell.

Stan: I admire Jon. He seemed to be a person who dealt with it all as it came along. I never heard Jon complain, never a self-pity, poor me thing. I'm sure he took a beating playing a character like that. People outside the industry have no idea of where you come from or what's been expected of you. Goals in life sometimes aren't totally realized—for everyone—but because we play ours out in the public eye, we always feel like somebody is measuring us, rating us. Why weren't we doing more?

The family.

William and Vivien were married in Malibu.

May 14, 1995

I was sitting next to Stan in the ballroom of a hotel in L.A. talking with fans at an autograph show when a cute redhead stopped to say hello to him. She was signing on the other side of the room, not photos, but books; she wrote books about Hollywood. I never do this, but I had to meet her. I used a reliable move from the old days. I kicked Stan under the table until he introduced us. Her name was Laurie.

January 13, 1996

Laurie: I thought he was adorable. He came over the next night and we talked and talked. I was working on a book about the Strip. We looked at old photos and he told me all about the scene in the '60s—the clubs, a woman named Genie the Tailor and seeing Jimi Hendrix at the Whisky. We had so much fun. When he left, I thought, "Too bad he doesn't live here." Four days later, I got a letter from him saying that our evening felt more like old friends getting together and that was special. "I want to get to know you better and I'm willing to put a great deal of effort into it. Please tell me if you feel the same way or if you don't." I felt the same way.

Thanks for the Dog, Jeff . . .

February 14, 1996   Deane Rettig called me in the early evening. I was pleasantly surprised. I hadn't picked up on the tone in his voice yet. "Jon, I didn't want you to hear it on the radio or TV . . . Dad died." I was blown away. Tommy was gone at just fifty-four.

Deane Rettig: About two months before he died, around Christmas, Tom and I talked about how Dad was deteriorating, destroying his body. We were concerned. Tom went and had a talk with him. Dad realized that, yes, he was driving his body into the ground. He started to try to turn everything around, but his body was so far gone. He had high blood pressure; he had high cholesterol. Dad smoked cigarettes and pot. He drank. He was a bit overweight, but not too heavy. He didn't abuse alcohol or drugs, but he abused his body. He was a computer geek. He got no exercise at all. It was total arterial sclerosis.

My brother called me at work and said, "Dad died." I said, "Yeah, right," thinking he was joking or something, and then I heard him start to cry. Tom was up in the Bay Area. I was in L.A. County, but an hour away from Marina del Rey, where Dad was. I told my boss and he said, "Get going, don't worry about anything." I hopped in my car and started driving. That's when it actually hit me, when I was alone and driving in traffic . . . that's when I just broke down.

There were police there and the medical people . . . some kind of medical examiner. They hadn't moved my dad's body and had me go and identify him before they moved him. He was walking to his bathroom and fell in the hallway between that and the sink and the counter space. He was on his side and his stomach. I couldn't tell if he fell to his knees or if he fell backwards and rolled over. I identified him and waited for them to roll him out. Then he was gone and I was there, and we had to lock up the place.

That night, I called everybody that I felt had any kind of a significant part in my dad's life, Jon being one. Later, I sat at home and went through his entire address book and called people. . . . It was hard, but I wanted everybody who knew him to know about it and anybody that could be at his services to attend. It was packed with computer people, too. It was almost split 50/50 computer friends and Hollywood friends.

Paul Petersen: For the burden he carried—and Jon would know this more intimately than anyone—and the fact that he had a checkered legal past, he did fine. The fact is, he turned his life around in the world of computers before anybody knew anything about it and created a whole new core of friends without losing his old friends.

Bob Weatherwax: Tommy was a major actor when he was young. It's a tough deal. Paul Petersen was out there on the ocean when we were spreading Tommy's ashes. He was on another boat spreading Rusty Hamer's ashes. He knows how it is with that life; and then you grow up and maybe can't make the transition; or in a lot of instances, their money had been spent. That was the real shame. Tommy didn't have any money. Although Tommy ended up very successful before he passed away, the boy worked all his life and ended up not having any money. Besides losing your life to working everyday, not having anything to show for it is a rotten shame.

Darlene: Bob brought Lassie in the boat to scatter Tom's ashes on the ocean . . . we all loved that.

Tom Jr.: When I was cleaning out his apartment, I was surprised to find he was still getting fan mail several times a week. It was just kind of amazing.

Bob Weatherwax: Bill Gates had just hand-picked him for his board. No one knew that, either. He would have been a millionaire at last.

In Loving Memory Of
Thomas Noel Kettig

Born
December 10, 1941
Jackson Heights, NY

Passed Away
February 14, 1996
Marina Del Rey, CA

Memorial Service
Thursday, February 22, 1996
2:00 pm
Marina Del Rey, CA

Private Interment

Darlene: Tom really loved getting into computers. The guy was brilliant. He wrote a book the size of a large dictionary on d-base. He wrote four of those on DOS. Sweden, Holland, Germany, England, he spoke all over the world. When the Gulf War ended, a General wrote to him to say that if it weren't for him, the war might have turned a different way. Apparently, something went wrong with their computers and they called Tom, who was able to fix it. He never even told me or the boys. We found this out through old e-mail files. . . . I'm sorry for Tom because I know he had a terrible childhood. He changed a lot. We went through a lot together. Tommy wasn't the best husband, but he was my best friend.

February 1996
28: Fran is a grandmother! Michelle gives birth to a daughter, Emma Jane.

Deane: It was really a great thing to be his son; it really was. It was a lot of fun.

Laurie

1997

Laurie and I visited each other. We faxed and called and e-mailed, and as the months passed, we fell in love. The first time I told her, it felt great. There had been a time, at the bottom of that well, when I could not imagine ever feeling this way again.

Laurie, being a historian, encouraged me to reconnect with my past. Over the next few years, she helped me track down Lloyd Nelson, Roger Nakagawa, Flip Mark, Mary Badham, even Sherry. One of the first people we visited was Hugh Reilly. I hadn't seen him since Rudd's funeral. We had a wonderful visit, reminiscing and catching up. I told him about autograph shows and eventually persuaded him to do one with me. He was so modest. "Who would care about seeing me?" He found out. Hugh spent a busy day signing autographs and shaking hands, delighted with his fans and their warm memories of his strong, solid work as Paul Martin. He was a great dad, on-screen and off, and a good and kind man. It was a great day.

Over dinner one night with Ryan and Katie, I shared my feelings for Laurie with them. "I'd like to ask her to marry me, but I wanted to make sure that would be OK with you." They both gave her an enthusiastic "thumbs up." On June 12, I proposed to her, and she accepted. Soon afer, she left L.A. for Santa Rosa.

June 1998

Lloyd: [Hugh and I] were always in contact after the show, never lost touch. Cigarettes got him. He was a heavy KOOL smoker, lost his voice. It was tragic, a genuinely nice person.

July 1998
17: Hugh Reilly dies at seventy-two of emphysema.

Laurie picked a beautiful and historic spot for us to be married, high on a hill above Hollywood in a Japanese restaurant called Yamashiro's—mountain palace. On this beautiful spring day, friends and family gathered in a Japanese garden to celebrate our wedding. Ryan served as my best man and William, my groomsman. Laurie chose Katie as her maid of honor and dear friend Patti Propper Aretz as her matron of honor. Our ring bearer was our nephew, Alexander, and our almost flower girl, our grandniece, Emma Jane.

March 28, 1999

Friend and former kid star Johnny Crawford conducted a six-piece 1929 jazz band. Johnny, in a top hat and tails, sang "The Way You Look Tonight" into a large, old-fashioned microphone right out of a Fred Astaire-Ginger Rogers RKO film. My beautiful bride was in heaven. June, the very first person to RSVP when the invitations went out, arrived glowing. Laurie called her her other mother-in-law. "And that's forever, darling," June replied. Jeanne Russell was there and Paul and Stan along with kid stars Brandon Cruz and Larry Mathews and old friends Laurie Ackerman, Bruce Dzieza, and Arnie Cohen. And my family was there. It was a perfect day.

August 1999
22: Michelle and Keith welcome a son, Max.

Mom

2000 | Mom suffered a stroke. She told Laurie, "The reason I'm not bouncing back like people think I should is because I'm older than I say I am." Laurie asked how much older, but Mom just rolled her eyes and said she'd never tell. She never did.

October 11, 2001 | Only Fran was with Mom in the hospital, curled up with her on the bed telling her she loved her when Mom slipped quietly away.

> *Fran*: My mother lived two different lives. She was definitely two people. She got her fame. I think she lost one son, my older brother, William. She lost a daughter, too, in order to get it. She gave her whole life to Jon, and he made her a very, very famous, respected person; that's the way she saw it. She could walk on *The Merv Griffin Show* or any show, strut across that stage, sit down in that chair, and she was Jon Provost's mother. She was a very special person whom a lot of people admired. But, she sold herself.

I know there are many people who would disagree with that. There's no question Mom did a lot of good in this world. She was so generous and giving to kids she never knew and so unavailable to the ones closest to her. It's almost as if she felt she had a bigger cause and we all had to sacrifice to help advance that cause. It was that "cause" Mom devoted her life to, not me; my fame only helped further her dreams. The clubs and charities she presided over raised thousands of dollars. The words *no* and *can't* were not in her vocabulary. She adored Dad, saying over and over, "I got the best one." She was a pioneer and the best mother she knew how to be. Did she make some mistakes? Of course . . . some we may never find out about. Mom was a mystery; and she was nothing short of amazing.

> *William*: I'm a little distant now, as an adult, because of the way I handled it all when I was young—which was to keep moving and seeking something new until I found what I wanted. That is where I am now. I'm happy, and I'm glad things worked out the way they did as far as for me. I do wish at times the whole family was a little closer. On the other

hand, would it be any different if our lives had been different? I don't know.

That's the question, isn't it? What would our lives be like today if I had never been famous, if Mom had never seen Hedda Hopper's column? But we make do with what we are dealt. My sister Fran has a full and happy life with Bruce and their beautiful family. William found true love with Vivien and he and I have walked a long road back to close friendship. My children, Katie and Ryan, continually amaze me. I'm so proud of them. And my wife, Laurie . . . I owe her more than I can ever say.

"Being Timmy" has acted like a universal passport, gaining me immediate entry into hearts around the world. Wherever I am, when people realize I was Timmy, they travel right back in their minds to that warm, happy time where, for thirty minutes every week, they were transported by the adventures of a boy and his dog; and I am greeted with warm smiles, hugs, and even some tears along with many stories about what it all meant to them. And today, I love it. I am proud of my legacy and grateful for the opportunity to have left such a mark. My wife and I continue to correspond with fans around the world—except this time, it really is me; and we've even invited a few to be guests in our home. Somewhere, Mom is smiling.

I could never possibly have imagined what my work would mean to people over the years; or even that *Lassie* would still be on the air in sixty countries fifty years after we made it. Yes, it was hard work; and yes, there have been many wells to climb out of along the way. And yes, I would do it again.

In a Hollywood minute.

With my beagle, Barney.

Epilogue

The day after I met Laurie, I went to her apartment in Beachwood Canyon in the shadow of the famous HOLLYWOOD sign. We talked comfortably and laughed easily. I looked at the things she collected and treasured . . . pieces of Hollywood's rich history. She loved it. It was part of her. It's why she wrote about it, worked in it. I told her I was thinking about writing my autobiography, hoping she'd leap at the chance to guide me through the process. She said she thought it was a great idea, that I should do it, and wished me luck with it. In other words, she brushed me off.

I had to marry her to get her to write it with me. She knows me now possibly better than I know myself and she still loves me. She's devoted to my kids; and she is head-over-heels about our dog, Barney. She tells me I was meant to play second fiddle to a dog my whole life long. That suits me just fine.

Photo Credits

Warner Bros.
3, 6 left, 7

Author's collection
6 right, 7, 9–13, 24, 25, 29, 30 left top, middle far right 32 top, 35, 37, 38, 39, 45 top, 46, 52, 53 middle, bottom, 54, 55 bottom, 57, 60 left, 63 top, 65, 66, 71, 76 right, 78 top, 79, 83, 84 top left, right, 87, 90, 91, 101, 102 bottom, 106 bottom left, 112 middle left, bottom left, middle, right, 117, 118, 121–23, 128 left , 130-4, 136, 140, 142, 144, 148, 150, 156, 159, 161, 162, 165, 167, 173, 177, 178, 181, 184, 185, 187, 189, 193–96 197 top, bottom, 198 middle, 201, 204, 208, 210, 212, 213, 214, 216, 218, 219, 221, 223–25, 233, 235–39, 249, 252, 254, 255, 257–58, 259–61, 265–77, 272, 274–75, 284, 286 right, 289, 290, 296 top, bottom, 301, 305, 308, 309 bottom right, 311 right

Courtesy of Paramount Pictures
15, 198 top, bottom

Courtesy of RKO Pictures
19, 20, 21, 24, 26–28, 30 left bottom, 47 bottom

The Wrather Corp.
32 bottom, 36, 45 bottom, 61 bottom, 62, 76 left

Courtesy of CBS
39, 40, 41, 42, 43, 44, 48, 49, 51, 55 top, middle, 56, 59, 60 right, 61 right, 63 bottom, 72, 73, 78 bottom, 84 left bottom, 93, 98, 99, 100, 102 top, 106 top left, right, 108, 109, 112 top, 116, 119, 127, 128 right, 137, 152–53, 158, 160, 174, 311 left

Robert Weatherwax
53 top, 85

Jeanne and Bryan Russell
107, 120, 126 bottom

Frank Conflenti
118

Stan Livingston
125, 126 top

Paul Petersen
143

Courtesy of *TV Guide*
147

Belinda Marcum
197 bottom

Susan Ladin collection
226, 229–30, 247

Deane Rettig collection
286 left

Courtesy of Al Burton Productions
293, 295, 296 middle

Photos by Steve Kerekes
309 bottom left, middle, top right

Photo by Lori Laube
313 right

Jonas Mohr Photography
313 left

Bibliography

Collins, Ace. *Lassie: A Dog's Life*. New York: Cader Books: Penguin Books, 1993.

Darvi, Andrea. *Pretty Babies: An Insider's Look at the World of the Hollywood Child Star*. New York: McGraw-Hill, 1983.

Mazarakis, Polly. "First Betsy, Then Natalie," *Deep South Magazine*, Vol. 15, #6 Nov/Dec 1965.

Mills, Diane. *TV Times*. Television Publications, Inc., St.Paul, MN Vol. 4, #40 February 15, 1964.

Wood, Lana. *Natalie: A Memoir by Her Sister*. New York: Putnam's, 1984.

Index

A

Aaker, Lee, 39–40, 80, 90

Ackerman, Laurie, 94, 184, 212, 253, 291, 304, 309

Ackerman, Warren, 94

Alberoni, Shari, 184

Alexander, Shana, 60

Ali, Mohammad, 281

Allen, Steve, 240

Allman, Gregg, 217

Altenes, Dan, 66

Ames, Leon, 185

Andes, Keith, 19

Andrews, Julie, 225

Archainbaud, George, 89

Armstrong, Robert, 132

Arnaz, Desi, 33, 68, 125

Arnaz, Desi Jr., 178, 258

Arno, A. J., 259

Aschauer, Ann, 75

Astaire, Fred, 103

B

Bacall, Lauren, 16

Badham, Mary, 187–188, 191–192, 194–195, 199, 200–201, 205–206, 308

Baer, Max Jr., 178

Bakalyan, Dick, 259

Ball, Lucille, 33, 68, 96, 125, 233

Bancroft, Anne, 40

Bankhead, Tallulah, 71

Bard, Rand M., 207

Barkley, Lillian, 80

Barry, Gene, 19

Barrymore, Drew, 298

Beatty, Warren, 201–202

Beaudine, Bill Jr., 33, 69, 73, 78, 97

Beaudine, William, 97–99, 106, 153, 155, 170, 194

Belafonte, Harry, 124

Bendix, William, 14

Benedict, Polly, 32

Benner, Ralph, 208, 209, 220, 241–242, 247, 262

Benny, Jack, 61

Bergen, Edgar, 95

Betz, Carl, 115, 143

Beymer, Richard, 6

Bingenheimer, Rodney, 242

Blake, Robert, 187, 192, 197, 200, 202

Coppola, Francis Ford, 187

Corby, Ellen, 127, 137

Corcoran, Kevin, 95

Corcoran, Noreen, 76

Corey, Stuart, 171, 179

Corrigan, Lloyd, 137, 170

Coville, Janice, 162

Cowsill, Paul, 258

Crane, Jeanne, 117

Crane, Steve, 142

Crawford, Johnny, 152, 309

Crosby, Bing, 14–15, 38, 225

Crosby, David, 224

Cruz, Brandon, 309

Custer, Bob, 220

D

Dana, Bill, 171

Dandridge, Dorothy, 304

Darvi, Andrea, 169, 317

Darwell, Jane, 135, 216

Davis, Ann B., 17

Davis, Bette, 236

De Wilde, Brandon, 14

Dean, James, 225, 248

Del Rio, Dolores, 304

DeMille, Cecil B., 193

Denham, Carl, 132

DeShannon, Jackie, 111

Diamond, Bobby, 152

Dillaway, Dana, 18

Disney, Walt, 34, 107, 258

Dixon, Willie, 223

Dolenz, Micky, 219, 241

Dolloff, Cherrie, 122

Donahue, Ed, 66

Douglas, Donna, 178

Dow, Tony, 130, 178, 208

Dozier, Ann Rutherford, 32–33

Dozier, William, 17, 32, 46, 47

Duke, Patty, 259

Dylan, Bob, 224, 227

Dzieza, Bruce, 278, 280, 284–285, 309

E

Eastwood, Clint, 31, 95

Ebsen, Buddy, 178

Eden, Barbara, 19

Edwards, Blake, 17

Edwards, Vince, 77, 134

Eisenhower, Dwight D., 16, 62

Ekberg, Anita, 19–20

Elgin, Johnny, 15

Estes, Will, 292, 294–296

Ewell, Tom, 93

F

Fabares, Shelley, 80, 130

Farrow, John, 19, 117

Farrow, Lisa, 117

Ferber, Edna, 4–5

Fernandez, Abel, 68–69, 135

Ferrell, Todd, 71–72, 94, 109

Field, Sally, 167

Fields, Jimmy, 131, 160

Finnigan, Joe, 185

Fitzgerald, Geraldine, 64

Flynn, Joe, 259, 261

Folger, Abigail, 223, 264

Foran, Dick, 135

Ford, Tennessee Ernie, 90–91

Forrest, Steve, 6–7

Forsythe, John, 286

Frawley, William, 115

Frazier, Joe, 281

Freeman, Kathleen, 93

G

Gable, Clark, 71

Garland, Judy, 32, 62, 124

Garner, James, 18

Gates, Bill, 307

Genie the Tailor (Jeannie Franklin), 182,
    224–225, 235, 241–243, 249, 255–256,
    262, 306

Gernreich, Rudi, 240

Gish, Lillian, 71

Gobel, George, 167

Gonroski, Cheryl, 233

Goosens, Sandy, 283

Gordon, Barry, 131

Gordon, Gale, 294

Gordon, Susan, 159

Grable, Betty, 62

Grady, Don, 126, 129

Graham, Sheilah, 245

Grant, Johnny, 304

Greene, Lorne, 162

Greene, Ron, 118–119

Griffith, D. W., 98

Guy, Buddy, 223

H

Hagen, Wendy Cox, 292–293

Hale, Alan Jr., 136

Halliburton, Jeanie, 14

Hamer, Rusty, 297, 307

Hanson, Jack, 250

Harlow, Jean, 55

Harrison, Bernie, 133

Hart, Bobby, 258

Hartman, Phil, 222

Hawkins, Ruthel, 234

Hayden, Sterling, 6

Hayes, Helen, 16

Heflin, Van, 40

Hendrix, Jimi, 222, 306

Hepburn, Audrey, 128

Herbert, Charles, 18, 93, 131, 136, 156, 184

Hill, Lonnie, 66

Hilton, Paris, 227

Hines, Connie, 185

Hinsche, Billy, 117, 178, 213

Hoffman, Abbie, 222, 266

Holden, William, 15, 18

Hope, Bob, 15–16, 112, 234

Hopper, Dennis, 95

Hopper, Hedda, 4, 95, 174, 311

Houseman, John, 187, 194

Hovey, Tim, 297

Howard, Ron, 100, 130, 131, 301

Howe, James Wong, 16, 193–194

Hughes, Bill Sr., 153

Hughes, Billy, 81, 126–127, 137, 153

Hughes, Howard, 17, 21, 35

Hughes, Whitey, 97, 152–155

Humphrey, Hubert, 129

Hunter, Jeffery, 95

Hutchings, Ashley, 262

Hutton, Betty, 69

I

Inn, Frank, 43–44, 289

Insley, Darlene Rettig, 40, 87, 111, 114, 124, 155, 233, 265, 276–277, 280, 289, 307–308

J

Jackson, Anne, 71

Janssen, David, 115

Jaye, Don, 189, 217–218, 254, 267

Johns, Glynis, 21

Johnson, Don, 208, 247

Johnson, Erskine, 48

Johnson, Rafer, 146

Johnson, Russell, 93

Jones, Brian, 211, 222

Jones, Davy, 220–222, 224, 241, 254, 266, 299

Jones, Shirley, 213

Joplin, Janis, 252

Jurado, Katy, 304

Juste, Samantha, 241

K

Keach, Stacy, 135

Keaton, Buster, 112, 193

Keeler, Donald, 41, 72

Keeler, Ruby, 41

Kelly, Gene, 142

Kelly, Grace, 14–15, 17, 158, 305

Kennedy, Bobby, 255

Kennedy, Caroline, 160

Kennedy, Jackie, 158

Kennedy, John F., 139, 160

Khan, Sajid, 205, 221, 241, 242, 258

Kiel, Richard, 152

King, Martin Luther Jr., 236, 254

Kirk, Phyllis, 19

Kirk, Tommy, 95, 178

Knight, Ted, 93

Koshikawa, Hideko, 30–31

Koufax, Sandy, 188

Kovacs, Ernie, 112, 193

Kuhn, Grace, 14–15, 17, 74, 77, 114, 134, 158, 173, 305

L

Laine, Frankie, 18

Lamble, Martin, 262

Lancaster, Burt, 212

Landau, Dov, 232

Lay, Beirne Jr., 18

Leachman, Cloris, 49–50, 54, 55, 64, 65, 93, 106

Lear, Norman, 58

Lee, Annabelle, 251

Lehman, Trent, 297

Lennon, John, 227, 285

Lerner, Alan Jay, 41

Lerner, Robert, 41

LeRoy, Mervyn, 18

Lesser, Sol, 34

Lewis, Linda, 197, 267

Lindsay, John, 94

Lindsay, Mark, 241, 244

Mitchell, Cameron, 21–23, 26

Mitchell, Joni, 223

Mitchum, Robert, 39, 298

Mobley, Roger, 131

Monroe, Marilyn, 39

Montecillo, Karen McCoy, 129

Moore, Clayton, 62, 92, 285

Moore, Lola, 5, 13, 34, 62, 72, 82, 268, 301

Moore, Mary Tyler, 93, 170

Morrison, Jim, 222

Morse, Hollingsworth, 109

Moses, Anne, 208–210, 220, 224, 226, 241, 243, 262

Mountford, Diane, 161

Mumy, Bill, 186, 205, 217

Murphy, Harold, 53, 105

N

Nakagawa, Roger, 22, 26, 48, 164, 179, 277, 308

Nelson, Lloyd, 38, 40, 51–55, 63–66, 70, 72, 74–76, 79, 86, 89, 93, 97, 100–103, 106, 112, 114–116, 123, 133, 135, 137–138, 152, 170–171, 173, 240, 268, 289, 308–309

Nelson, Nels, 79, 86, 95

Nelson, Ozzie, 95

Neri, Adrianne Conflenti, 118, 166, 273

Nero, Danny, 90–91

Nhut, Tan Son, 217

Nicol, Simon, 262

Nitzsche, Jack, 262

Niven, David, 16

Nixon, Richard, 95, 108, 280

Nogle, Wally, 53, 114

Normand, Mabel, 98

North, Jay, 41, 81, 94, 119–121, 126, 136, 142, 146–147, 151, 156, 178–182, 205, 212, 216, 240, 249, 258, 264, 298, 305

Novak, Kim, 16, 18

Nyby, Chris, 114

O

O'Brien, Cubby, 184

O'Brien, Hugh, 281

O'Connor, Donald, 62

O'Malley, J. Pat, 93

O'Sullivan, Maureen, 19, 117

Ochs, Phil, 221

Odets, Clifford, 14

Osmond, Ken, 130, 255

P

Paritz, Jack, 171

Parsons, Louella, 47

Parsons, Michael, 236–237

Peach, Ken, 84

Petersen, Patty, 210

Philpot, Ford, 234, 236, 254

Pickford, Mary, 98

Pittman, George, 113

Pitts, ZaSu, 95

Plato, Dana, 298

Platz-Petersen, Rana, 298

Polanski, Roman, 264

Pollack, Sydney, 287–188, 192–195, 202

Porter, Cole, 138

Portwood, Darlene, 111

Potterville, Jerri, 66–67

Power, Tyrone, 55

Presley, Elvis, 149, 255

Price, Vincent, 108

Priest, Pat, 186

Priore, Dom, 244

Provost, Katie, 289, 301, 309, 311

Provost, Ryan, 288, 302, 309, 311

Prud'homme, Cameron, 19

Pryor, Richard, 223

Pyle, Denver, 135

R

Raitt, John, 41

Ramsey, Betty, 71

Ramsey, Bruce, 71

Reagan, Ronald, 35

Redding, Otis, 215

Redford, Robert, 187–188, 192, 195, 200–201

Reed, Donna, 80, 115, 143, 148

Reid, Kate, 187, 192, 202

Reiner, Carl, 240

Remick, Lee, 225

Rettig, Deane, 155, 286, 295, 306

Rettig, Tom, 7, 32, 32, 39, 40, 41, 51, 86, 111, 155, 205, 233, 266, 276–277, 280, 289, 295, 308

Rettig, Tom Jr., 286, 306, 307

Reynolds, Debbie, 16

Riley, Dexter, 259

Roach, Hal, 14, 117

Robbins, Trina, 182

Robinson, Maureen, 186

Rogers, Ginger, 103

Romero, Cesar, 112, 122, 124, 259

Ronstadt, Linda, 208

Rooney, Mickey, 13, 32, 62, 300

Rooney, Teddy, 108, 131

Rubin, Jerry, 222

Russell, Bryan, 57, 59, 126, 315

Russell, Jeanne, 57–60, 71, 81, 87, 102, 107, 117, 119–120, 130–132, 142, 171, 181, 290, 298–301, 303, 305, 309, 315

Russell, Kurt, 126, 258

S

Saunders, Tony, 22

Saxon, Skye, 215

Scafide, John, 191

Schallert, William, 135, 259

Schoenfeld, Don, 53, 84, 101–102

Schultz, Evelyn, 254

Schultz, Kevin, 254

Scott, Gordon, 34

Scott, Joey, 131, 136

Seaton, George, 14

Sebring, Jay, 264

Selby, J. E., 110

Selznick, David O., 16

Sennett, Mack, 98, 106

Shaw, Rosemary Hilb, 107, 206

Shepherd, Mike, 119

Shepodd, Jon, 49, 69, 268

Shepodd, Lynne, 65

Sherman, Bobby, 229

Shore, Roberta, 178

Silverman, Joyce, 145

Silverman, Marvin, 139, 145, 164

Simmons, Richard, 62, 151

Sinatra, Nancy, 225

Singerman, Gary Alan, 250